WOMEN'S VOICES
FROM THE
WESTERN FRONTIER

Another title by
Susan G. Butruille
published by Tamarack Books

Women's Voices from the Oregon Trail

WOMEN'S VOICES
FROM THE
WESTERN FRONTIER

by
Susan G. Butruille

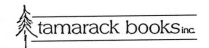 tamarack books inc.

PUBLISHED BY:
Tamarack Books, Inc.
PO Box 190313
Boise, ID 83719-0313

Cover Design and some original illustrations by:
Kathleen Petersen

About the cover: Quilt "Wheel of Fortune" used with permission of Mollala Area Historical Society and "Shared Memories" photo courtesy Washington County Museum, Portland, Oregon.

Author's note: The recipes printed in this book are intended for reading only, not necessarily for eating. I take no responsibility for any food prepared according to these "recipts."

Excerpts from: The letters of Kate and Eunice Robbins published by permission of Crook County Historical Society, Prineville, OR; The transcript of Elizabeth Burt's manuscript at Fort Laramie, Wyoming published by permission of Merrill J. Mattes publications; The diary of Angie Mitchell Brown from the Angie Mitchell Brown Collection reprinted by permission of the Archives of Sharlot Hall Museum, Prescott, AZ; *Daughters of Copper Woman* by Anne Cameron reprinted 1981 by permission of Press Gang Publishers, Vancouver, Canada; *The Life of An Ordinary Woman* by Anne Ellis, copyright 1929 by Anne Ellis, renewed 1957 by Neita Cary and Earl; E. Ellis, reprinted by permission of Houghton Mifflin Co., all rights reserved; *Conversations of Pioneer Women* by Fred Lockley reprinted by permission of Mike Helm, Editor, Rainy Day Press, Eugene, OR; *Daughters of Dakota, Vol. 2: Stories from the Attic,* Sally Roesch Wagner, editor, reprinted by permission of Sky Carrier Press, P.O. Box 2135, Aberdeen, SD 95402; The Holt Family Letters published by permission of Elizabeth Calef Howells from her private collection; The Mary Richardson Walker papers, Mss. 1204 and Bethenia Owens Adair papers, Mss. 503 published by permission of Oregon Historical Society, Portland, OR; "An Address to the People of the Year 2000" by Arvazena Spillman Cooper published by permission of Phyllis Klindt, Klindts' Booksellers, The Dalles, OR; *One Woman's West* by Martha Gay Masterson reprinted by permission of the editor, Lois Barton; *Let Them Speak for Themselves: Women in the American West* © 1977 by Christiane Fischer, reprinted by permission of Archon Books, North Haven, CT; "Mary Richardson Walker: The Shattered Dreams of a Missionary Woman" by Patricia V. Horner, *Montana The Magazine of Western History* published by the Montana Historical Society, by permission of the editor; *Memories of St. Elmo* by Charlotte Merrifield with Suzy Kelly reprinted by permission of Suzy Kelly; *Covered Wagon Women* series edited by Kenneth L. Holmes, reprinted by permission of The Arthur H. Clark Company, Spokane, WA; *Pioneer Women* © 1981 by Joanna L. Stratton, reprinted by permission of Simon & Schuster Inc.; *They Saw the Elephant* © 1990 by Jo Ann Levy, reprinted by permission of Archon Books, North Haven, CT; *The Sacred Hoop* © 1986, 1992 by Paula Gunn Allen, reprinted by permission of Beacon Press; *Saloons of the American West* © 1979 by Richard Erdoes, reprinted by permission of Alfred A. Knopf, Inc.; and *Ten Thousand Goddam Cattle* © 1976 by Katy Lee, published by Katydid Books & Records, P.O. Box 395, Jerome, AZ 86331. Verses from "Weaving and Quilting" and "Dandelion Song" from *Washington Notebook;* "Overland, 1852" from *October Roses* by permission of Linda Allen. Recording available from Rainbow Dancer Productions, P.O. Box 5881, Bellingham, WA 98227. Selected excerpts from *American Indian Prose & Poetry* © 1946 Margot Astrov. Copyright renewed. Reprinted by permission of Harper Collins Publishers, Inc.

DEDICATION

To John—my romance.

Special thanks to:
  Molly Van Austen, Michael Claypool, Mary Cross, Bonnie Jo Hunt, Judy Mann DiStefano (in memoriam), Win Blevins, Lillian Schlissel, Kathy Jones, Audrey Scott, Suzy Kelly, Bryce Kelly, Deborah Olsen, George Olsen, Kathleen O'Neal Gear, Mary Kramer, Fritz Kramer, Jim Considine, Paula McKenzie, Mary Worthington, Kathy Gaudry, Faye Simpson, Kathleen Petersen, Tony Butruille, Frank Butruille, R.J. Greffenius (in memoriam).
  The two people who made the writing of this book possible were my husband, John, and my mother, Ruth Hendricks Greffenius.

TABLE OF CONTENTS

Prelude 1

Chapter One
    A Wagon Full of Hope: Women's Dreams....... 9
Chapter Two
    Oh Woman Remember
    Women Who Were There First 21
Chapter Three
    Strong-Hearted Indian Women 43
Chapter Four
    Westward I Go Free? 69
Chapter Five
    Women Who Were Free................................. 89
Chapter Six
    Whiskey, Oysters, and Wild Wimmin:
    The Carnival Frontier.................................... 111
Chapter Seven
    Sporting Women 133
Chapter Eight
    Over There: The Search for Home.................. 155
Chapter Nine
    Stories Entwined:
    Weaving and Quilting the Fabric of Home 171
Chapter Ten
    The Hush Was So Loud:
    Frontier Dangers and Delights........................ 195
Chapter Eleven
    Tea, True Womanhood,
    and Uppity Women 221

Chapter Twelve
    Is Western Romance an Oxymoron? 243
Chapter Thirteen
    To Everything There is a Season:
    Rituals and Celebrations 267

Endnotes 299
Acknowledgments 303
Illustrations and Photographic Credits 304
Bibliography 305
Index 317

PRELUDE

Wait, there's so much I haven't said, so many voices to be heard.
—from *Women's Voices from the Oregon Trail*

When I reached the closing pages of my first book, *Women's Voices from the Oregon Trail,* I knew it was time to let it go. But the voices pulled me back, those voices of the women on the verge of settling the western frontier of the United States. So here they are, in their singularity and in their connectedness. Along the way, I've picked up many more voices than the ones I evoked from the Oregon Trail. And I know that when I reach the end of this journey, I'll feel the same way—so much not said, so many voices not heard.

How does one begin to envision what the western frontier looked like? We can imagine vast pastel-colored vistas in scrim-covered mists, like an old-fashioned painting. Snow-tipped mountains descend onto gold plains, with a river running through. A log cabin with a little window and a smoking chimney presents a perfect, tranquil picture.

But wait. The picture moves. The log cabin fades to reveal a tipi. The mountains dissolve into an endless horizon of prairie. Look again. Into the hill someone has built a home. Prairie grass grows on its roof.

Rivers flow across the picture in ribbons of blue and green and brown.

If we could step back and watch the flow of people as well as the flow of rivers, we first would see rivulets of clans and tribes flowing with the seasons.

Then we would see sod and wood cabins grow to settlements. Settlements fade with bad luck or grow with good luck to towns and cities. Some grow and fade again.

Colors quietly blend and noisily crash. The green of vast forests yield to patches of earth brown, making way for farms and ranches and towns. Knee-deep mud streets lead to glowing saloons decorated with painted faces and scarlet skirts over stripe-stockinged legs.

Gold winks and beckons from all directions, and mountainsides open in gashes and wounds to the gold seekers.

Burnished waves of free-flowing bison disappear. They yield to orderly herds of longhorns, eastward bound on new railroad tracks.

Listen. You can hear the giggle of a child playing hide and seek in tall grass. The distant drum of an Indian ghost dance dreams the time the lands will once again be theirs. The steady clank of a placer mine coaxes minerals from the earth to make some dreamers rich and more of them poor. A brassy band plays "The Girl I Left Behind" as it accompanies a gaudily decorated casket bearing the body of one more prostitute who found her way out with morphine.

There are the smells of fresh earth waking up in spring, of smoke from campfires and rock chimneys, of decaying oxen and cholera-infested garbage marking the way of the westward trails.

And there are the smells of pinon bread baking in an adobe oven, of wheat bread baking in a dutch oven, of jelly cake for a wedding, and dandelion wine.

What you are sensing are the many western frontiers: the disease frontier, which killed millions of the first Americans; the mining frontier, the carnival, military, agricultural, and urban frontiers. There was the frontier many women dreamed of, and the frontier they found.

Focus the lens on the lives of the women. There you will find etched into the picture, like a carefully-pieced quilt, the finely-embroidered details of many lives on the many western frontiers, in varied colors and textures. In my own mind, there are so many stories they sometimes flow together, a misty mix of lives.

One story, though, has imprinted itself in my gallery of mental pictures. The story was told by a woman who never was a real westerner, as we Real Westerners say. Anna Howard Shaw made it as far west as the Michigan frontier and did most of her life's work in the settled East. Unlike most nineteenth-century women, she built her own career and became famous.

Anna Howard Shaw's story of her mother speaks for legions of women who landed somewhere on the western frontier, not by choice, but simply because the thing for a woman to do was to follow her husband.

Anna Howard Shaw was born in Scotland. Hard times brought the child Anna and her family first to Massachusetts, then to the Michigan frontier on a 360-acre claim, nine miles from the nearest settlement. Anna, who was then twelve, later remembered arriving with her mother at their new frontier home. It was a crude cabin with dirt floors and holes for the door and windows.

It was late in the afternoon when we drove up to the opening that was its front door, and I shall never forget the look my mother turned upon the place. Without a word, she crossed the threshold and, standing very still, looked slowly around her. Then something within her seemed to give way, and she sank upon the floor. She could not realize even then, I think, that this was really the place father had

prepared for us, that here he expected us to live. When she finally took it in she buried her face in her hands, and in that way she sat for hours, without speaking or moving . . .. [Her face] never lost the deep lines those first hours of her pioneer life had cut upon it.[1]

Anna's mother never recovered, and retreated into invalidism. Anna Howard Shaw never married, perhaps because she didn't want to repeat her mother's experience in marriage. She went on to become a minister, lecturer, and activist working for a woman's right to vote—a right her own mother never had, not even within her own family.

While the story of Anna Howard Shaw's mother spoke for thousands of women, her story was not typical because there was no typical frontier woman. Just when you focus on her determined and careworn face, her calico dress and white apron, Calamity Jane swaggers into the picture, dressed in her trademark men's pants with a swig of whiskey in her hand. Paiute leader Sarah Winnemucca searches for the magic key, the one that will open the minds and hearts of the white men who keep making promises to her people and then breaking them, along with her people's hearts and bodies.

Here is Anne Ellis, coming of age in a Colorado mining town, longing to be a Lady but unable to contain her free spirit. Lalu Nathoy sails east to Gold Mountain, *Gum San,* over the Great Ocean of Peace, dreaming of picking up enough gold on that mountain to buy her way back home but instead finding herself sold into prostitution. Seventy-year-old Stagecoach Mary drives a stagecoach through the scene, expertly working the reins of the horses with her strong, chocolate-colored hands.

Here is Buffalo Bird Woman, remembering the childhood songs she sang to the corn in the fields with the mothers. And Julia Archibald Holmes defying the Cult of True Womanhood by wearing bloomers, which come in handy when she climbs 14,000 Pikes Peak in 1858. And Doctor Bethenia Owens Adair paying tribute to the woman who inspired her to test her own limits, the woman who boldly galloped her horse across the prairie lassoing cattle, hair flying free.

Many frontier women's stories are inspiring, even heroic, hilarious, shocking, and exciting. Yet through the vastness of landscape and language and culture are timeless connections in rituals and customs, in the food they shared, the dreams they dreamed, and the stories they told, commonalities within the diversity.

Most women's lives, like the men's, were made of strung-together moments of everydayness, and it is these moments that become the stuff of lives lived and stories told.

Within the diversity, I invite you to explore this everydayness with me, through women's stories, journals, songs, and recipes—receipts they called them. Look over the shoulder of frontier women wearily recording thoughts and receipts and secrets in letters and journals so they wouldn't be forgotten. Dance to the wail of a fiddle or the beat of a drum. Smell the hope, taste the sweetness, touch the despair, and feel the joy of moments that make up the stories of the many American western frontiers.

The main focus is on the early frontiers, before settlement, when women and men improvised their lives before re-establishing the order of the lives they had left back home. We'll invoke the voices of women mainly from the Pacific Northwest, Wyoming, Colorado, and the Southwest. I've chosen these parts of the West because they're the places I know best. Sometimes, though, we'll stray outside these boundaries to pick up a good story.

That's the who, the what, and the where. The when is harder, because the western frontiers happened at different times in different places. Pioneers would settle one place while the first Americans would still be living on their own lands in other areas. Most stories in this book don't go beyond 1900, but a few do because the frontier was still left in a few places into 1910 and even beyond.

What was the western frontier?

Bill Bullard, former Administrator of the National Frontier Trails Center in Independence, Missouri, warned that "Everyone who writes about the trails disagrees with everyone else." You could say that about the western frontier as well. As historian Glenda Riley says, "Whatever question you're talking about, there's never a simple answer."

The classic definer of the American western frontier was Frederick Jackson Turner, who saw it as a series of moves westward, leaving at each step convention and restraint to find freedom Some Place Else. In Turner's eyes, the western frontier was a world of men who could start over, make up their own rules, maybe do it better than they did before. He didn't seem to take much notice of the women who came along, most of whom saw their future there much differently. Nor did he take into account the people who were already there.

> **Ho! Westward!**
> **Soon the world shall know**
> **That all is grand in the western land;**
> **Ho! Westward Ho!**[2]

While Turner described the frontier as freedom from the order of civilization, others have described it as advancing civilization, bringing the ways of "civilized" cultures ever westward. Both are right, and both have a lot to do with men and women and the meaning of frontier. On the early frontiers, it was mainly the men who sought freedom from civilization, and the women who were assigned to bring civilization with them. It was the crack between these worlds, and the cultures they replaced, that was the frontier.

Some historians now call the frontier the place

where different cultures met one another and clashed, even crashed.

Many who came to the western frontier didn't move westward at all, but across oceans and continents toward the east, the south, and the north.

Whatever and wherever the frontier was, it transformed the women who came and the women who were already there. For many women, the frontier experience caused them to redefine who they really were after being told by the Experts who they were supposed to be. For some, it was their first taste of freedom.

Whatever their experience, women relied on other women to help them in their journey. In my journey traveling and writing about the Oregon Trail, many women were there, especially my mother, Ruth Hendricks Greffenius. I relied on her to help me complete that journey. She was there for this journey as well, sharing her perspectives on the women who have gone before, and linking me with customs and experiences of past generations, my grandmothers and great-grandmothers. Mother also is a link with the lands she and I claim as our home, the mountains of northwestern and southwestern Colorado.

Through the sharing and connections and remembering, listen to the voices that tell the stories of women from the western frontier.

CHAPTER ONE

A Wagon Full of Hope:
Women's Dreams

[W]hen you leave each home with nothing but a wagon full of hope and a new baby after each move everything finally gets lost or broken—even your dreams sometimes.
—from *Skagit Schoolma'am: A Pioneer Teacher in the San Juans* by Elizabeth Duncan

A wagon full of hope. These wistful words from Inger Dahlen, a Norwegian immigrant to Puget Sound, are packed with history and meaning for many, maybe most frontier women. The moving on, the life-goes-on part of frequent births, the lost dreams, renewed hope.

Hope was one of the common threads weaving together the lives of the women who lived and traveled and dreamed there. Even

End of the Trail Museum,
Oregon City, Oregon

when dreams were lost and broken, the women packed their hope with them for the next move, placed it in the next child.

Above my bed is a dream catcher, a lovely web of thread woven inside a ring. According to Indian spirituality, the dream catcher catches the bad dreams and lets the good dreams filter through to the dreamer. So maybe it should be called a nightmare catcher instead of a dream catcher.

The Indian women shared with the pioneer women hopes and dreams of home and community. Their nightmares came with strangers on their lands and forced migrations away from their homes.

> **Where the mountain crosses,**
> **On top of the mountain,**
>   **I do not myself know where.**
> **I wandered where my mind and my**
>   **heart seemed to be lost.**
> **I wandered away.**[1]
>   —Dream Song of a Woman (Papago)

Indian people, men and women, would wander away to dream, to know the way they were to go, to know where their spirit, their power, would come from. The spirit would reveal itself in the dream song. The spirit of the dream would reveal itself as a helper to guide the woman to live in the best way to help her community survive, to keep going the cycle of birth, life, and death. This meant showing respect to the earth and all they took from it.

In her elegant book, *Ishi: In Two Worlds,* about the last California Indian to emerge from the old ways in 1911, Theodora Kroeber imagined the dreams of the Yana people in winter. Safe in their earth-covered houses, wrapped in rabbitskin blankets, watching their food baskets empty, "the Yana dreams turned to a time, not far off, when the earth would be covered with new clover."

It was simple, really. The Indian people ultimately dreamed of a world lost, while those who came into their lands dreamed of a world to be found.

And in the end, the shared dream would be of clover in the spring.

Those who came into the land believed it to be free—empty and free. They had their own dreams—dreams of a better life than what they knew. Some dreamed of fabulous wealth, streets of gold. The Spanish explorers believed they would find the Fabled Seven Golden Cities of Cibola. Chinese called it *Gum San*—Gold Mountain. Argonauts dreamed of chunks of gleaming gold waiting to be plucked out of the streams and hillsides.

Many saw the new land as the place where they would work hard and grab their fortune and return home triumphantly to claim their bright future for themselves and their family. Others figured they'd make their fortune, stake out their own piece of land, and live free. Others saw it as the place where they would finally have enough rich land to plow and plant and raise a family on it. Many proclaimed themselves chosen by God to have dominion over this fertile land.

'The star of empire,' poets say,
Ho! Westward Ho!
'Forever takes its onward way!'
Ho! Westward Ho!
That this be proven in our land,
Ho! Westward Ho!
It seems Jehovah's great command,
Ho! Westward Ho![2]

It's all there in an 1872 painting called *Manifest Destiny,* widely seen in the settled lands to the east. Bathed in a golden glow, men are prospecting, driving a stage coach, plowing the land, coaxing oxen pulling a covered wagon, and chasing buffalo on a galloping horse. Ships and a train bring more men into the picture. Indians dance in the distance, while other Indians flee the scene. It is a male scene, except for a bare-breasted Indian woman leading a horse dragging a travois bearing a woman and her child.

A mystical barefoot goddess-looking woman dominates the picture. She floats in the air, blond hair flying free, her flowing white robes barely covering her seductive body. She holds a school book and strings telephone wire across the golden land.

The mystical woman leads the way to a waiting paradise. The land of Eden, they called it. Industrialists, hucksters, patriots, promoters, politicians, artists, writers spun tales and painted pictures of a shimmering, virgin land just waiting to be taken, subdued, conquered, tamed.

Let's widen the lens here. Not all immigrants to the new land went west, though most did. Not all were of European ancestry, though most were. Not all were men, though most were. While the "virgin-waiting-to-be-taken" image was a best seller to an eager audience to the east, images of different shapes filtered through the webs of people's dreams, especially the women's.

While most Indian women dreamed of staying on

or returning to their lands with their people, dreams of most immigrant women looked a lot like home. Their paradise was a safe home, their Eden a garden of fruits and vegetables and flowers.

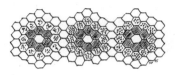

The people in quest of their dream were not pioneers until they got there. Until then, they called themselves immigrants or emigrants, depending on whether they thought of themselves as coming or leaving.

Phoebe Judson was twenty years old when she journeyed to Oregon Country with her husband and two-year-old child in 1853. She bore their second child on the trail two months later. Phoebe recalled how as a child she passed many delightful hours "building, re-building and furnishing the 'ideal home' that should some day be mine—little dreaming that 'to find it I would travel over two thousand miles in an emigrant wagon, through a country inhabited only by Indians and wild animals.'"

The couple wanted to become "independent," to have a home "we might call ours."

She described the "ideal home" she built of "air castles":

It should be built by a mountain stream that flowed to the Pacific, or by some lake, or bay, and nothing should obstruct our view of the beautiful snow-capped mountains.

True, it would be built of logs, but they would be covered with vines and roses, while the path leading to it should be bordered with flowers and the air filled

with their sweet perfume. Phoebe wrote in her journal, as though writing the words would bring it closer:

> '**Home, home, sweet home;**
> **Be it ever so humble,**
> **There's no place like home.'**

The journey "nearly cured" Phoebe of building her
"air castles." It became so difficult, with fearful river
crossings, Indian threats, leaving precious belongings
behind, and the birth of her second child, that her
hopes for the journey were only that their little family would "escape being caught in the snow of the
Cascade mountains."

After many moves and less-than-ideal homes,
Phoebe had her ideal home in Washington Territory. It
was "not a mansion by any means, but a commodious,
comfortable and pretty home" in "an enchanting
spot."

Lodisa Frizzell, one of 5,000 women and 42,500
men who bolted to California in '49, dreamed of a
place to rest as her party approached South Pass in
what is now Wyoming, less than halfway to her desti-
nation:

> **O the luxury of a house, a house! I felt**
> **what some one expressed, who traveled**
> **this long and tedious journey, that, 'it**
> **tires the soul.'**

Mary Ann Hafen was a six-year-old hand cart pioneer to Utah with her Swiss family in 1860. Theirs
was the tenth and last Mormon hand cart company to

cross the plains from Nebraska. Besides caring for
Mary Ann, her two-year-old sister, and nine-year-old
brother, Mary Ann's mother was nursing a six-month-
old baby.

> **Some must push and some must pull**
> **As we go marching up the hill,**
> **As merrily on the way we go**
> **Until we reach the valley, oh!**[3]

When Mary Ann's mother would get discouraged,
her father would tell her that "we were going to Zion,
that the Lord would take care of us, and that better
times were coming." Theirs was one of the most fortu-
nate of the hand cart companies. Others before them
had become stranded in Wyoming snows and many
had died.

Bertha Josephsen Anderson and her family were
part of the "Great Dakota Boom" of the late 1870s and
1880s after the railroad opened an easier path to
homesteading the land of the Dakotas and Montana.
She and her husband simply couldn't get ahead on
their little farm in Denmark. America beckoned.
Bertha and her husband and their three small children
traveled by ship, train, and lumber wagon to a place
they called "The Badlands" of what is now eastern
Montana. There, they scraped by the first winter, and
avoided starving only because of strangers' generosity.

"We had but one aim," she remembered: "to struggle along as best we could, planning in five years to
have enough money made so we could go back home
to Denmark and buy back the little home we sold to
come over here."[4]

She never returned to live on her native soil. The
family would file their Homestead claim and become
U.S. citizens.

Nineteen-year-old Della Holt fled the devastation
of the Civil War in Georgia with ten family members
in 1866. Her father must have looked around at the
grieving land and despaired of taking care of his fam-

ily. "It is all that Pa can do to get bread for us to eat.
. . . Then we have no home here and never can have
one." The Holts also were among thousands of non-
slave owning southerners whose move westward was
influenced by slavery.

Before she left on the journey that would take the
family by ship and rail through the Isthmus of
Panama, Della wrote to her aunt, who had begged the
family to stay.

> **Aunt Sally you say that it would
> change the subject if we had husbands
> to go with us. That is about half that I
> am going for, for don't you know how
> hard I have been trying to get one these
> many years. So I am going out there
> and try my best to deceive some
> man. . . . If we could get there without
> going I would be very glad indeed but I
> think it is right for us to brave our
> hardships and make the attempt for the
> Uncles have promised to do more for us
> than we can ever do for ourselves in
> this old country.**[5]

Della was successful in her plan to "deceive some
man." After becoming a teacher, she married within
four years after she arrived in Oregon.

Anne Ellis traveled as a child to the Colorado gold
fields in a covered wagon with her parents and
extended family from Missouri in 1879. Her father
was a charmer with great ideas, but not much on fol-
low-through. "My father was the kind who traveled,"
Anne wrote, "trusting to Fate to provide, and it did—
but Mama was Fate!"

Janus-faced, "She would look forward and be
happy, thinking of the home she was going to have
'out there,' and then look back and cry, thinking of the
friends she had left."

By 1879, the trip west was easier than in earlier

years, with real roads beneath the wagon wheels, and places to stop along the way for rest and provisions. Anne recalled, "With all the work and hardships, [Mama] was 'eating her white bread' then, although she did not know it." ("Eating her white bread" meant that times were easier.) Evenings brought singing, laughter, and dancing—something Anne's mother didn't have before or after the journey.

When the family arrived at the edge of Pueblo, Colorado, they had nothing to eat. Fate—Anne's mother—stepped in. She walked into town with a prized pieced quilt and sold it to buy food for the family.

How many dreams were in that quilt? How many hours and tears and laughter and family lore? Now gone, like the dreams. Anne Ellis' mother never did have that home she dreamed of.

> **Guide me, O Thou great Jehovah**
> **Pilgrim through this barren land**
> **I am weak, but Thou art mighty**
> **Hold me with Thy powerful hand**
> **Bread of heaven, Bread of heaven**
> **Feed me till I want no more**
> **Feed me till I want no more.**
> —Old Methodist hymn from the Welsh

This hymn must have comforted many an immigrant to the west. Both Phoebe Judson and Anne Ellis recalled its words during their journey westward.

Lalu Nathoy didn't go west. Kidnapped by bandits and shipped off to America from China, she traveled east in a bruising, cramped voyage across the "Great Ocean of Peace" to *Gum San,* Gold Mountain. There, she had been told, people could just gather up the gold. Her dream was to pick up enough gold to win her freedom, become rich, and return home.[6] Instead, she was sold, like livestock, into prostitution. Her story, however, had a happy ending in a lasting marriage to an Idaho gambler and saloon owner after she saved his life.

Elinore Pruitt, a widow with a young daughter, was working in Denver as a laundress, a housekeeper, and a furnace tender in 1909. Ill and discouraged, she heard about homesteading land in Wyoming. "[N]othing but the mountains, the pines, and the clean fresh air seemed worthwhile . . . and I wanted to homestead." Two days later, she headed north and soon fulfilled her dream.

A black woman named Laura fled violence when some men in town thought her Creek Indian husband walked too proud.

Westward bound black women, whose ancestors had moved freely in their villages and forests, sought a kind of freedom known only to those who had known slavery and its aftermath. Black women were more likely than white women to move westward by choice. Some began their trek as early as the 1840s. Some traveled by themselves, some with communities, some as servants, and a few as legal slaves.

And so the women and men and children came. They came from many directions, by many different means.

**Moses Speese family near Westerville,
Custer County, Nebraska, 1888.**
Solomon D. Butcher collection, Nebraska State Historical Society

During the 1500s, women were among the Spanish who moved from Mexico into the desert lands to the north, searching for gold and silver. The Spanish began to establish chains of missions through the Southwest and into California, forcing Indian people who were already there to work in the missions and become Christians.

Distinct cultural groups, the mestizo and metis, grew from intermarriages of Spanish and Indian in the Southwest, and French and Indian in the North. African slaves brought by the Spanish added to the racial mix.

For two centuries, Spain, France, England, Mexico, and the United States fought over control of the lands to the west of the Mississippi. By mid-century, the U.S. had bought and otherwise taken over roughly the area of what are now the lower forty-eight states.

The nineteenth century brought a surge of settlers and wanderers into these lands, as worldwide drought and crop failures, depressions, disease, wars, plain bad luck, religious and racial persecution, and sometimes incurable restlessness pushed people to move on. In 1843, yellow fever killed 13,000 in the Mississippi Valley. The devastating Civil War in the States uprooted thousands of lives.

A chance to run, to start over, and maybe even strike it rich was worth the risk of losing everything, maybe even your life. Many of the U.S. citizens who moved westward already had been moving westward in a series of moves. Many moved as families, and this is where most of the first western frontier women came from.

Agricultural lands in Oregon and California were the first to open officially to settlement, followed in the 1850s by tall grass prairie country of what is now Kansas and Nebraska. The California Gold Rush set off a chain of gold strikes that spread throughout the western lands, bringing gold seekers, farmers, merchants, and other fortune and home seekers from all directions and in many colors.

The green earth and gleaming gold pulled the men and women and children from foreign lands until nearly half of the non-Indian immigrants were foreign-born. They had good reason to leave, most of them. In 1845 alone, a potato fungus triggered a famine that killed two and a half million people from Ireland to Moscow. There were famines in Peru, Chile, Italy, China, Brazil, Mexico, and Nicaragua. Smallpox and cholera stalked populations by land and sea.

They came in streams, in torrents, in trickles, overflowing here, drying up there, and changing direction on a whim. Each came with a dream, a dream full of hope.

> **[F]or forty years . . . people have lived on the hope of 'things opening up in the spring.'**
> —Anne Ellis

And for many, the dream was as simple as the Yana dream of clover in the spring.

CHAPTER TWO

Oh Woman Remember
Women Who Were There First

**She Who Watches, Columbia
River Gorge, Washington**

Listen to the Grandmothers tell the story of Tsagaglalal.

Long ago, some say, the Grandmother came out of the waters and created the earth and the animals and the people and the spirit beings in it. The Grandmother watched over her creation from the rocks above the place where her people lived beside the rushing waters.

One day Coyote, the Trickster, came down the river's edge to the village. "How are you being treated?" he asked the people. "We live well," they told him. "We live in strong houses and catch lots of fish."

They pointed toward the rocks. "Go ask our chief," they told him. "She lives up there. Her name is Tsagaglalal."

Coyote climbed up the rocks and asked the chief, "How are you treating your people?"

"My people live well," replied the chief. "They live in strong houses and catch lots of fish."

"Soon the world will change," Coyote told the chief, "and women will no longer be chiefs or hold power."

Coyote used his magic and changed Tsagaglalal to stone. "You will stay there forever, up there on the rocks. And you will watch over your people."

And so Tsagaglalal became She Who Watches. She is still there, on the rocks over the Columbia River. Many still tell her story. Calm waters now cover the rushing falls where her people once caught lots of fish and lived in strong houses.

Tsagaglalal's people painted and etched her face on stone hundreds—some say thousands—of years ago. The huge unblinking eyes now watch over the interstate highway that lines the gorge where the people's strong houses used to hug the river's edge.

As you gaze on She Who Watches, listen. Hear her voice. Remember the women throughout the millennia whose voices once were heard and then were silenced.

Like She Who Watches.

Many American Indian tales tell of the creation of the earth and its people and spirits. Most begin with water, and it is the birth-giving Mother or life-continuing Grandmother who is most often associated with life-bearing water. The Blackfeet of the north say the animals and people came from a great womb. The tale is told of the Creator Grandmother weaving and thinking and dreaming the earth and its peoples and its spirits into being. In most creation myths, male and female are there.

She is there. She is the beginning, the one whose womb birthed the world, the one who always was there. To some, she is Thought Woman, who with her two sisters, generates and regenerates life. To others, she is Changing Woman, who forms a sacred trinity with her twin sons. She is Corn Woman, whose body and spirit nourish the fields. She is Grandmother Spider, who weaves together the strands of earth and spirit. She is Earth Woman, Yellow Woman, First Woman.

To the Lakota (Sioux), she is White Buffalo Woman, who brought her people the Sacred Pipe. The pipe is wakan. It contains power, the power of creation and regeneration. Without this pipe there can be no magic. Some say White Buffalo Woman lives in a cave, where she directs the four winds.

> **From beyond time,**
> **beyond oak trees and bright clear**
> **water flow,**
> **she was given the work of weaving**
> **the strands**
> **of her body, her pain, her vision**
> **into creation, and the gift of having**
> **created,**
> **to disappear.**[1]
>
> —from "Grandmother"
> by Paula Gunn Allen

Within the circle of the Grandmothers, touch the wisdom of age and living a long life. Remember the wisdom of the Grandmothers, handed down in songs and dances and weaving and clay pots and memory.

The hands of my own grandmothers and great-grandmothers were not brown like those of the first grandmothers in this land. The hands of my grandmothers and the first grandmothers did not intertwine. My grandmothers and great-grandmothers did not, could not, hear the voices of the first grandmothers. I mourn those losses.

But all of us can claim some of the lost voices, the lost wisdom. For if we go back far enough in our collective histories, we know that all the ancestors lived close to the earth. Mother Earth belief systems are found in indigenous cultures world wide, as are counterparts to kivas and sweat lodges and rituals of song

and dance and food preparation. We are all con-
querors and conquered.

I offer what I have learned through written and
spoken words, knowing that still there is much that I
don't understand. I evoke the voices of the first grandmothers so that we may better hear our own voices in
those of others, walk another's path with our own
footsteps. So we may know that we walk the ancient
path together. So we may re-think, perhaps re-dream,
what we mean by tradition.

From the bark of a willow tree, a Yakama[2] woman
of the Northwest shapes her time ball. Each day she
ties a knot on the cord, marking with colored beads
the seasons and ceremonies and important events in
her life, so that she may remember.

You may notice that when I write of Indian people
and their culture, I sometimes change tenses. Now
we're in the present, now in the past. This is by design
because in traditional Indian culture, time itself is cir-
cular, like the rolling ball, moving between past, present, and future. Also, many Indian people still hold
ancient beliefs and rituals.

"The Dreamer is the center, the hub of the wheel,"
wrote Paula Gunn Allen. "It is through her dreams
that the women keep children safe in war, that heal-
ings are made possible, and that children are assured
a safe passage through life."

Indian people would wander away to dream, to
know the way they were to go, to know where their
spirit, their power, would come from. The spirit, often

the spirit of an animal guardian, would reveal itself in
the dream song.

> **Where the mountain crosses,**
> **On top of the mountain,**
>   **I do not myself know where.**
> **I wandered where my mind and my**
>   **heart seemed to be lost.**
> **I wandered away.**[3]
>   —Dream Song of a Woman (Papago)

The first westerners knew themselves not as
"Indian," but as The People. Most tribal names familiar today are those given them by Europeans who
came into their lands, not the names known by The
People themselves. For example, *Lakota* (or *Dakota,*
depending on the dialect) means Alliance of Friends,
explains Bonnie Jo Hunt, Lakota founder of Artists of
Indian America. When the French trappers heard the
people they knew as Chippewa calling their rivals
"Nadawe Sioux," the French began to call the Lakota
people "Sioux."

Now many Indian people are claiming their
ancient names. For example, the ancient name of the
Pima is *Akimel.* The Papago are *Tohono O'odam,* and
the Navajo are *Dine* (DEE-neh). I will continue to use
mainly European names, however, only because they
are what I know.

The swastika is an ancient symbol, known
throughout the world. To the Hopi, the swastika represents among other things migration routes to the
four directions and back again. As Colorado historian
and mythologist Michael Claypool explains, "It's like
a ripple in a pond. The migration waves move outward, touch the boundaries, and come back."

The Hopi consider their home in the North

American Southwest to be the center, the navel of the earth. The Hopi swastika centers on and revolves around their home, the place of Emergence, or Shipap. The migration journey also is a metaphor for life's journey, back to Shipap.

Picture, then, a continent of peoples moving inward and outward in different directions, slowly migrating and intermixing for thousands of years, and living according to tradition and the cycles of the seasons where they lived.

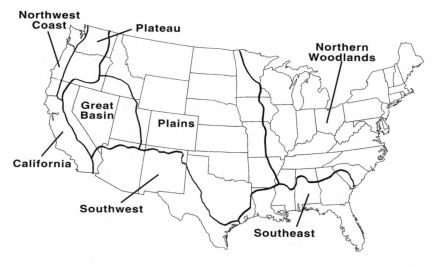

When the Spaniards, French, and English first came into the lands of the People, they encountered bands, clans, and tribes of varying sizes, many languages, and many cultures.

The best-known culture group is that of the Plains people, who lived on the land roughly between the Mississippi River and the Rocky Mountains. They were the fierce horsemen of movie fame. Yet the horse culture lasted only about 100 years, from the late 1700s to the late 1800s. The Plains Indians were a diverse people. They included the Sioux, Cheyenne, Shoshone, Arapaho, Comanche, Crow, and Blackfeet, and they ranged from peaceful farmers, gatherers and

hunters, to horse-mounted buffalo hunters and
raiders.

The bands and clans of the desert Southwest also
were both settled and mobile, from the Apache and
Ute horse people to the Pueblo apartment dwellers to
the Navajo horsemen-turned-herders and the Paiute
gatherer-hunters.

Along the Pacific coast, the living was easiest,
with abundant food from the sea and, on the north
coast, dense rain forests. East of the Cascade Range of
present-day Washington and Oregon to the Sierra
Nevadas of California, lay the high desert plateau and
great basin. Here, most bands and clans moved from
summer to winter camps, making the seasonal rounds
of fishing and food-gathering for their generally-
peaceful living.

**Women
cleaning fish**

From the
collection of the
Jefferson County
Historical Society,
Port Townsend,
Washington
#14.074

I try to listen for the voices of the women who
lived before the coming of the white people. But the
voices are not clear. They have faded or died with
time. The stories that told their history, their medicine, their wisdom, their language, were forbidden
and many died. Their written history survived mainly
through the eyes and ears and pens of white men and
women. Those who came into their lands didn't know
the ways of the people, and saw the women only as

domestic workers, not as community leaders or sources of history and wisdom.

But the people's voices didn't die. They are still there, in the hearts of the people, their songs, their history, and traditions.

Sarah Winnemucca

Courtesy Nevada Historical Society, Reno, Nevada #78 Bradley & Rulofson

As a little girl, Thocmetony, or Shell Flower, gathered seeds and roots with her sister and mother in the high desert country that was their home in what is now called the Humboldt Sink country of western Nevada. Little Shell Flower delighted in singing and dancing and "being happy" with her people.

Shell Flower, later known as Sarah Winnemucca, adored her grandfather, Chief Truckee. He had told his people the prophecy of the coming of his white brothers, who had separated from the dark people long ago. And when the white people came into his people's land seeking California gold, he welcomed them, crying, "My white brothers—my long-looked for white brothers have come at last!"

Chief Truckee guided some of the Gold Rush emigrants through his people's lands, and fought with General John C. Fremont's army in California against Mexican control.

"[Y]ou will not hurt a hair on [the white people's] heads," Chief Truckee told his people, "but welcome them as I tried to do."

But little Shell Flower cried when she first saw them. "Oh mother, the owls!" she screamed.

"I saw their big white eyes, and I thought their faces were all hair," she would write later.

> **Very much also**
> **I of the owl am afraid,**
> **Sitting alone in the wigwam.**[4]
> —(Chippewa)

Shell Flower's mother had heard terrifying stories about the white people, some crazed by this time in their long journey from far away over mountains and deserts on the California Trail.

Sarah Winnemucca, Shell Flower, cried when her mother buried her to keep the white people from finding her. Her mother and aunts couldn't move fast enough with the children to get away from the white people, so they buried the children in the sand, covered their faces with sage bushes, told them not to cry, and came back for them that night.

Little Sarah cried with her people when her father dreamed the same dream for three nights: "I saw the greatest emigration that has yet been through our country. I . . . saw nothing but dust, and I heard a great weeping. I saw women crying, and I also saw my men shot down by the white people."

The old women talked about it and said it was true. It was not a dream. "We shall no longer be a happy people, as we now are; we shall no longer go here and there as of old; we shall no longer build our big fires as a signal to our friends, for we shall always be afraid of being seen by those bad people."

Little Sarah cried when they burned up her people's winter supply of food. She cried when they shot her uncle.

As little Sarah grew older and became a leader of

her people, she cried many more times as she saw the white people invade the lands where her people traveled with the seasons, where they knew where to find roots and berries and fish and antelope.

Mesa Verde National Park, Southwestern Colorado

There was no one Indian Way. Different bands, clans, and tribes had their own traditions, their own way of living and loving and believing. But they shared much. They shared a commitment to their community of people and animals and plants. They shared a recognition of individual skills and talents that contribute to that community. And they shared the living on the land, paying close attention to the cycles of the seasons.

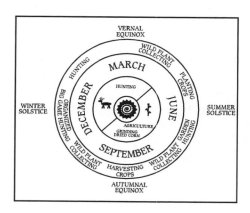

Diagram showing the seasonal calendar of the Anasazi people of the Southwest. The social calendar is adapted from the modern Tewa of north central New Mexico

Adapted from a calendar at Dominguez and Escalante Ruins, Anasazi Heritage Center, Bureau of Land Management, Dolores, Colorado

When you have no shiny watch to tell you the hour and minute of each day, when you have no calendar with names assigned to clusters of days, when you have no store where you can buy supplies of flour and sugar and bacon, you know you must be attentive to the earth around you that yields life and wields death.

You watch the skies. You pay attention to where the roots and berries grow, and you learn how to keep them growing. You learn the ways of fish and animals whose flesh and sinew and bones and skin keep you and your children fed and warm and sheltered. You know when to expect the life-giving rains, when to gather food, when to store it. You know how to respect the spirits of the plants and animals to keep the food growing, the animals near, and the rains coming.

They saw that what died (like the plants) or went to another place (like the bear or the snake) in winter came back in the spring, to be part of their lives in the summer and preserved for the winter when they went away again. They saw the sun warm their days and go away at night, to come back the next day. They watched the moon grow in light every twenty-eight days, then die, and come back again.

Because their lives and living depended every day on the things and beings that surrounded them, they saw all beings, all things connected by what some would call spirit, some God, some soul. In the far north, the Inuit people called this spirit Inua. When the Inuit men made cooking utensils and hunting implements, they would endow them with faces or symbols of this soul that was in every thing. It was a sign of respect and, they believed, part of survival.

In the cycles of the days and nights and the seasonal rounds, they saw the cycles of their own lives—
birth, life, death, and regeneration. According to
Paula Gunn Allen, author of *The Sacred Hoop,* most
American Indian tribes recognized the primary power
of the universe as female. Mother-power "is not so
much the power to give birth, . . . but the power to
make, to create, to transform."

Mother-power simply is. The Navajo word *shima*
and its multiple meanings embrace one's own mother,
the living earth, the sheep flock, the corn field, the
sacred bundle.[5] Mother-power is everywhere.

It was women who birthed new life, who nurtured
the living, and assisted and mourned the dying.
Mother-power was theirs as centers and leaders of
community.

In societies that were matrilocal, where families
lived with the mother's clan, mother-power was
strong. In societies that were matrilineal, where clans
traced their lineage and inheritance through the mother's family, mother-power was strong.

Western matrilineal tribes included the Apache,
Navajo, Mandan, Hidatsa, Crow, some northwestern
tribes, and many Pueblo tribes, according to author
and historian Valerie Sherer Mathes. All Southwest
Pueblo people were—and remain—matrilineal,
according to Michael Claypool. In such tribes, the
women owned the dwellings and their contents, any
fields they cultivated, food they gathered, and any
food grown by the men in their fields.

In the most peaceful societies, women's and men's
roles, while separate, complemented one another.
Both women and men valued nurturing, and family
units extended beyond the mother, father, and children, to include aunts and uncles and grandmothers
and grandfathers. Often the mother's brother influenced the lives of her children more than the children's father. Women and children sometimes lived
separately from men, and in many tribes, the husband
was considered a guest in the wife's house.

Indian women, like Anglo women on the early frontiers, were valued for the work they could do. Buffalo Bird Woman, a Hidatsa of North Dakota, described the skills she learned in her mother's lodge:

> **My father's lodge, or better, my mother's lodge—for an earth lodge belonged to the women who built it— was more carefully constructed than most winter lodges. . . . I learned to cook deer skins, embroider, sew with awl and sinew, and cut and make moccasins, clothing, and tent covers. . . . My father did the heavy lifting. . . . He was a kind man, and helped my mothers and me when we had hard work to do. . . . For my industry in dressing skins, my clan aunt, Sage, gave me a woman's belt. . . . Only a very industrious girl was given such a belt. . . . To wear a woman's belt was an honor.[6]**

The men were to hunt, establish the community's territory, and protect their boundaries and their clans.

Women and men drew power from rituals, separately and together. As Paula Gunn Allen wrote, women's rituals focus on "maintenance of life over the long term," while men's rituals deal with "risk, death, and transformation—that is, all that helps regulate and control change."

Gaspar Perez de Villagra wrote in 1610 about the people of the Kuaua pueblo in what is now New Mexico. "They live in complete equality, neither exercising authority nor demanding obedience. . . . The men spin and weave and the women cook, build houses, and keep them in good repair. . . . They are quiet, peaceful people."[7]

Women's hands built many dwellings. They fashioned tipis by stretching cured buffalo hides around pole frames or by wrapping tule (a marshy grass) mats around a frame, bound with hemp or rawhide strips. The women used wood, bark, willow branches, grasses, and mud for their houses, from the Plains tipi to the Apache stick wickiup, to the complex mud brick pueblos of the Southwest.

Dwellings, no matter how they were made, were more than places to live. They were also places for teaching, story telling, and ritual.

To many Indian people, their dwellings were sacred. A woman of the farming northern Hidatsa people remembered the earth lodge of her childhood as alive, with "the door for a mouth."

The Navajo deity Changing Woman gave instructions for building and caring for the hogans (one-room huts), "which are personified in myth, song, prayer and 'ordinary' conversation—they are alive; they need to be fed, cared for, spoken to, and shielded from loneliness."[8]

The ruins of the Kuaua pueblo still stand at Coronado State Monument, just north of Albuquerque, New Mexico. It is a compelling combination of remnants and reconstructions of the lives of the people who were living in this land of sage brush and sky when the Spaniards first came in 1540.

Coronado came through here with 1,200 people,

Remaining walls of Kuaua Pueblo, Coronado State Monument, Bernilillo, New Mexico.

searching for the fabled Seven Golden Cities of Cibola.
All the Spaniards found were peaceful people living
in mud brick apartment-style complexes. Some pueblos reached as many as seven stories high, many with
window openings and terraces. The walls were so
strong that pieces of them still stand, hundreds of
years after the Kuaua people mysteriously left.

Women and men built these structures together.
The men brought wood supports and put them in
place. The women built the walls of bricks they made
of ashes, coals, dirt, and water.

> **They gather a great pile of twigs and
> grass and set it afire, and when it is
> half coals and ashes they throw a
> quantity of dirt and water on it and mix
> it all together. They make round balls
> of this, which they use instead of stones
> after they are dry, fixing them with the
> same mixture which comes to be like
> stiff clay.**[9]
> —Pedro de Castaneda 1540–41

Inside these walls was sacred space. Here, the people carried on the rituals of everyday living—cooking,
eating, birthing, dying, and invoking the spirits to
guide their paths. "On the walls of the rooms where
we were quartered were many paintings of the demons
they worship as gods," wrote Gaspar Perez de
Villagra. "Fierce and terrible were their features. . . ."

Among the Indian people was the common thread
of knowing that all life is sacred and connected. Food
itself is sacred—imbued with power—and whatever
composes food is to be nurtured and respected, whether animal or plant. And the cycle
continues.

**This corn is my heart and it shall be to
my people as milk from my breasts.**[10]
—Corn Mother, as she planted the first fields

To many Indian people, the trinity of staples (corn, beans, and squash), are known as "The Three Sacred Sisters." In the southwest, corn is the most sacred to physical and cultural survival. Before the Spanish landed, Indian people had developed two to three hundred varieties of corn on the North and South American continents.

In an intricate mythology, corn is both food and a source and symbol of magic and power. In sacred rituals, birth to death, Corn Mother is there. Corn Mother, symbolized by an ear of corn, "maintains the connection between individuals in the tribe as well as the connection between the nonhuman supernaturals and the tribe."[11]

To Keres Pueblo people, Corn Mother is one of three aspects of the great Creatrix. To the northern Arapaho, an ear of corn is regarded as a sacred tribal possession. To the Pawnee, Mother-Corn is Mother-Evening-Star.

Listen to the words of Waheenee, known also as Buffalo Bird Woman, the Hidatsa woman who lived along the banks of the Missouri River in what is now North Dakota. Waheenee was born in 1840. Her own childhood was a metaphor for her people. She grew up in the freedom of working and singing with the women in the corn fields. On the reservation, she had to learn the white ways of farming, where the men were in charge, and the women's voices no longer were heard in the fields.

As a child, Waheenee "liked better to watch the birds than to work." She remembered how families would build "watchers' stages" in their fields. There the young women and girls would watch the corn fields and chase away the crows. The older women would work in the fields and come to the stage and sing.

We cared for our corn in those days, as we would care for a child; for we Indian people loved our fields as

**mothers love their children. We thought
that the corn plants had souls, as
children have souls, and that the
growing corn liked to hear us sing, as
children like to hear their mothers sing
to them.[12]**

But all of that changed. Years later, Buffalo Bird
Woman still heard the women's voices of long ago.

**I cannot forget our old ways. Often in
summer I rise at daybreak and steal out
to the cornfields, and as I hoe the corn
I sing to it, as we did when I was
young. No one cares for our corn songs
now.[13]**

Credit: Carol Claypool,
Heart of the Earth.

Pueblo women bake bread from corn meal in bee-
hive-shaped outdoor ovens called *hornos* (OR-nos).
Sometimes they shape the bread in beautiful symbols
like the squash blossom, an ancient symbol of female
sexuality. Colors of corn and corn meal have meaning:
white and yellow for the female principle, blue and
red for male.

Across the land, the buffalo, deer, antelope, fish,
birds, and bighorn sheep provided meat for food;
hide, sinew, gut, and bone for shelter, clothing, containers, and tools. The women and men fashioned
cooking utensils of wood, stone, bone, and antler;
women wove bowls, bags, and baskets from grass or
bark.

The pots and baskets and jars that held food for

cooking and storing were sacred. The fibers, tree bark, and clay that would make them were to be treated with respect.

Scar on western red cedar north of Trout Lake, Washington on the Gifford Pinchot National Forest bears witness to long-ago basketmaker.

Photo by W.T. Schlick, courtesy Mary Dodds Schlick.

Look at me, friend!
I have come to ask for
    your dress . . .
I have come to beg you
    for this,
Long-Life maker,
For I am going to
    make a basket for
    lily roots out of you.
I pray you, friend,
    not to feel angry
On account of what I
    am going to do
    to you . . .
Keep sickness away
    from me,
So that I may not be
    killed by sickness
    or in war,
O friend![14]
    —from "Prayer to the
        Young Cedar"
            (Kwakiutl)

As the ones who controlled the food supply, Indian women knew many ways to work with materials the earth provided. It was the women who were to do the digging and the cooking in the ground. For men to be in women's cooking space was tabu for many Indian people.[15]

Using hot stones in pits covered with earth, grass, or leaves, the women roasted or steamed meat, fish, and roots. Or they cooked the meat on spits over fire.

Woman clam digging, Scow Bay, Washington.

From the collection of the Jefferson County Historical Society, Port Townsend, Washington #14.012.1.

Plains Indian women cooked food in a "stomach pot," a buffalo stomach suspended like a pouch from four poles, or fitted into a pit. By dropping hot stones in the water-filled pouch, the women could boil water or boil soup. When they were finished cooking, they would hang up the pouch to dry. When the pouch began to leak, they could eat it.

Over the vast prairies, the women with their digging sticks dug from the earth the roots of many plants, especially the camas, a lily with onion-like roots. With their toes, the women dug in swampy earth for the wapato, or swamp potato. They dried and pounded the roots, often with fish, meat, or berries to make a flour or meal to shape into cakes to be dried or baked.

Anna Moore Shaw, a Pima woman of southern Arizona, described how her mother prepared food for winter storage.

Molly's huge storage baskets were filled by the time winter came. Besides wheat, saguaro [Southwestern cactus] syrup, cholla [cactus] fruit, caterpillars, mesquite cakes, parched corn, melon strips, and squash, they contained dried salt bush leaves to flavor winter foods in the cooking pot. Next to the great storage baskets, animal skin bags held the jerky Molly had put up for the winter meals. There was honey for sweetening and salt for seasoning. From the ceiling hung bunches of willow twigs, cattails, and devil's claws for weaving baskets on winter days.[16]

Indian women knew well how to make portable food. Most of them traveled at least part of the year, usually to and from well-established summer camps to winter camps. To make jerky, they dried and smoked meat or fish in thin strips. To make pemmican, they combined dried berries, fish, or meat with melted plant or animal tallow.

Pemmican
Pound dried meat into powder and mix it with dried berries. Put it into a basket or other container. Pour melted plant or animal tallow over the powder and stir it. Let it harden. You can also make sausage by stuffing the mixture into animal intestines.

To the European emigrants and pioneers, much of the food prepared by Indian women seemed bizarre and creepy. Grasshoppers, ants, caterpillars, crickets, locusts, mice, lice, and snakes often went into soup, pemmican, or dried cakes.

Oregon Trail emigrants wondered at the greenish-black lichen that hung like webs from the branches of evergreen trees of the Blue Mountains.

**Then we came upon huge trees from
which hung long clumps of blackish
moss. The Indians call this Spanish
beard. When they have nothing else to
eat they pound up this moss and make
a kind of bread with it.**[17]

The Flathead Indians of Montana enjoyed a "highly prized soup delicacy" of blood soup mixed with
powder from camas and lichen.[18]

From the bark of the cedar, soaked and fringed,
Indian women of the Northwest made skirts. From
animal skins and intestines, bark, and grasses, they
made coats and dresses and hats.

**Twined hat with
traditional design
arrangement of three
triangles at top and
bottom.**

Photo by W.T. Schlick,
courtesy Mary Dodds
Schlick.

In 1851, Harriet Talcott Buckingham's party
encountered "Nez Percies" (the Nez Perce people)
near the Blue Mountains of what is now Oregon. She
described with fascinated detail what she saw.

**The women are all dressed in native
costumes of dressed antelope skins—
fringed & ornamented with moccasins
on their dainty little feet. They came to
see us mounted astride of great sleek
horses, & laugh & chatter among
themselves like just so many gay school
girls. Their long black hair is braided
into two long plaits that hang down &**

> on top of the head is a gay little hat
> shaped like a flower pot—made of
> woven grass—it serves to pick berries
> in or to drink out of, as it holds water
> it being so closely woven. . . . One
> pretty squaw took my knitting & very
> proudly took a few stichs . . ..[19]

As the worlds of Indian and European began to merge, the women who looked with their eyes and their hearts could see that the work of the women was the work of making home and sustaining their people and their community.

It was the hands of the mothers and grandmothers, sisters and daughters and aunts, that planted and dug and ground the roots and seeds of life that nourished the body. It was their hands that wove the fabric of life and the fabric of home.

Remember the Grandmothers. Remember how it was.

> some make potteries
> some weave and spin
> remember
> the Woman/celebrate[20]
> —from "Womanwork" by Paula Gunn
>   Allen (Laguna/Sioux/Lebanese)

Sikyatki, "Shalako Mana" (Corn Maiden), after Tewa design.

Bowl by Carol Claypool, 1994. Photo by author.

CHAPTER THREE

Strong-Hearted Indian Women

I am about to sing this song of yours,
This song of long life.
Sun, I stand here on the earth with
    your song;
Moon, I have come in with your song.[1]
    —from "Puberty Rite Dance Song"
                (Apache)

The spring of a young girl's life was a time of celebration and solemnity. It was a time for showing that she could do the hard work of a woman. It was a time for long periods alone, time to fast, time to raise her voice to the sun and moon and spirits, appealing for help.

Isolation, hard work, singing, dancing, and feasting greeted most girls' journeys into womanhood (and most boys' into manhood). The budding woman often would be confined to a menstrual hut, or "moon hut," or sent away on a spirit quest to fast and wait for messages from spirit helpers.

In Sarah Winnemucca's Paiute tribe, the young woman "is set apart under the care of two of her friends" and sent to a special tipi. For twenty-five days, "three times a day, she must gather, and pile up as high as she can, five stacks of wood." Then she returns to her family lodge for celebration.

A large round cake, baked all night in an earthen oven while songs are sung, celebrates a Navajo girl's womanhood. In the morning, the girl distributes pieces to the people gathered for the ceremony.[2]

Maria Chona, a Papago woman of the Southwest, remembered that when she became a young woman, her mother cut her long hair "so it came just to my shoulders, for we women cannot have hair as long as the men; it would get in our way when we work."[3]

A girl coming into womanhood would learn that she was to stay away from men and their rituals during the time of menstruation. "Girls are very dangerous at that time," said Maria Chona.

"The menstrual taboos were about power, not about sin or filth," explained Paula Gunn Allen, author of *The Sacred Hoop.* That power was so strong that it could stand in the way of a man's power, and that's why a woman had to be careful.

As for the menstrual hut where she was banished, some women deliberately kept the secrets of the cycle from their husbands so they could be "banished" more often.

As Clarissa Pinkola Estes wrote in her book *Women Who Run With the Wolves:*

> **All women know that even if there were such a forced ritual exile, every single woman, to a woman, would, when her time came, leave the village hanging her head mournfully, at least till she was out of sight, and then suddenly break into a jig down the path, cackling all the way.[4]**

The taboo/celebratory attitude toward menstruation reflects an ancient fear and awe of woman's power to procreate. Menstrual power was both taboo and sacred, depending on who held the power. Women, when they held power, used their sexuality to create their own taboos and scare men away. Men, when they held power, used the same taboos to keep women away from their places, and to "prove" that woman's power was evil and therefore to be controlled.

There was no one way of loving and marrying among Indian people, to whom family means kin and clan and community. Women and men often spent more time with their own sex than with the other. Arranged marriages, love marriages, dowry, polygamy—all were ways for women and men to be together depending on what seemed to work best for the community.

In the sacred cycle of life, women used their knowledge of plants for medicine power. As they watched the plants grow and die, tasted and smelled them, and learned from their mothers and grandmothers, they learned the secrets of leaf and bark and root and bud for eating and drinking and for healing.

The roots of the furry cattail relieved diarrhea, sores, and inflammation. Fruit of the evergreen shrub manzanita made cider, flour, tobacco, and remedies for stomach ache, cramps, bronchitis, and dropsy. Tea from a variety of berries eased poison oak infection, cuts, and burns.

Credit: Carol Claypool,
Heart of the Earth.

In my native southwestern Colorado, the shimmering white-barked aspen blankets with gold and crimson whole mountainsides in autumn. But Indian people knew them for more than their surface beauty. They knew the tender buds and seeds as food, that eating the inner bark prevented what we know as scurvy. From the bark, buds, seeds, and leaves, they could relieve pain, fevers, urinary infections, diarrhea, and burns. And, in their rituals, they could smoke the young leaves.[5]

Midwives knew secrets of birth control and abortion, some ancient, and some effective. Indian women of what is now Nevada effectively used the hard seeds of the stoneweed to suppress fertility. From thistles, yarrow, squirrel, seneca, beans, yam, mesquite, and pennyroyal, they made potions to work their magic. Long periods of nursing and abstinence limited pregnancies. Rarely, women resorted to infanticide.

> **Ho! Ye Sun, Moon, Stars, all ye that**
> **move in the heavens,**
> **I bid you hear me!**
> **Into your midst has come a new life.**
> **Consent ye, I implore!**
> **Make its path smooth, that it may**
> **travel beyond the four hills.**[6]
> —from "Prayer for Infants" (Omaha)

When a child was born, the whole community welcomed and cared for it. "We like children, you know," said Maria Chona, the Papago woman. "We talk to them quietly and tell them what to do, but we do not scold."

Mothers made cradle boards for their infants in varying sizes to fit them as they grew. They carried the cradle boards on their backs or propped them up against a tree while they worked, or swung them in the tree branches.

The women filled the bottom of the cradle boards with material like dried moss, rotted or crumbled wood or bark, cattail, powdered buffalo chips, or soft leaves or grasses—the original disposable diapers. When the diaper matter was dirty, the mothers simply threw it away and replaced it. Menstruating women also used many of the same materials.

Washington pioneer Phoebe Judson wrote that her Lummi neighbor Sally's newborn baby "was already strapped to its little baby board and swaddled in a quantity of soft moss, which takes the place of the linen used in civilized life."

> **Old Woman is watching**
> **watching over you**[7]

Many Indian women's lives increased in power and adventure after their child-bearing years. In many tribes, a woman could be a healer, shaman, tribal elder or leader, story teller, or religious leader only after reaching menopause.

In her book, *Life Among the Piutes,* Sarah Winnemucca wrote of the Paiute women's participation in decision making:

> **The women know as much as the men**
> **do, and their advice is often asked. We**
> **have a republic as well as you. The**
> **Council-tent is our congress, and**
> **anybody can speak who has anything to**
> **say, women and all.**[8]

Many tribal leaders (Europeans called them "chiefs") inherited titles through the female line or were chosen by the women's council. Some women became leaders themselves, often after menopause. Few leaders—male or female—had sole power because most tribes had several leaders or sub-leaders, according to their skills.

The people who came into their lands called the women squaws. They didn't know that before the world changed, a squaw was a queen or a lady.

According to Paula Gunn Allen, a sunksquaw was a "hereditary female head of state."

> **Behold, I go forth to move around the earth,**
> **Behold, I go forth to move around the earth,**
> **I go forth as the puma that is great in courage.**[9]
>> —from "A Warrior's Songs from the Mourning Rite" (Osage)

Among some Indian people, women were allowed to be "like a man." Women could dress as men and take on their assigned roles as warriors and protectors. Some were shamans and medicine women. Some were lesbian, some not, and most were respected. One anthropologist identified tribes of California, the Southwest, Northwest, and the Great Basin as the ones most commonly allowing women to be "manly-hearted," "strong-hearted," or warrior women.

The Plains Indians also had warrior women. Since men's status in most of these tribes was much higher than women's in the nineteenth century, a woman who was brave enough to be a warrior was held in especially high esteem.

Many women warriors were past menopause. Strikes Two, a Crow woman, rode into battle at age sixty, armed only with her root digger.[10]

Sarah Winnemucca once rode horseback more than

two-hundred miles in two days to sneak into enemy camp and rescue some of her people captured by the Bannock Indians. As a scout and interpreter in the front lines of battle, Sarah also helped the army defeat the Bannock, the Paiutes' old enemies. Her father named her leader of her people, and white soldiers called her the "Amazonian champion of the army."

Running Eagle of the Blackfeet wore men's leggings into battle, cooked for the men, and mended their moccasins. She led war and buffalo hunting expeditions and sang her war song:

> **Sun, I am not a man**
> **But you gave me this power**
> **to do what I desired**[11]

One night Running Eagle walked into a rival tribe of Flatheads. The sentry, watching for any woman who might be the legendary woman warrior, asked her name. She couldn't answer because she didn't know the language. They shot and killed her.

Crow raiders captured a Gros Ventre child who grew up to become known as Woman Chief of the Crows. An excellent horsewoman, rifle shot, and buffalo hunter, Woman Chief stole enemy horses, led war parties, counted coup (claimed credit for courageous acts of touching enemies in battle), and became known for her bravery in war. She had four wives, "adding to her standing and dignity as a chief; for after successes at war, riches either in horses or women marked the distinction of rank with all prairie tribes."[12]

Whether they were "manly-hearted" women or not, many women actively participated in sports. Sarah Winnemucca wrote that when her people were on their way home after hiding in the mountains from the white people, they celebrated for five days, with dancing, hunting, fishing, singing, and sports. "My people were so happy during the five days. The women ran races, and the men ran races on foot and on horses."

Horse racing, snow sledding, swimming, wrestling, and forms of badminton and hockey were among the women's competitive sports. Often the women and men bet on the winners. Women played several ball games, some as a form of ritual. A contemporary Ojibway woman describes "Throwing the Ball" as wisdom-gathering.[13]

Papago women of the Southwest loved to play double ball, a game played by opposing sides with hooked sticks and two balls attached by a string. Women would travel from village to village looking for competition, neglecting their household duties. Mission nuns periodically confiscated and burned the women's beloved game balls.

Many women and men gambled, sometimes for high stakes. Maria Chona told about winning a foot race with a woman who already had lost her red dress and Mexican scarf, then bet her sleeping mat, a basket, and a big winter jar. "I heard her crying that night in the desert, because she had lost everything."

Gambling and games often had a sacred aspect, connected with the whimsies of the spirits. Many games involving animal spirits could be played only in the winter when the animals slept. Remember playing the "cat's cradle" game with string as a child? Its roots are in an ancient sacred game of the Navajo people.

> **Spider Woman and Spider Man exhale webs to hold back the waters during emergence. Spider Woman teaches weaving and cat's cradle; the discipline and thought/breath required in both the craft and the game constitutes continual, ritual re-creation of cosmic**

**and human harmony. . . . Navajos
protect spiders and rub their webs on
girl babies' hands and arms so they will
learn to weave without tiring."**[14]

The re-creation of cosmic and human harmony was
in every part of their lives. I saw and felt it as I
descended the ladder into the reconstructed semi-
underground ceremonial lodge or kiva at the Kuaua
pueblo in New Mexico.

**Inside Kuaua kiva replica,
Coronado State Monument,
Bernalillo, New Mexico.
Museum of New Mexico,
Santa Fe.**

Photos by author.

**No Girls Allowed—Except If
Bringing Food**

From the time I was a kid scrambling on ladders
down into kivas and up into the cliff dwellings of
Mesa Verde near my home in Durango, Colorado, I
understood that the kiva was the men's place. Women
weren't to go there—sort of like the boys' tree house
with the "No Girls Allowed" sign. Since then I've seen
kiva-like ceremonial lodges in many parts of the
world.

Like the women in the moon huts, the men often
would stay there for a long time. At the Kuaua pueblo,

the young men lived in the kiva, which the Spaniards called the *estufa.*

The womb-like ceremonial lodge is a place for connecting body with spirit, earth with sky, male with female. The men believed they needed special help to make this connection. Women, through menstruation and child birth, already had this spiritual link. That's why women often didn't enter the "boys' club"— because they didn't need to. At the Kuaua pueblo, women could enter, however, if they were bringing food.

Lakota activist Russell Means explains that "indigenous peoples worldwide began to develop their ceremonies so that the men would come into balance with the female, because she is in rhythm with the universe, capable of creating life itself."

Credit: Carol Claypool,
Heart of the Earth.

The sweat lodge, which men heated with steam from water poured over hot rocks, is a "sacred purification lodge," Means says. "It's a man's ceremony so that we can become in balance with the female. It represents the womb, and you're reborn when you come out of the purification lodge. You start again, spiritually clean."[15]

In the soft light of the Kuaua pueblo kiva, I slowly turn around, mesmerized. The ladder symbolically links the world above with the world below. The small hole in the floor leads to the underworld. The altar stands behind it.

Painted on the walls all around are murals of skirted, mythical human-like figures and sacred symbols, painted in blue, gold, red, black, and white. The figures, according to *Book of the Hopi,* represent journeys of Hopi clans and of the sacred girl and boy

Replicas of Kuaua murals, Coronado State Monument, Bernalillo, New Mexico.

Museum of New Mexico, Santa Fe. Photo by author.

twins. Most figures are in the form of Kachina (or Katcina) dancers, who wear skirts "to honor womanhood and acknowledge the female roles in their society," according to Michael Claypool.

> O our Mother the Earth, O our Father
>   the Sky,
> Your children are we, and with tired
>   backs
> We bring you the gifts you love.
> Then weave for us a garment of
>   brightness;
> May the warp be the white light of
>   morning,
> May the weft be the red light of
>   evening,
> May the fringes be the falling rain,
> May the border be the standing
>   rainbow.
> Thus weave for us a garment of
>   brightness,
> That we may walk fittingly where birds
>   sing,
> That we may walk fittingly where grass
>   is green,
> O our Mother the Earth, O our Father
>   the Sky.[16]
>
> —Song of the Sky Loom (Tewa)

The most mysterious figure on the kiva wall represents Qaletaqa, or Kwa-Taka, the traditional Hopi guardian.

The macaw mask and form of the entire figure represent the SKY FATHER, whose all-seeing eye beholds everything that transpires. The scalloped skirt represents water and thus bespeaks rain necessary for the fructification of the earth, while the dun-colored garment itself symbolizes the EARTH MOTHER.[17]

The mediating figure, often represented as Sky Father/Earth Mother, is central to Indian people's spirituality. The mediator links earth and sky, male and female, the spiritual and the temporal.

In some tribes, important mediating figures were men the French called *berdaches.* These "men-women" or "two-moon men" dressed as women and took on women's assigned role. Often, they were medicine men or shamans. They did not fit the standard definitions of transvestite or homosexual, though many were. They were more like a third sex—between the strict roles and expectations of male and female.

When we encounter a man singing or weaving or spinning with the women, or a symbol of both male and female, it may be a clue that here is the man-woman tradition.

Maria Chona spoke affectionately of Shining Evening of her clan.

> **We girls used to spend all day with that man-woman, Shining Evening. She went off with us to gather plants and she could carry more than any of us and dig longer. She ground corn with us, all taking turns at my mother-in-law's grinding slab. . . .**
>
> **Shining Evening was good to me . . .. She was stronger than we women and when I was tired she carried my baby for me. No man could do that; it would not be right. Shining Evening was a great help.[18]**

The man-woman tradition seemed to be strongest in the tribes where women were most respected. The tradition was weakest where women and women's power were most feared and subordinated.

Until European contact, men-women generally were respected as special, sacred people with extraordinary spiritual powers. Europeans, beginning with the Spanish, were horrified with the "perversion" they saw. Some Europeans tortured men-women as "sodomites" and pointed to the "evil" practice to justify extermination of the Indian people.[19]

The Navajo word for man-woman is *nadle,* meaning "changing one" or "one who is transformed." In Omaha, it is *mexoga,* meaning "instructed by the moon." The Lakota Sioux *winkte,* roughly translated, means "one who becomes woman."

"From the beginning of the world," said a Mohave elder, "it was meant that there should be [men-women], just as it was instituted that there should be shamans. They were intended for that purpose."[20]

The shaman mediated between the human and the spirit world through his or her own journey of the spirit-soul. The journey was like the cycle of seasons of life—birth, life, death, rebirth.

Two universal symbols, the spiral and the labyrinth, represent aspects of the shamanic journey,

and both symbols connect with the kiva, where many shamanic rituals took place.

When the U.S. government took over Indian lands, it banned traditional rituals, songs, and dances. The Indian people saw their dreams dying. And they began to dance. All across the western lands, they danced the Ghost Dance, based on an ancient Northwest prophet dance. It was said that anyone wearing a sacred Ghost Dance shirt could not be harmed. It was said that if they kept dancing, the Messiah would return with their dead ancestors, the buffalo would return, and the lands would be restored.

> My children,
> When at first I like the whites,
> I gave them fruits,
> I gave them fruits.
>
> Father have pity on me,
> I am crying for thirst,
> All is gone,
> I have nothing to eat.
>
> I'yehe! my children —
> My children,
> We have rendered them desolate.
> The whites are crazy—Ahe'yuhe'yu!
>
> We shall live again,
> We shall live again.[21]
> > —from "A Sequence of Songs of the
> > Ghost Dance Religion"

Tension over the forbidden dance fed the flames that erupted in 1890 at Wounded Knee on the Pine Ridge Reservation in South Dakota. There, cavalrymen shot down an estimated 150 men, women, and children. Some of those cavalrymen received the Medal of Honor for what they did at Wounded Knee.

> **A people's dream died there. It was a beautiful dream. . . . the nation's hoop is broken and scattered. There is no center any longer, and the sacred tree is dead.**[22]
> —Black Elk, remembering Wounded Knee

> **He dreamed that a strange race had woven a spider's web all around the Lakotas, and he said, when this happens you shall live in square gray houses and you shall starve.**[23]
> —Black Elk's grandfather's dream

The lives of the people come to us only through a filter of time and interpretation and lost language and memory. How can we know who these people were and how they lived before the coming of the Europeans, before the coming of disease and chaos and dying?

Imagine the North American continent with communities of millions of people on the land, thousands of small bands, tribes, some city-sized communities.

The coming of the Europeans brought diseases that invaded water supplies and camp sites, and traveled with trappers, traders, and with the Indians themselves. Smallpox, plague, typhus, influenza, malaria, measles, yellow fever, and venereal disease killed millions.

Estimates of pre-contact native populations range from nine million to an astounding 120 million. Based on archeological evidence, the most currently accepted figure is that forty to fifty million native Indian people lived on the North American continent. This is according to archeologist Kathleen O'Neal Gear, co-author of the *First North Americans* series. Up to ninety percent of the Indian people died within one-hundred years at each point of contact, mostly of European diseases, according to Gear. We will never know the real numbers, or the depth of disruption caused by the coming of the Europeans.

The riding horse, introduced by the Spanish from the South and the French from the North, dramatically changed many Indians' ways. The horse increased mobility, increased the spread of disease, and propelled some agricultural peoples into migratory patterns.

The coming of the horse had devastating effects on the lives of most Plains Indian women. In the space of less than one-hundred years, the horse enhanced men's status and diminished women's.

With his horse, a man could go farther and bring in more meat. Since it was the woman's work to tan and cure the hides, her work increased. Horse stealing and war-making increased. As mythical, romanticized images of the warrior and hunter grew, so did the status of hunters and warriors. "The myths themselves reflect the heightened emphasis on male domination and concurrent loss of female power that accompanied the social and economic revolution brought by the use of horses."[24]

Polygamy also increased with horses. A man's horses and ability to hunt game increased his wealth. He needed more wives to do the work, and could afford them.

Some pre-contact American Indian practices were anything but peaceful: slavery, war, human sacrifice (rare, but real), and persecution of witches or others perceived as dangerous to the community. Some tribes took defeated enemies as slaves. Especially prized were female slaves because of the work they could do and the children they could bear. In some culture groups, men would raid other tribes and kidnap young women for their wives. We don't know the extent of these practices before the Europeans came, or how they changed because of the disruption caused by the invasion.

The coming of Europeans changed forever a way of life that was never perfect, but one that provided more balance and understanding of the people's places in the world than the ones that supplanted it.

> **Spanish civilization crushed the Indian; English civilization scorned and neglected him; French civilization embraced and cherished him.**
> —Francis Parkman

Although it wasn't that simple, nineteenth-century historian Francis Parkman was right in his observation that different groups of early incoming Europeans had different agendas for the people who were already there.

One could say that the Spanish conquistadors tended to see the Indians as workers and slaves while the French and, to an extent, the British, saw them as potential trading and marriage partners. Missionaries viewed them as converts and emigrants from "The States" regarded them as impediments. The Indian people were all these things to those who came into their lands. But never were they regarded as equal, as co-creators of mutual destinies.

Early trappers and traders, many of whom were French, Scot, British, and Spanish, saw many advantages to living with Indian people. Many owed their lives and fortunes to Indian women who lived with them, some as legal wives. The Indian women knew the ways of survival and caring for furs and other trade items. Mixed-race metis to the north, and mestizos to the south changed old cultures and formed new ones.

Pioneer men often either brought their families or

planned to send for them. Most had no intention of bonding their lives to the people who already were there. Pioneer women, who desperately needed help, often saw the Indian people as useful servants. Many believed the Indians would be better off working for them and learning Anglo ways.

> **During our residence in Olympia peace reigned throughout the territory. The Indians were finally subjugated. . . . The women learned to wash, clean house and do garden work. They made very useful servants for the white settlers, and were usually the only help obtainable in those days.**[25]
> —Phoebe Judson, Washington Territory

As more Anglo immigrants came into the country, their journals reflected their cultures' prejudices against the Indians. In their need to set themselves apart from the Indians, men and women repeatedly referred to them as lazy and dirty and "nauseous-smelling creatures [emphasis added]."

But they had little understanding of what they were seeing. They were seeing through the lenses of their own culture. And they were witnessing many people who were dying or mourning their dead.

> **I am on the way, traveling the road to where the spirits live, at Shipap.**
> . . .
> **When a cloud comes this way, you will say, 'That is he!' When I get to the place of spirits, I will hear everything you ask. You must always remember me.**[26]
> —from "Song of a Child's Spirit"
> (Santo Domingo)

As they mourned their children, their loved ones, they would wail and cut their hair, and sometimes cut their skin. They would smear themselves with dirt or wear old ragged clothing.

Missionaries, trappers, and pioneers persisted in describing American Indian women as inferior, exploited slaves of men. They saw the women chopping wood, transporting heavy loads, building houses, and harvesting crops. They called the Indian women slaves of men, conveniently ignoring the fact that pioneer women had few legal rights, and most worked longer hours and lived shorter lives than the men.

Missionaries, Catholic and Protestant, believed their sacred duty was to convert the "heathen" Indian men and women into proper Christians. Some even believed Indian extinction to be justified to make way for those "destined" to occupy western lands. More than one minister told his people that the "hand of Providence" was removing the Indians to make room for a "more worthy" people.

Missionaries told the women they must no longer practice their magic to heal. They must not talk about the Grandmothers if they are to go to this place in the sky they call heaven. Their people must stay in one place and not follow the seasonal round of food harvest and production. Now the men, not the women, must plant and harvest. The women must sew.

"When an Indian woman ceases to do a man's work, she learns the household arts," reported one Oregon missionary approvingly. "It is an interesting sight to see her seated upon the ground with a child on each side whom she is teaching to sew."[27]

Those who came into the land of She Who Watches had been told the "squaws" were unclean, uncivilized, promiscuous. They were what True Women were not supposed to be. They had dark skin, sometimes dressed immodestly, often lived on the ground, worked outside, made and transported their houses, and dug in the earth for their food. The pioneers, in their struggles with the land and the elements, had to believe they were more enlightened and more civilized than the "heathens," who would be better off if only they became civilized.

Yet many pioneers—especially the women— changed their attitudes toward the Indians as they lived side by side with them and even came to rely on them. Many expressed gratitude and admiration as their familiarity increased. Many owed their survival to the Indians who showed them how to live on the land and gave or traded desperately-needed food.

> **[An Indian woman] told me the Indians were getting ready to fight the whites. . . . Usually an Indian woman told the whites when the men were preparing for war. I think they preferred peace to war.**[28]
>
> —Martha Gay Masterson, Oregon

> **The Indians were mighty good to the whites when we came here. They used to bring us clams, salmon, game, and big bladders of whale oil for our lamps.**[29]
>
> —Rhoda Quick Johnson, Oregon

Women were more likely to see the commonalities they shared with Indian people they encountered, while clutching to their convictions of superiority. Phoebe Judson, an early pioneer in Washington Territory, wrote of her Indian neighbors:

> **In all my experiences with the Indians, I have never known of an offensive word or act offered to a white woman. They were so respectful and solicitous of my comfort, appearing more like innocent children than adults, that I was never afraid to travel alone with them.**[30]
>
> —Phoebe Judson, Washington Territory

Anglo men were more likely to stick to their ideas of who Indians were: not-to-be trusted hellions meant to be conquered. I sometimes wonder if the men, no matter the race or tribe, had been closer to tending the ordinary food-in-the-mouth, dirty-bottom, skin-to-skin survival, perhaps they too would have built stronger bonds with people with whom they shared the same physical needs.

Sarah Winnemucca wrote that when she was a child, "a whole band of white people perished in the mountains, for it was too late to cross them."

> **We could have saved them, only my people were afraid of them. We never knew who they were, or where they came from. So, poor things, they must have suffered fearfully, for they all starved there. The snow was too deep.**[31]

The women cried for their lost people. They cried for the old ways. Washington Territory pioneer Phoebe Judson wrote about Polly, an Indian woman, "recalling the bygone days."

> **Presently she raised her voice in mournful wails of sorrow, and continued to utter her cries of grief for an hour or more. . . . This lovely valley had been her father's favorite camping ground. Here, a little child, she had played with her brothers and sister. This valley had been covered with her father's ponies. A trap in the creek supplied them with an abundance of salmon and trout, and here she had, as a wife and mother, passed many happy years. Now they were all gone and she was a lonely 'lummai' (old woman), obliged to pack for a living.**
>
> **Poor old Polly! My heart went out in sympathy for the poor lonely old soul.**[32]

So much was lost. So many lives and souls and
friendships. So many opportunities to learn from one
another, to co-create a way of living that would have
benefitted all.

But working together would have depended on
government policies different from the ones that supported Indian subjugation, removal to reservations,
and even extinction. And working together would
have required the full participation of women.

> **If women could go into your Congress I
> think justice would soon be done to the
> Indians.**
> —Sarah Winnemucca

But Anglo women had no voice in Congress, and
little voice in their own families. And Indian women
were losing their power with increasing Anglo presence.

As the old ways disappeared, Indian women lost
their ancient voice in their councils and communities.
They lost the power to trade, to grow food and control
its distribution. They lost the power to divorce and to
keep their own property and their own children.

> **A nation can not be conquered
> Until the hearts of its women
> Are on the ground.
> Then it is done,
> No matter how brave its warriors
> Nor how strong its weapons.**
> —Traditional Cheyenne saying

The Indian people were colonized by the taking of
their lands and their buffalo and their knowledge of
how to live on the land, and the power of the women,
so that Indian women—and men—were left dependent, like Anglo women.

After she had helped the U.S. Army defeat the
Bannock Indians, Sarah Winnemucca saw that there
was no reward for her people.

"Oh, Major! My people will never believe me again," she cried when she learned that her people would be forced to march hundreds of miles north in winter to the Yakama reservation in what is now Washington state.

On that march Sarah Winnemucca watched hungry children die in the biting cold, and saw her sister, Mattie, weaken. At the reservation, the Paiute were penned up "like horses and cattle," with no heat and rags to wear. And there, Mattie died. "Oh, how she did suffer before she died! And I was left all alone."

The woman now known as "the Amazonian champion of the army" went to Washington, D.C., and won the hearts of the eastern elite as the "Indian princess" pleading for justice for her people. But she could not win back her people's land. She died when she was not yet fifty years old. Her fear of the people her beloved grandfather had told her to love had turned to bitter disappointment. The women had lost their power. Her people had lost their power.

Sarah Winnemucca wrote in her book, *Life Among the Piutes:*

> Oh, for shame! . . . Yes, you, who call
> yourselves the great civilization; you
> who have knelt upon Plymouth Rock,
> covenanting with God to make this land
> the home of the free and the brave. Ah,
> then you rise from your bended knees
> and seizing the welcoming hands of
> those who are the owners of this land,
> which you are not, your carbines rise
> upon the bleak shore, and your so-
> called civilization sweeps inland from
> the ocean wave; . . . leaving in its
> pathway marked by crimson lines of
> blood, and strewed by the bones of two
> races, the inheritor and the invader;
> and I am crying out to you for justice,—
> yes, pleading . . . for the dusky

**mourner, whose tears of love are
pleading for her husband, or for their
children, who are sent far away from
them. . . .**[33]

Sarah Winnemucca's angry courage stayed with
her people, and in the 1940s they recovered some of
their Nevada land, where many of her people remain.

She Who Watches blinks. The Squaws, the
Grandmothers, are watching. They weave their healing patterns, connecting past and present and future,
woman with woman, man with man, woman with
man, community with children, people with people.

Lillian Pitt

When contemporary Oregon artist Lillian Pitt
began her work in clay, she searched her soul and her
surroundings for authentic images that would express
her self and offer respect to her people.

But she felt lost. "I knew I needed to find out who
I am," she says.

Lillian went to the grandmothers. They told her
that her people's houses used to hug the river's edge
beneath the rocks where She Who Watches gazes over
the Columbia River. Lillian had seen the beautiful,
strong image of She Who Watches. But she had to go
see her up on the rocks.

"I went around the bend, and there she was in all her magnificent glory," Lillian remembers. "I had a profound sense of identity when I saw her and I thought, 'I know who I am now.'

"Many people don't know their heritage. When people know their past, they can know more of their future and have a sense of direction."

Lillian Pitt has since produced more than 5000 masks—most of clay, some of bronze. And she has made more images of She Who Watches than any other artist. Her images are strong and beautiful, like She Who Watches. They capture the spirits of her people's stories, their history.

In one of her latest pieces, Lillian made hundreds of small clay images of She Who Watches to honor the salmon. "If we make enough She Who Watches maybe the salmon will come back," she says.

And if we listen enough to She Who Watches, maybe we will hear the shared voices of all our people.

> **Old Woman is watching**
> **Watching over you**
> > **In the darkness of the storm**
> > **she is watching**
> > **watching over you**
>
> > **weave and mend**
> > **weave and mend**
> > **. . .**
> > **I have been searching**
> > **Old Woman**
>
> > **and I find her**
> > **in**
> > **mySelf**[34]
> **—from** *Daughters of Copper Woman*

CHAPTER FOUR

Westward I Go Free?

You cannot know the perfect freedom
and independence that characterizes all
our relations. Society if it exists at all
is freed from the multitude of
prejudices and embarrassments and
exactions that control the Eastern
cities.[1]
> —John McCrackan, lawyer, California

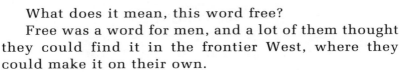

Free:
Ease or facility of doing
    anything, as, he speaks
    or acts with *freedom.*
Being at liberty.
Unconstrained, unrestrained, not under
    compulsion or control; as, a man is
    free to pursue his own choice.
> —Webster's Dictionary

What does it mean, this word free?

Free was a word for men, and a lot of them thought they could find it in the frontier West, where they could make it on their own.

Westward I go free.

> **Free:**
> **Not subject to the rule or control of**
>   **another.**
> **Subject only to fixed laws, made by**
>   **consent.**
> **Invested with franchises.**
> **Not subject to the arbitrary will of a**
>   **sovereign or lord; as, a *free* state,**
>   **nation, or people.**
> **Liberated from the government or**
>   **control of parents or of a guardian or**
>   **master, as, a son or an apprentice,**
>   **when of age, is *free*.**
>   —Webster's Dictionary (1953)

When a young American man reached the age of twenty-one, the women of the family would present him with a freedom quilt they had made to celebrate his liberation from the family and his freedom to make his way in the world. There was no such freedom celebration for women.

I don't recall a woman saying she was going westward to be free.

Of the women who journeyed westward to the frontier, most went because their husbands did, and the law decreed that the husband would determine where home was.

> **Beloved sister:**
>   **I have seated myself for the purpose**
> **of writing a few lines to you to inform**
> **you that we are all well as usual**
> **excepting I am pretty much tired out a**
> **fixing for California we expect to start**
> **next monday . . . it looks like a great**
> **undertaking to me but Clifton was**
> **bound to go and I thought I would go**
> **rather than stay here alone with the**
> **children . . ..[2]**
>   —Martha S. Read, Norwich, NY, 1852

But to go westward to be free?

Free was men's language. When applied to women, the word free just didn't come out sounding right.

> **Free:**
> **Immoderate; unrestrained;**
> **inconsiderate; going beyond due limits**
> **in writing or speaking; as, she was too**
> *free* **in her behavior.**

In the nineteenth century, free was something women were not supposed to be. It was rather like the sardonic observation of a character in Ursula Le Guin's novel *Searoad:* "I guess we think when a woman's free she's wrong."

In eastern "civilized" society, where most frontier women came from, women were expected to be dependent, not independent. They were to be married and follow their husbands' dreams, not their own. Women were supposed to be pious, pure, domestic, and submissive—the four virtues of what came to be called the Cult of True Womanhood, defined by Barbara Welter in her classic 1966 essay of the same name.

The True Woman's proper role, as man's moral superior, was to civilize the world and man, woman's intellectual superior. Without the True Woman virtues, according to Welter, "no matter whether there was fame, achievement or wealth, all was ashes. With them she was promised happiness and power." If happiness was not there, it was her own fault; she just wasn't doing it right. Besides, it was her lot in life to suffer. Deliverance would be in heaven.

Mary Richardson was twenty-two, a teacher, and trying to be a True Woman. Her problem was that she also was smart, ambitious, and what might be described as proud. No wonder she couldn't figure out her life's direction.

> **But I have been thinking to day that the**
> **ties that bind me to earth can never be**

> **weaker than they seem now. It seems to
> me that I do no good in the world. . . . I
> can think of nothing that is worth
> living for. . . .**[3]

Mary's problem was that she wanted to be free. By the time she was twenty-five, she had devised a plan.

> **By night and by day I scarcely think of
> any thing but becoming a missionary. I
> think I feel more engaged in religion
> than I have ever befor. At least I have
> more freedom in prayer May God grant
> that I may not mistake the path of duty.**
> —Mary Richardson, Maine, 1833

Excited, she applied to the American Board of Commissioners for Foreign Missions to become a missionary. In her application, Mary confessed to having "an aspiring mind," but, ladylike, she assured the Board that hoped to cultivate "a spirit of humility: to be willing to do some thing and be nothing if duty required."

They turned her down. Women must be married to go on a mission.

Mary was at a crossroads. She had an offer of marriage from a farmer who was a decent man. But he

Mary Richardson Walker

Courtesy Eastern Washington State
Historical Society, Cheney Cowles
Museum, Spokane, WA #L94-9.87

wasn't the missionary sort and she would have to give up her dream of being a missionary in order to marry him.

> **Ought I to bid adieu to all my cherished hopes and unite my destiny with that of a mear farmer with little education and no refinement. In a word shall I to escape the horrors of perpetual celibacy settle down with the vulger I cannot do it.**

Enter Elkanah Walker, a Christian man, also burning to be a missionary. He needed a wife to go with him and asked her to be the one. Here was the answer to her prayers. Mary wasn't sure she could love him, nor he love her, but she decided to marry him. If it was Mary's destiny to be a missionary, it was her duty to marry Elkanah Walker. "[C]oncluded the path of duty must prove the path of peace."

In a letter to "W" expressing her concerns, she confessed she liked to "tread a devious path," the path of learning and ambition.

For Elkanah, this would never do. He responded with his recommendations on what she should study and how she should behave in order to be worthy of him.

> **You speak of attending some study. I would rather recommend to you to read some good book in Female Education & some more refined authors. You need more of refinement than you do of solid sciences. You have the foundation well laid. All you need is a little more finishing to make you an honor to your sex & a worthy prize to your intended.**

Trying to reconcile her duty to please him with her wish to "retain [her] personal identity," Mary wrote:

> **I will always try to improve myself—for your sake, my dear E. I could wish myself beautiful as houris (sic) and graceful as Venus. But I never did. . . . When I intended to be an old maid one consolation I had was that it was nobody's business whether I was lovely or not.**

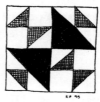

The wedding day, March 5, 1838, arrived. Dressed in black, her mind full of "thunder showers," Mary Richardson married Elkanah Walker, despite her misgivings.

A week later, she wrote ominously:

> **Nothing gives me such a solitary feeling as to be called Mrs. Walker. It would sound so sweet to have some one now and then call [me] Mary or by mistake say Miss Richardson. But that one expression Mrs. W. seems at once to indicate a change unlike all other changes. . . . The name W. seems to me to imply a severed branch. Such I feel myself to be. . . .**

A month after the wedding, Mr. and Mrs. Elkanah Walker set off from Missouri on horseback with three other couples for a mission among the "heathen" Indians in Oregon Country. Mary, by then a month pregnant, would be among the first white women to cross the Rocky Mountains.

Mary Richardson Walker tried to be free within nineteenth century expectations of what women were supposed to be. "May God help me walk discretely, do right and please my husband." But women were not supposed to be free and Mary was wrong.

Through the dangerous, beautiful, fearsome two thousand mile journey, Mary was fascinated by plants and minerals she wanted to examine. But ladies were not to mount and dismount their horses by themselves. So she had to observe from a distance the intimate world she longed to explore.

In the years that followed, Mary helped her husband establish a mission in what is now Washington. Her dream of teaching and ministering to the Indians got lost in caring for the eight children she would bear. Their mission ended after the massacre of neighboring missionaries Narcissa and Marcus Whitman.

Mary tried to please her God and her husband, and to protect the purity of her thoughts and her home. She expected appreciation and affection in return. She tried so hard, but judging from the journals into which she emptied her heart, she believed she failed at all she was supposed to be and do.

If I stir it is forwardness, if I am still, it is inactivity. I keep trying to please but sometimes I feel it is no use. I am almost certain more is expected of me than can be had of one woman.

I some times feel discouraged & fear I shall never do anything to benefit the heathen & might as well have stayed at home.

For the Mary Richardson Walkers who tried to be True Women, there was no promised happiness, no dreamed-of freedom. In fact, there was no such thing as a True Woman. No human being could possibly have lived up to the expectations of True Womanhood. It was a masquerade.

**But I am too often treated as tho my
convenience & wishes were not to be
regarded. The thought often occurs, I
am glad my friends do not witness &
can never know it.**

In her forties, Mary Richardson Walker even
doubted her faith. "Fear my heart is not right & I do
not love God cincerly but serve him through fear."

In the next two years were two sad entries: "Am
loosing my reckoning. Have so much to do find no
time to report."

"How I wish, wish, wish."

Wish what? Having failed at the impossible job of
being both the True Woman she was supposed to be
and the free woman she longed to be, she hardly knew
herself what she wished.

Old age brought Mary Richardson Walker resigna-
tion and retreat into insanity. Perhaps there she found
some kind of freedom.

**Free:
Not subject to the rule or control of
    another.
Subject only to fixed laws, made by
    consent.
Invested with franchises.
Not subject to the arbitrary will of a
    sovereign or lord; as, a free state,
    nation, or people.**

In the mid-nineteenth century, when wagons began
moving westward and ships landed on the west coast
unloading passengers seeking freedom and riches,
women were subject to laws made without their con-
sent. They were not invested with franchises, and
most, if married, were subject to the arbitrary will of
their husbands, who decided where the family would
live, had sole custody of any children, owned any
property and money, even money made by the women.

The Cult of True Womanhood grew out of the chaos of the nineteenth century. The industrial revolution disrupted families and farms and produced periodic booms and depressions. Epidemics of illness and violence and a great civil war marched across the hills and valleys, reaping death and sorrow and confusion.

Amid the turmoil, the center of economics and activities were moving away from the family-centered farm, where women played a central role. A separate work place and cash-based economy was taking men away from the home, separating the worlds of men and women.

Out of the chaos, aided by a wave of evangelism, grew a stricter set of rules and beliefs than they had known. The rules began in part as a practical reaction to a changing world. But they became an obsession, and evolved into a cult-like set of elaborate prescriptions for the behavior of men, and especially for women.

Women were to be everything men were not. Men's sphere was the public one, women's the private one. Men were thinking, women emotional. Men's work was outside the home, women's inside. Men were to be the doers, the initiators, and women the followers.

The Cult of Individualism propelled men away— away from home, away from security, away from rules and women and community. The Cult of Individualism meant male freedom. The Cult of True Womanhood meant female restriction, a cage of rules directing women away from freedom and into dependency.

A True Woman was to remain anonymous, silent, and home. Her name was to be in the paper three times: when she was born, married, and died (the last as Mrs. Husband).

Oregon pioneer Phoebe Newton was mighty proud that "I have been here . . . for more than sixty-five years and I have never done anything yet to get my name in the papers."[4]

In a complex web, the Cult of True Womanhood wove its threads through every facet of a woman's life to make sure she behaved as "Nature" intended. Many women supported and aspired to True Womanhood, believing that there they would find happiness, and safety from criticism.

Instant Experts, especially preachers and doctors, inflamed the Cult. Songs, sermons, stories, novels, medical books, and women's magazines contained detailed instructions on how to behave, how to act, dress, sew, love, speak, laugh, eat, pray, clean, wash dishes, care for children, faint, set a table, listen, go on a picnic, sleep, dream, wake up, stand, sit, wash clothes, hold a parasol or a fan, obey, prepare food, serve, care for the sick, walk, smile, and think. The True Woman received instructions on how to please everyone. Everyone but herself.

If the instructions didn't fit the reality of women's lives, the Priests of the Cult of True Womanhood would impose it, for, as Plato instructed, "Passion must be ruled by philosophers."

Experts—the "philosophers"—used sacred text, fear, science, and flattery to convince women of the "naturalness" and truth of the Cult. They delivered a wealth of wisdom to teach women that their only true mission—and protection—was to bring order to society through childlike obedience, self-denial, and religious practice.

> **Let the woman learn in silence with all subjection. But I suffer not a woman to teach, nor to usurp authority over the man, but to be in silence.**
> —Paul the Apostle, I Timothy: 2, 11

Woman has a head almost too small for intellect but just big enough for love.[5]
—1848 text book

The man bears rule over his wife's person and conduct. She bears rule over his inclinations; he governs by law; she by persuasion. . . . The empire of the woman is an empire of softness. . . . her commands are caresses, her menaces are tears.[6]
—from "Matrimony," The Lady's Amaranth II, 1838

[Woman's] great mission is self-denial . . .. She is to rear all under her care to lay up treasures, not on earth, but in heaven.[7]
—Catharine Beecher and Harriet Beecher Stowe

Religion is exactly what a woman needs, for it gives her that dignity that best suits her dependence.[8]
—Caleb Atwater, Esq.

Yours it is to determine whether the beautiful order of society . . . shall continue as it has been . . . [or whether] society shall break up and become a chaos of disjointed and unsightly elements.[9]
—Rev. Mr. Stearns

In truth, woman, like children, has but one right and that is the right to protection. The right to protection involves the obligation to obey.[10]
—George Fitzhugh, defender of slavery and the Cult of Domesticity

Drawing from Biblical and classical tradition, the Experts spun fantastic tales to prove that women must be controlled. Women who were "naturally" weak and mild were also "naturally" in danger of falling under the influence of the devil if they didn't conform to True Woman rules. As one preacher sagely explained this seeming contradiction, a woman is "a dunghill covered with flowers."[11]

Experts reminded women that they bore the guilt of Eve, who was tempted by the devil and brought evil into the world. All women were, of course, capable of committing Eve's sin of disobedience in seeking for herself the forbidden fruit of the tree of knowledge.

A perfect God made [Eve] a perfect woman, to be the companion of a perfect man, in a perfect home, and her entire nature vibrated in accord with the beauty and song of Paradise. But she rebelled against God's government, and with the same hand with which she plucked the fruit she launched upon the world the crimes, the wars, the tumults, that have set the universe a-wailing.[12]
                —Rev. T. De Witt Talmage, D.D.

**How sad by state our nature is
Our sin bow deep it stains
And Satan binds our captive souls
Fast in his slavish chains.**
                —Old Methodist hymn

In written and spoken sermons, even in songs, women and girls were warned against self-indulgent pleasures like dancing.

> **No, my folks wouldn't let me go to dances. They held that the devil was in the fiddle and that if a girl danced, she was dancing her way to hell.**[13]
> —Catherine Thomas Morris,
> Oregon immigrant, 1849

Dancing was a favorite entertainment on the frontier. Those who believed dancing to be a sin got around it with the Midwestern custom of "play parties," where participants merely pantomimed movements to sung instructions. Many on the frontier, though, made up their own rules and decided that they may as well call what they were doing dancing.

Birth control and abortion, according to the Experts, were twin evils practiced only by "loose" or "free" women. Dr. William Goodell wrote about these two "sins"

> **which defile every class of society—sins which, like the plague of the frogs, creep into our houses . . ... To these detestable practices do I attribute, in a great measure, the general ill health of our women . . . and . . . much, if not most, of the wretchedness and misery of this land.**[14]

Women who listened to the Experts lived in constant fear that they would say a bad word, show a bare limb, be in the wrong place, do the wrong thing, and fall off their pedestal into the abyss with the devil. If a woman felt sad, angry, or depressed, it was the work of the devil. If she didn't want more children, she was a bad woman. Did she want to be by herself for a while, have some fun? It was her evil nature. Did she feel like yelling at her husband? The devil again. Was she lonely out there in the middle of that prairie, with nothing but the wind and crying children to listen to? It was her fault.

> **I was very wicked all day both in thought and deed. I do believe that I was possessed of an evil spirit that day if such things are (which I think there is no doubt as to the theory).[15]**
> —Carrie Williams, Sierra mining town,
> 1858

> **Ever thing looks dull to me I cannot look on the bright side for their appears to be no bright because I am naughty and ever thing else appears so to . . .[16]**
> —America Rollins Butler,
> Oregon Territory, 1853

Elinore Pruitt Stewart, alone with her daughter after the men had left for a roundup, "kept wanting to go *somewhere.*"

> **I got reckless and determined to do something real bad. So I went down to the barn and saddled Robin Adair, placed a pack on 'Jeems McGregor,' then Jerrine [her daughter] and I left for a camping-out expedition.[17]**
> —Elinore Pruitt Stewart, Wyoming, 1909

Mary Richardson Walker blamed herself for her failures, and constantly feared that something bad would happen to punish her for her sins.

> **I tremble in view of afflictions because I know I need chastisement. Why I have hitherto received so many mercies I do not know. One thing I know, it is not**

**because I have deserved. I have been so
ungrateful I have reason to fear they
will all be taken from me.**

There were many ways for a woman to demonstrate
that she was a True Woman. One was to control her
language, keeping it free of slang lest she slip into
slangy behavior—a veiled reference to prostitution.

**The girl who is slangy in her manner is
the girl who commenced by being
slangy in her speech, and who is to-day
the worst specimen of bad manners in
existence. . . . The girl who is slangy in
speech, dress and manner is very apt to
grow slangy in her amusements.[18]**
—*Ladies' Home Journal,* 1893

Anne Ellis, who lived in Colorado mining towns in
the late 1800s, tried hard not to be slangy. Her mother, her teacher, her husbands, all cautioned her about
it. But sometimes she would forget and say something
like "You bet!"

**All this winter, George is trying to train
me. . . . One day we have a time over
my saying 'darn.' He didn't intend to
have his woman swearing.**

One of Anne Ellis' worst offenses happened at a
Christmas dance when two miners started throwing
apples at each other.

**I am not going to stand for any rough-
house, as I had set out to have a
ladylike, refined affair, so I jump up on
a chair and yell—'HERE, YOU TWO
STIFFS, CUT OUT THE APPLE
THROWING!' At this, George drags me
down and takes me home, but I guess it**

**was just as well, as the dance ended up
in a free-for-all.**[19]

The True Woman was to present a proper appearance to display her husband's wealth and her dependency and station. Fashionable women's corsets, when tightened, could exert pressure on the torso from twenty to nearly ninety pounds, causing shortness of breath and fainting spells to severe indigestion, broken ribs, and deformed internal organs. Winter clothing of skirts, petticoats, and coats could weigh nearly forty pounds.

"Ladies with Faces to Wall."

From the collection of the Jefferson County Historical Society, Port Townsend, Washington #619-JC.

Most nineteenth century white women wore their hair long, often parted in the middle and tightly bound to avoid the appearance of looseness or slanginess. Indian and Hispanic women, as they were colonized, were expected to tame their hair in the same way.

From ancient times, unbound women's hair signified power, and it was believed that witches could raise storms by letting their hair fly free.

> **Brown hair flying free,**
> **Short skirt flowing with her body**
> **The girl races her brother**
> **To the edge of the meadow.**
> **Heart thumping, breath pumping,**
> **Her moccasin-covered feet**
> **Pound the contours of the grass-covered**
> **earth.**

She nears the edge of the meadow
   where the little creek flows
Bet you can't jump it!
   her brother yells

Bet I can!

Reaching the edge
Ahead of her brother
   she
      flies
           through the air
Brown hair flying free

Giggling
   at the feel of the wind on her face
   and the twinkling water beneath her
She reaches the other side
   breathless
     laughing
       grinning

Still laughing, the girl runs
   brown hair flying free
   to tell her mother
How she ran through the meadow,
Flew over the twinkling water.

The mother looks sad.
It is time to tell her daughter
The meaning of becoming a woman.

Now my daughter
You must not run,
   brown hair flying free
You must cover your limbs
   with long skirts and petticoats
You must cover your feet
   with tight leather shoes
You must lace up your waist
   to make it small.

And your brown hair
You must fasten it down tight,
     not let it fly free.

Otherwise
What will people think, my dear?

And who would want to marry a girl,
     brown hair flying free,

Who thinks she can fly?
                    —"Brown Hair Flying Free"
                    ©Susan G. Butruille, 1994

A woman's indoctrination into True Womanhood began early. An 1885 medical manual warned that at puberty, "a girl is vulnerable to insanity, epilepsy and a score of other affections" if she subjects herself to too much intellectual stimulation.

"[A]t thirteen, the woman is born," the Experts intoned, "and for four years should have nothing to do which can interfere with her growth into woman-hood." Being smart was the worst thing she could do. "Too often the success of her school life is purchased by the sacrifice of her sexual perfection. It is the unanimous experience of physicians, that such cases of imperfect sexual development are usually found in girls with brilliant school records."[20]

Experts even knew how to spot a girl with brilliant school records by looking at her. She was the one with small breasts, a result of devoting her energies "to study and mental accomplishment. Her blood has been devoted to her brain; the development of other organs and of other powers has been sadly neglect-ed."[21]

As Mary Richardson Walker's story shows, it is true that young women were subject to insanity and other afflictions. But the problems came from trying to be who the Experts said they should be instead of being free.

In the either-or world of the nineteenth century, The Cult of True Womanhood divided women into two species. True Women or Ladies, and Others. Others were those who deviated from True Woman instructions on how to behave and who to be. Others, then, were farm women who worked outside, pioneer women, factory workers, slave women, dark-skinned women, non-Christian women, single women, Indian women, and immigrant women. Women with independent thoughts and ideas, anger, loud voices, slangy language, and ambition also were Other.

Those who wore their masks well thought they would be rewarded with status, a good reputation, and physical protection. But True Womanhood was a danger zone where a woman was vulnerable to physical abuse, injury from restrictive clothing, depression, and insanity.

In "civilized" societies, ideal True Women were valued for their supposed weakness and *helplessness,* plus their piety, purity, domesticity, and submissiveness. But on the early frontier of dirt and hard work, a woman who feigned weakness was out of place. The frontier modified the ideal. Women were valued for their *helpfulness* (or, more accurately, their horse-like work) plus their piety, purity, domesticity, and submissiveness.

Frontier women themselves recognized the masquerade of True Womanhood—the ridiculousness of trying to be helpless and submissive when the very lives of your family depend on the swiftness of a blow, the accuracy of a gunshot, and the strength to butcher a whole hog or heft countless loads of wet wash.

They took seriously their commitment to taming the west and its wild men to make it safe for family, children, and community. If, then, they saw through the charade of True Womanhood, most women honored the Cult of Domesticity.

In the circles of church groups, sewing bees, and woman-to-woman friendships, they spoke of their dreams and their disappointments, and shared secrets of how to avoid having babies. They shared their lives and their loves, and how they would fulfill their assignments as the civilizers of men. And there, within the circles of women, they planted the seeds of their own longings for freedom.

With money earned from selling quilts, butter, cheese, and eggs, they bought shoes and clothing and food and windmills for their families, and raised millions of dollars for their communities.

And into their quilts and fine linens, they sewed their hearts.

> **I'd rather piece as eat, and I'd rather patch as piece, but I take natcherally delight in quiltin' . . . Whenst I war a new-married woman with the children round my feet, hit 'peared like I'd git so wearied I couldn't take delight in nothing; and I'd git ill to my man and the children, and what do you reckon I done them times? I just put down the breeches I was patchin' and tuk out my quilt squar'. Hit wuz better than prayin', child, hit wuz reason.[22]**
>
> —Aunt Cynthy, c. 1900

CHAPTER FIVE

Women Who Were Free

**At last I understood why the birds sing.
. . . The real life is to be free . . ..**[1]
—Grace Gallatin Seton-Thompson

I believe that many women did go westward to be free. They just didn't say it. Maybe they didn't know themselves that freedom was what they were going for.

**I have desired to become a missionary
& why? Perhaps only to avoid duties at
home.**
—Mary Richardson Walker,
Oregon Country, 1839

On the early frontier, the frontier of improvising, of starting over in the wildness and the grit, there was more opportunity to defy the rules. As they moved into the West, the freedom seekers and gold seekers were moving backwards in time, from established homes and communities to starting over. Many had seen their agricultural and barter-based economies turning to cash-based industrial economies. On the early frontier, they were back to an economy based largely on growing, trading, and bartering, where women's work was central.

Anything could happen in this crack between the worlds—perhaps even new thinking about the meaning of freedom, especially for women. When survival is at stake, you suspend the rules. You do what needs to be done.

Freedom meant defying the Cult of True Womanhood, breaking the rules, even living independently. Many women probably believed they were so evil anyway (being merely normal) that they might as well have some adventure while they were at it.

But a woman who tried to be free of True Womanhood rigidity wasn't free either. A woman who broke the rules risked poverty, criticism, loneliness, and perhaps violence.

Take Calamity Jane.

Now there was a woman who thumbed her nose at True Womanhood. But even Calamity sometimes bowed to convention to try to look respectable. As a child in Missouri when the little girls wouldn't play with her because of her slangy language, Martha Cannary decided that it was more fun playing with the boys. Orphaned at age fourteen, she headed west and kept on playing with the boys. Her main claim to fame was that she was a woman doing man things.

Calamity Jane (Martha Jane Cannary).

Courtesy Wyoming State Museum, Cheyenne, Wyoming #8883/13395.

As Calamity's fame spread, so did tall tales about her. She herself said she lied all the time, so her story is as much legend as fact.

In a world where beauty was a relative thing, Calamity was described as looking like a "busted bale of hay," a "beautiful and dangerous courtesan," and a "ministering angel."

Calamity Jane drifted around the West, from Colorado to the Dakotas to Oregon, and was at various times a teamster (ox or horse team driver), army scout, gambler, prostitute, camp follower, journal writer, and volunteer nurse who saved lives. She could out-drink, out-gun, and out-ride a lot of men, and she could for sure out-cuss any bullwhacker. And she was an excellent cook. She wrote in her journal:

I am proud of my cooking, especially of my fish dishes, cakes & pies. I make up receipts & try them out on these outlaws a cross the way.

Calamity took up with at least thirteen men, including, she claimed, Wild Bill Hickok. But to make it sound more ladylike, she called each one her husband.

According to one tale, she reported to a judge that she wanted a divorce because her husband had run away.

"Why was he running away?" asked the judge.

"I was after him with an axe," she replied.

People didn't know what to make of this "strange, nomadic creature" whose "misfortune it was not to have been born a man."

"[W]hile her masculine traits were abnormal, her womanly traits of kindness and charity would have done credit to any of her sex," wrote one awed and charitable writer.

"The spirit of original sin itself possessed the girl," wrote another.

Calamity Jane would have been miserable trying to

be a True Woman. But beneath the swagger of the life she chose was a lonely woman for whom there was no place. She longed for love and even respectability so much that she apparently invented the daughter to whom she addressed her journal.

Close to death at age fifty, Calamity Jane wrote to her imagined daughter:

> **Dear Janey**
> **I guess my diary is just about finished. I am going blind—can still see to write this yet but I cant keep on to live an avaricious old age. . . .**
> **I hate poverty & dirt & here I shall have to live in such in my last days. Dont pity me Janey.**
> **Forgive all my faults & the wrong I have done you.**[2]

Other women broke enough rules to be free. But, like riches or abundant crops or love, freedom could be a mirage and fade just as quickly as it came.

The gold mining frontier of masquerade and indulgence was the perfect stage for a woman with a talent for performing and the audacity to defy the bounds of proper behavior. The carnival frontier of California was the perfect place for the final burst of flame in the blazing career of the famous dancer/revolutionary/mistress/world traveler Lola Montez. Born in Ireland, Marie Dolores Eliza Rosanna Gilbert put on the mask of a Spanish dancer and danced her way through affairs with a string of lovers, including Franz Liszt, Alexander Dumas, and the King of Bavaria, whose devotion to the luscious Lola enflamed a revolution and toppled him from his throne.

Toward the end of her dancing career, Lola Montez wowed California audiences with her famous, writhing, spider dance, and then retired to lecture on women's rights and study religion. When she died in New York at age forty-three, her fortune and beauty were gone. She described the classic dilemma of the nineteenth-century woman wanting to be free.

> **The great misfortune was that there
> was too much of me to be held within
> the prescribed and safe limits allotted
> to woman; but there was not enough to
> enable me to stand securely beyond the
> shelter of conventional rules.**[3]

On the frontier where invention was a necessity, improvised laws were more likely to grant women rights to their own money, property, divorce, and child custody. Improvised laws also were more easily changed, lost, or not enforced.

While some women on the early frontiers had more varied work roles and opportunities than their eastern sisters, most had more children and more work to do. The make-it-up-as-you-go also meant that women on the western frontier were more likely to move in and out of marriage, homes, and jobs.

Malinda Jenkins did just that. She left a husband and married another, lost custody of her children and got them back, lost and regained her health, started businesses, lost them, and started again.

> **I knew I could make some money
> [taking in boarders] . . . and . . . got six
> day boarders, at five dollars and a half
> each week. I bought dishes, tablecloths,
> towels and such things as I needed.
> And them men went crazy over my
> baking-biscuits—they was used to sour
> dough all their lives and they thought
> my biscuits was wonderful.**[4]

Malinda Jenkins eventually became a millionaire breeding race horses. Looking back on her life, she concluded:

Do you know what I'd do if I was to get broke up? I'd go into business tomorrow. Yes sir, . . . and I'd make good like I always done.

In the frontier West of the 1870s, perhaps as many as twenty-five percent of women may have worked for wages at some point in their lives, but the numbers varied wildly depending on time and place. Many women understood that their path to freedom depended on making enough money to live on and being able to control it.

The frontier service economy increased opportunities for some, from farm wives who sold butter and eggs, to entrepreneurial women who started cottage industries and became business and property owners. The service economy enslaved others, like Indian people and other minorities, most prostitutes, and indentured servants.

Most money-earning women were domestic servants and many were prostitutes or madams. It seems that many prostitutes got there simply because they were seeking freedom; they believed it to be a way of controlling their own lives. "I don't say that whoring is the best way of life," said a San Francisco courtesan, "but it's sure better than going blind in a sweatshop sewing, or twenty hours work as a kitchen drudge or housemaid with the old man and the sons always laying for you in the hallways."[5]

Many other women were teachers, laundresses, seamstresses, nurses, missionaries, midwives, saleswomen, postmistresses, cooks, boarding house keepers, waitresses, and dance hall girls. On the early western frontier, women were more likely than their eastern sisters to be actresses, authors, photographers, artists, lawyers, doctors, and journalists.

An estimated quarter of a million western women were running their own farms and ranches by 1890. Most were spinsters or widows.

**She made her start in cattle, yes, made
  it with her rope;
Can tie down every maverick before it
  can strike a lope.
She can rope and tie and brand it as
  quick as any man;
She's voted by all cowboys an A-1 top
  cow hand.[6]**
  —"The Pecos Queen," cowboy ballad

There were more than a hundred cattle queens in Colorado alone around 1875, with herds ranging from a few head to hundreds. When the first cattle woman in the area near Durango, Colorado dared to wear divided skirts and ride her horse astride, someone took a shot at her.

**Women of the Tatum family 1880s along Salt Creek,
near Bernard, Kansas.**

From the collection of Molly Wullstein Van Austen.

After claiming her own Wyoming homestead, Elinore Pruitt Stewart married, bore four children in four years, raised all of the ranch's food, and proved up her own homestead. There she found her freedom and recommended it to other women who would be free.

**[A]ny woman who can stand her own
company, can see the beauty of the
sunset, loves growing things, and is
willing to put in as much time at
careful labor as she does over the
washtub, will certainly succeed; will
have independence, plenty to eat all the
time, and a home of her own in the
end.**[7]

Necessity and desperation, combined with frontier inventiveness and loneliness, urged some women on to unthinkable thoughts and acts of courage and defiance. Some were driven by a pure sense of adventure.

Some women, unlike Mary Richardson Walker, used religion and spirituality as their path to freedom. Women were prohibited from speaking and teaching in most churches, and Experts insisted that women's power rested in the emotional, intuitive, and moral domains. Many women then embraced a mystical spirituality that they claimed transcended the power of men.

Early frontier teachers sent by the National Board of Popular Education had to prove membership in an evangelical church and a conversion experience. Many women used that requirement to justify a decision to go west, insisting that obedience to God took precedence over obedience to a man, usually a father, who might oppose the decision.[8]

Some women claimed mystical and spiritual powers. Indian women taught their daughters what we might call self-hypnosis—how to "leave" their bodies if something bad was happening to them.

With roots in Spanish-Moorish and Indian traditions, Hispanic women of the New Mexico frontier cultivated mystical powers through veneration of the Virgin of Guadalupe, grounded in the tradition of the Aztecan Goddess Tonantzin. In the New Mexico frontier of the 1600s, many women became followers of the "Lady in Blue," believed to be a nun who had mystically transported herself from Spain to New Mexico.[9]

Cipole School, Sherwood, Oregon, 1890s.

Courtesy Washington County Historical Society and Museum
#LP72-12-47/1307-26.

A group of Texas housewives claimed religious, sanctifying power to escape abusive husbands and build their own economic power. Aided by what we would call consciousness-raising sessions and led by a housewife, Martha McWhirter, the "Sanctified Women" pooled their butter and egg money and eventually bought a hotel, which prospered. The commune, sometimes called the Woman's Commonwealth, thrived and became a powerful force in the community as well as a refuge for women longing to be free.[10]

Among the frontier missionaries were thousands of nuns who answered the call of their God to establish missions, schools, and hospitals across the West. Usually traveling alone or with other sisters of their orders, often from across the sea, these women had to be tough and independent—outside the bounds of True Womanhood.

Sister Blandina Segale, an Italian Sister of Charity,

accepted a mission to New Mexico and found herself filling the roles of administrator, spiritual advisor, architect, diplomat, and teacher while she worked in schools, hospitals, and other projects. She used the mystique of her mission and spirituality to command the respect of the community and the priests alike.

> **I wish I had many hands and feet, and
> a world full of hearts to place at the
> service of the Eternal. So much one sees
> to be done, and so few to do it. I have
> adopted this plan: Do whatever
> presents itself, and never omit anything
> because of hardship or
> repugnance. . . .[11]**
>
> —Sister Blandina,
> in a letter to her sister, 1872

Informed one day that there was no food for her hospital patients, orphans, and sisters of her order, Sister Blandina contemplated the abundant vegetables in the archbishop's walled garden. "I made one athletic spring (old habits die slowly) and landed near the cabbage patch." She helped herself to some of the archbishop's vegetables, throwing them in a flurry across the wall. She immediately made a confession to the archbishop, who instructed her to take the rest.

Mother Joseph, a Sister of Providence from Quebec, became the "Department of Health, Education and Welfare in the Pacific Northwest," as well as the Northwest's first architect after her arrival there in 1856. Often wielding her own tools, Mother Joseph established more than two dozen hospitals, academies, Indian schools, and orphanages throughout the Northwest. Conditions were so terrible in the beginning that she wrote back home, "Beginnings are always trying, and here the devil is so enraged he frightens me."[12]

In all frontier cultures, medicine women were powerful and respected. They knew the lore of herbs

**Statue of Mother Joseph,
St. Vincent Hospital, Portland, Oregon.**

Photo by author

and medical care handed down through their own mothers and elders. Women healers often had more skills than male doctors, who were not required in the early years to have medical training. Many of the medical training and licensing procedures of the nineteenth century were designed to keep women out of the practice.

Women were the first on call in child birth and emergencies, and often the only healers in far-flung communities. Utah had the highest number of women doctors on the early frontier.

Among the most powerful and influential women in Hispanic communities were the *curanderas* and *parteras,* the healers and midwives. The *curandera* tradition is rooted in two cultures, the Indian medicine women, and the healers with roots in Moorish culture who came with the Spaniards to the New World. The *curandera* has healing powers and spiritual powers as an intermediary between earth and spirit, and between cultures and religions, like the Aztecan goddess Tonantzin, who preceded the Virgin of Guadalupe.[13]

> **There was a woman in each generation who became a healer. This woman had a closeness with her predecessor. From their relationship the healer novice was trained and taught through many informal experiences.[14]**
>
> —Grerorita Rodriquez

Author Fabiola Cabeza de Baca Gilbert wrote about her village's old, mysterious *curandera*, Seña Martina.

> **The next morning, . . . Seña Martina
> came by with a sack full of herbs. She
> had been out in the fields since dawn
> gathering medical herbs which she
> shared with her neighbors. . . . Very
> often she went out to neighboring towns
> to heal persons from various maladies
> and her fame as a medicine woman
> stretched over many miles.[16]**

Bethenia Owens Adair came over the Oregon Trail in 1843 as a child. Married at fourteen, she divorced her abusive husband and supported herself and her son by washing, teaching, and running a dressmaking and millinery shop. She became a physician at age thirty-four and specialized in the treatment of women and children. In a speech to the Women's Congress, about 1920, Bethenia recalled a seventeen-year-old friend who gave her inspiration and courage as a child.

> **[Miss Ann Hobson] could row or sail a
> boat equal to a Columbia River
> fisherman. She could manage a canoe
> and swing a lasso equal to a cowboy.
> . . . I have seen her riding at full speed,
> swinging the lasso around her head, in
> hot pursuit of a wild cow, that would
> not be driven into the corral, when near
> enough away flew the lasso and the**

Girls on horseback in eastern Oregon.

Courtesy Peter Palmquist Collection.

**cows head or foot was caught!! . . .
There was not a man in those pioneer
days who could equal Miss Hobson in
riding and using a lasso. I was a little
girl in those days and was Miss
Hobson's special pet, perhaps because I
admired & loved her so much. Many a
time did she pick me up from the
ground . . . & go flying across the
prairie. Her examples of courage and
daring have been inspirations to me
throughout all my life. And I gladly pay
this tribute to her strong vigorous and
fearless girlhood.**[16]

Susan La Flesche Picotte became the first
American Indian woman doctor and a leader among
her Omaha people in Nebraska. She worked to free her
people of the alcoholism and disease that plagued
them because of the destruction of their communities
and economy.

Ethnologist and archeologist Alice Fletcher lived
and worked among Indian tribes from Nebraska to
Idaho and learn their culture. Dressed in long skirts

and petticoats, she directed surveys and allotments under the controversial Dawes Act, which she helped draft, believing it would help the Indian people stay on their lands. In effect, the Dawes Act took Indian people away from their traditional communal way of living into the white property-owning economy.

Jane Gay assisted and lived with Alice Fletcher for four years. Jane was cook, carpenter, and expert photographer for Alice Fletcher and the Nez Perce people of what is now Idaho.

Women sometimes lived together in close relationships known as Boston marriages. In the nineteenth-century culture of separate spheres, people judged close same-sex relationships far less severely than male-female relationships outside marriage. Whether or not these relationships were sexual, few seemed to need to know or care.

Biddy Mason's thoughts were on another kind of freedom as she herded cattle on foot the entire distance from Mississippi to California behind her "master's" wagon train. When he decided to return home, Biddy, still considered a slave, sued for and won freedom for herself and her daughters. Starting as a midwife and nurse, she built a $300,000 fortune. With it she helped build schools, churches, and nursing homes, and aided flood victims and people in jail.

The western frontier gave some women excuses to change their True Woman costumes for the freedom of more comfortable clothing, like bloomers. These Turkish trouser-like outfits were named after the eastern feminist Amelia Bloomer, editor of a women's rights newspaper. Bloomers made many activities easier and safer—tending fires, carrying children, working in the corral, riding horses, getting through mud.

Am wearing the Bloomer dresses now; find they are well suited to a wild life like mine. Can bound over the prairies like an antelope, and am not in so much danger of setting my clothes on

**fire while cooking when these prairie
winds blow.**[17]
—Miriam Davis Colt, Kansas, 1856

Julia Archibald Holmes headed west enthusiasti-
cally with her husband and brother from Kansas to the
Pikes Peak gold mines in Colorado in 1858. On the
trail, Julia's costume attracted curiosity and indigna-
tion.

> **I wore a calico dress, reaching a little
> below the knee, pants of the same,
> Indian moccasins for my feet, and on
> my head a hat. However much it lacked
> in taste I found it to be beyond value in
> comfort and convenience, as it gave me
> freedom to roam at pleasure in search
> of flowers and other curiosities, while
> the cattle continued their slow and
> measured pace.**

Julia's outrageous costume disgusted the only
other woman in the traveling company, but Julia
tramped on, undaunted, dismissing the woman's com-
plaints.

> **She proved to be a woman unable to
> appreciate freedom or reform, affected
> that her sphere denied her the liberty to
> rove at pleasure, and confined herself
> the long days to feminine importence in
> the hot covered wagon. . . . I cannot
> afford to dress to please others' taste.
> . . . I could not positively enjoy a
> moment's happiness with a long skirt
> on to confine me to the wagon. . . . I
> rejoiced that I was independent of such
> little views of propriety, and felt that I
> possessed an ownership in all that was
> good or beautiful in nature . . ..**[18]

When Julia reached Colorado, she and her husband climbed Pike's Peak, Julia no doubt in her outlandish costume, to a height of 14,000 feet.

Some women even let down their hair or bobbed it.

No, I didn't bob my hair to be in style, but because I believed it would be easier to care for if I bobbed it than if I left it long; and it is, too. There is no reason why a woman should be a slave to long hair or long skirts.[19]
—Martha Jane Spencer Janney, Oregon

Women out for a ride, Durango, Colorado.

Courtesy Center of Southwest Studies, Fort Lewis College, Durango, Colorado.

A remarkable number of women published frontier newspapers, including at least two black women. Many women-published newspapers focused on women's rights. Caroline Romney wore her True Woman costume to win respect and safety as the first newspaper publisher in Durango, Colorado. The petite widow brought the presses 350 miles over the Continental Divide in the middle of winter, the last 120 miles by horse-drawn carriage. She published her first issues in a tent in a foot and a half of snow. Caroline took on gangsters and vice and reflected the racism of the day toward the nearby Ute Indians.

In the pages of her newspaper, Caroline Romney urged women to come to Durango. "We want girls," began one article. It must have worked. Months later, a story appeared on "The Matrimonial Boom." As to her own matrimonial status, the publisher dispelled a rumor that she would soon be married. "In fact we can't afford to support a husband just yet," she wrote.

Asked by an interviewer if she wasn't afraid, the intrepid publisher's response explained one reason most women clung to their ladylike costumes.

> **A woman is safer in the roughest**
> **mining camp of the West, if she holds**
> **herself a lady, than in New York. . . .**
> **The women who get insulted are mostly**
> **women who one way or another, invite**
> **it. Inborn lady-hood . . . has nothing to**
> **be afraid of anywhere.**[20]

Throughout history, in wars, and on the sea, outrageous women have disguised themselves as men to ease their movement and widen their world. They could walk the streets at night and go places they wouldn't be allowed as women.

In her letters to her daughter, Calamity Jane explained why she favored wearing men's clothes. "You see, I wear pants so I can get around while these peticoted females yell for help."

Little Jo Monaghan first donned men's pants on the westward journey because it was safer. Then she discovered a new freedom and kept her masquerade for twenty-five years as a reclusive cowboy in Idaho. No one knew her secret until she died and the county coroner discovered her secret. A recent movie told her quiet, colorful story.

Elsa Jane Forest Guerin put on a man's costume to

go after her husband's killer and kept up the disguise for most of the next thirteen years.

> **I began to rather like the freedom of my new character. I could go where I chose, do many things which while innocent in themselves, were debarred by propriety from association with the female sex. The change from the cumbersome, unhealthy attire of woman to the more convenient, healthful habiliments of man, was in itself almost sufficient to compensate for its unwomanly character.**[21]

Elsa Jane, one of several women known as Mountain Charley, evidently was a lousy shot. She twice found her target, twice shot him, but never managed to do him in.

Another woman named Charley was Charley (or Charlie) Parkhurst, said to be the first woman to vote in a presidential election, in 1868. Charlotte, her apparent real name, escaped from an orphanage dressed as a boy, and spent the rest of her life masquerading as a man. She became a stagecoach driver in California.

"Black Mary" Fields packed guns and reportedly wore a white apron over her two-hundred pound frame on the mail coach route she won when she was past fifty. She was the only woman in Cascade, Montana allowed to drink in the town's saloons.

Pearl Hart was one of a number of women on the frontier who took their freedom to the extreme. She lost hers after she robbed a stage coach and went to jail. Then she went on stage and told of her adventures as a bandit her victims thought was a man.

Nellie Cashman was nearly seventy-five years old when she mushed a dog team seven hundred and fifty miles and became champion woman musher of Alaska. For decades, the Irish-born adventurer had freely roamed the west, from Tombstone, Arizona to Baja, California to the Yukon, helping miners and establishing hospitals, boarding houses, and restaurants. She struck it rich several times with her businesses and gold prospecting, and spent most of the money helping people, especially her beloved miners.

When Clara Brown arrived in Central City, Colorado, she had freedom on her mind—the freedom of her family still in slavery. She did laundry, worked as a nurse, and invested in mining claims until she had ten thousand dollars to buy her family's freedom. Clara returned to the South and searched in vain for her husband and children. She did locate some relatives and organized the first of several black wagon trains to go west. Shortly before she died, Aunt Clara Brown was reunited with her daughter.

Tabitha Brown, a sixty-six-year-old widow, was so enthusiastic about going west that she lined up her own ox team. Her 1846 Oregon Trail passage was a classic tale of hardship and adventure. After taking an ill-advised cutoff, Tabitha, with a lame hip and a broken arm, became stranded alone with her sick brother-in-law. Tabitha kept him going until they were found. She went on to start a glove-making business with a coin she found in her worn-out trail glove. In her new home in Oregon, she helped establish an orphanage, part of what would become Pacific University. Tabitha Brown is now known as the Mother of Oregon.

Maude or Pearl Zeigler, Kansas, 1880s.

From the collection of Molly Wullstein Van Austen.

Orphanages like Tabitha Brown's cared not only for parentless children, but for children whose parents were unable to take care of them. Many were children of men—and women—who had headed for the Gold Rush. On the western frontier, so many families were broken by illness, violence, divorce, or the search for Some Place Else, that many children grew up outside the "traditional" two-parent family.

"Traditional" families of the time allowed little room for freedom for women, and if they divorced, it was difficult to win custody of children. Women alone with children who had to support themselves often entrusted care of their children to relatives or friends.

Westward I go free?

Every woman who journeyed to the western frontier, every woman who was already there, struggled with what it meant to be free.

One western editor expressed the opinion of some men toward women who would be free.

The assurance of the strong minded women of the day is amazing. It has become insufferable. . . . Women have no business with affairs that do not belong to their sphere. When they depart from the limits of that propriety which should govern them, none but a dastard would refrain from speaking to them as they deserve!!![22]

Amazon Guards, c. 1890s.

Courtesy Museum of Western Colorado, Grand Junction, Colorado.

As for the men, although freedom—by definition—was for them, they weren't free either. True Men were not free to show compassion, sadness, or fear, or to look to women for advice and companionship. Most men, like women, were lonely and undoubtedly frightened in a world they found they didn't have much control over after all.

The western frontier, in the end, was simply a larger reflection of a world that wasn't yet ready to recognize that the real life is to be free. Truly free.

CHAPTER SIX

Whiskey, Oysters, and Wild Wimmin: The Carnival Frontier

We go to the circus! I am the owner of a balloon, quite the finest thing which has happened to me so far. When I returned to the house, I put it behind me for safe keeping. I hear a noise, look for my balloon—nothing there! This seems unbelievable, so wonderful just a moment ago, and now just a string! I cried.[1]

—Anne Ellis, age six
in a Colorado mining town

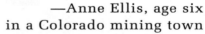

You reach for it, so bright and beautiful. You've never had anything like it. You feel like dancing, celebrating. You hold it in your hand and put it away to keep it safe. Suddenly, with a bang, it's gone. And you cry.

Young Anne Ellis didn't mention the color of her balloon. To me, it has to be red, the color of carnival, hope, and surprise.

Some say it was a carnival frontier, when the western frontier was new and full of promise and excitement to the people who came there. When I think of the carnival frontier, I think of red—the color of gold-bearing hills at the crest of a shimmering sunset. It's

111

the color of the queen of hearts and velvet curtains, painted lips and cold death.

Chet Orloff, Executive Director of the Oregon Historical Society, reflected on one meaning of frontier. "In military terms, it's the front line—the place you don't want to be when the shooting begins."

Some have called it the meeting place of desperate people. Others have said the frontier was the place where different cultures met and clashed. Both were true of the carnival frontier.

To the editors of *Far From Home: Families of the Westward Journey,* the carnival frontier was "a world of 'fool's day' where hunger, desperate effort, and fear could be transformed by hilarity."

Orloff described the stage between frontier exploration and the beginning of commerce and settlement as a "quick two-step." That's the dance of the carnival frontier—that brief, uninhibited fandango of unaccountability before you have to settle down and behave yourself.

Carnival means "flesh, farewell." It's Mardi Gras, the last wild fling before the discipline of Lent, when you give up pleasures of the flesh. It's a frenzied parade of dancing and feasting, a cacophony of brassy music, gaudy costumes, and lovemaking. Weaving through the revelry are the masked and costumed tricksters and seducers, who beckon you to wild adventure with one hand and rob you with the other.

And suddenly it's gone. So wonderful just a moment ago, and now just a string.

A carnival, with its mad parades of flamboyant characters and costumed magicians scheming ways to finagle somebody else's money, could be found on every western frontier—the cattle frontier, ranching frontier, farming, logging, railroad, and urban frontiers. But it was the gaudiest and most bizarre in the gold mining camps.

Anne Ellis, who with her husband pursued gold on the mining frontiers of Colorado and Utah, wrote of "seeing life in big gobs," the women more excited than the men. Fortunes were "made or lost each day on the stock exchange, in the saloons, at the mines, or at stealing, buying, and selling highgrade [ore from which gold could be extracted]. . . . [W]e put all the money we had left, not much, into mining stock—United Mines. Each day after we buy it, it drops, till it is taken off the board. This was our luck."

Calamity Jane gave this description of Billings, Montana in 1891.

> These are hectic days—like hell let out for noon. These human parasites prosper, both men & women. The respectable citizens of the town are power less they cant even control the elections & the police figure they would risk complete anihilation by attempting raids on the dens running at top-steam—block after block appropriated entirely to saloons & sporting houses.[2]

In their mad dash for gold, it was mostly young men who scrambled across the prairies or elbowed onto the first ship sailing toward the gold. They left behind parents and wives and children, rules and restrictions, to go to a golden land, find their gold, and return as rich heroes.

Some of the men already had moved their families west over two-thousand miles of dust and mud and death—and then left them there while they clamored after gold.

> Half my children gone
> and the winter comin' on
> We came to California
> nearly starved, our money gone
> John went to pan for gold

> **and soon forgot the kids and me**
> **And now I take in washing**
> **and I curse his memory.**[3]
> —from "Overland 1852"
> by Linda Allen ©1984

On the mining frontier was perhaps the most motley crowd of any of the frontiers. In the first year of the gold rush alone, an estimated 100,000 people flooded into California. They came from every direction and one in maybe ten was a woman or a child. Mary Ballou described her neighbors in Negrobar, California in 1852.

> **I am among the French and Duch and**
> **Scoth and Jews and Italions and**
> **Sweeds and Chineese and Indians and**
> **all manner of tongus and nations but I**
> **am treated with due respect by them**
> **all.**[4]

"There is every class of people here in California the rich and poor of every nation of the world," said another newcomer in 1852.

The mining frontier was the most moveable of the American western frontiers as miners streamed from one strike to the next. Gold mining didn't start with the discovery of gold at Sutter's Mill, near present-day

**St. Elmo,
Colorado.**

Photo by author.

Sacramento. Spanish and Mexican settlers and Indians had started small but unpublicized mining operations in California before that. They, in fact, showed some of the immigrants ways to mine for gold.

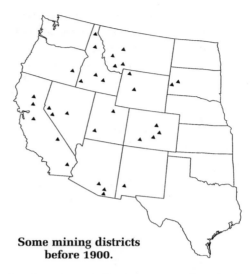

Some mining districts before 1900.

If you had before you one of those maps that lights up at different points to illustrate time and place of events, you would see lights flash on and off throughout the west with each gold rush, beginning in California. After the first light flashes at Sutter's Mill, lights soon begin to twinkle all along California's Sierra Nevadas. Soon lights flash in what is now Nevada, then Cherry Creek, Colorado and the central Rocky Mountains, but Colorado's lights don't stay on for long. You see lights flash in Montana, Idaho, Wyoming, and Eastern Oregon and Washington, and, finally, in South Dakota's Black Hills. Last of all, near the turn of the century, the lights go on in the Klondike. Lights keep flashing on and off all over the West with the mining of other metals and minerals such as silver, copper, coal, and lead.

Some early miners struck it rich, just as they dreamed. Some built their dreams and fancy houses right there. Others collected their dreams and went home to settle down. But behind the masquerade of strike-it-rich and happily-ever-after was the scummy reality of ramshackle shacks and tattered tents, disease-infested mud, worm-ridden food, gaudy come-ons, broken dreams, and broken lives.

Women who were left behind had to scratch out a living or move in with charitable relatives until the man either came home or sent for them.

They must have worried about their husbands' extracurricular activities. "Please write me about your business. . . ." wrote Maggie Keller Brown from Virginia to her husband in Colorado. "Have you bought any cloaths yet? Have you taken up a claim? Have you kissed any one since you did me? *I tell you you had better not.* Now answer *all* my questions."[6]

Maggie had reason for concern.

A Denver newspaper blustered at the masquerade he saw.

> **Men of decent appearance seen elsewhere, as soon as they reached Leadville jibed, sang low songs, walked openly with the painted courtesans with whom the town teems . . .. Secure in the fact that their boon companions would not 'give them away,' that their women folks were safe and snug in their distant homes, that their children, prayers said, were tucked in the little beds, these . . . gentlemen announced that they were going 'the whole hog or none.'[7]**

Mrs. Lee Whipple-Haslam, a child in California mining camps of the 1850s, remembered a surrealistic, now-you-see-it, now-you-don't scene.

> **In the early part of '53 strict laws and the vigilantes sent an ever moving stream of human microbes [coming] from the cities—gun men, gamblers, blacklegs, and all the low class of the sporting element (men and women) to this country. They considered our hard-working miners lawful prey and immediately introduced methods to**

> reap the harvest. . . . In the most
> unexpected places they started
> groggeries, where both men and women
> lived, sold whiskey, and gambled;
> sometimes with music and dancing.[8]

Luzena Stanley Wilson, a young wife and mother, described a bizarre scene of frolic and death side by side in a Sacramento hotel in 1849.

> [S]ome men were having a wordy
> dispute over a game of cards; a cracked
> fiddle was, under the manipulation of
> rather clumsy fingers, furnishing music
> for some half dozen others to dance to
> the tune of "Moneymusk".
> One young man was reading a letter
> by a sputtering candle, and the tears
> roling down his yet unbearded face told
> of the homesickness in his heart. Some
> of the men lay sick in their bunks, some
> lay asleep, and out from another bunk,
> upon this curious mingling of
> merriment and sadness stared the white
> face of a corpse. They had forgotten
> even to cover the still features with the
> edge of a blanket, and he lay there, in
> his rigid calmness, a silent unheeded
> witness to the acquired insensibility of
> the early settlers. What was one dead
> man, more or less! . . . The music and
> the dancing, the card-playing, drinking,
> and swearing went on unchecked by the
> hideous presence of Death. His face
> grew too familiar in those days to be a
> terror.[9]

It was a curious mingling of merriment and sadness, and danger. Malaria, cholera, and smallpox stalked the argonauts to the gold fields. Snakes lurked

in hidden places. People were on edge or looking for
a fight. Accidents, floods, and fires could happen at
any moment.

Imagine the first women arriving in this murky
world, dirt-caked and ragged. Their filthy clothes
hang in shreds. Part of them was lost somewhere back
on the trail, or on that rat-infested ship.

Luzena Stanley Wilson described her arrival with
her husband in Nevada City, California in 1849.

> **Our entrance into the busy camp could
> not be called a triumphal one, and had
> there been a 'back way' we should
> certainly have selected it. Our wagon
> wheels looked like solid blocks; the
> color of the oxen was indistinguishable,
> and we were mud from head to foot. I
> remember filling my wash-basin three
> times with fresh water before I had
> made the slightest change apparent in
> the color of my face; and I am sure I
> scrubbed till my arms ached, before I
> got the children back to their natural
> hue.[10]**

Luzena decided to set up a boarding house.

> **With my own hands I chopped stakes,
> drove them into the ground, and set up
> my table. I bought provisions at a
> neighboring store, and when my
> husband came back at night he found,
> mid the weird light of the pine torches,
> twenty miners eating at my table.[11]**

Luzena's enterprise was so successful that she took
her husband "into partnership." She "became luxuri-
ous and hired a cook and waiters." Within six months
the couple had twenty thousand dollars worth of
property and goods.

And then it all burned up in a fire and Luzena and her husband left for Some Place Else, where they eventually prospered again.

There were other ways for women to relieve the miners of their gold.

> **First came the miners to work in the mines**
> **Then came the ladies who lived on the line.**
> —mining frontier ditty

On the carnival frontier, it was a little harder to tell who was who since things were pretty slapdash there. But you could usually tell the ladies from the harlots by the costumes they wore.

> **Oh, the color of her hose was red and yeller.**
> **She says to me, 'You're a mighty fine feller.'**
> **I escorted her home under my umbrella—**
> **The girl with the striped stockings on.**
> —from "The Girl with the Striped Stockings" (traditional)

The most obvious harlots were the ones wearing the carnival costumes in the parade of thousands to the carnival frontier. These were the "painted ladies" of legend—the ones in the flashy colors and sparkling jewelry, the ones with painted lips and exposed legs.

Hangtown Gals are plump and rosy
Hair in ringlets mighty cosy
Painted cheeks and gassy bonnets
Touch them and they'll sting like
hornets.[12]

Hang-Town was the earliest name of Placerville,
California. Sarah Royce, who traveled there in 1849,
told how Hang-town got its name.

I had heard the sad story (which, while
it shocked, reassured us) of the
summary punishment inflicted in a
neighboring town upon three thieves,
who had been tried by a committee of
citizens and, upon conviction, all hung.
The circumstances had given to the
place the name of Hang-Town. We were
assured that, since then, no case of
stealing had occurred in the northern
mines . . ..[13]

Placerville wasn't the only Hang-town. They were
all over the frontier. A hanging could be a social
event. Montrose, Colorado "was a wild town for a
while with its landseekers, saloons, gambling houses,
and an occasional 'Hanging Bee.'" In Salem, Oregon,
"Hangings were public in those days [1865] and people drove in from 20 miles around to see . . .. It was as
big a crowd as a circus would have brought out, only
they were quieter."

Hang-Town, California gave its name to a carnival
frontier delicacy, Hangtown Fry. Its main ingredients
were eggs and, not surprisingly, oysters.

If there's a food that's a metaphor for the frontier,
it's oysters. Oysters in great variety were served with
flair on nearly all of the American western frontiers,
but especially in the California boomtowns. Oysters
on the frontier were a flamboyant extravagance, a delicacy that could be transported on ice with the coming

of the railroads to the later frontiers. Oysters were gentility in a world of swagger, swagger in an ungentle world.

A miner discovered a great way to eat the slippery mollusks in a San Francisco saloon after he accidentally spilled some oysters in his whiskey cocktail.[14]

Oyster Cocktail
Soak a bunch of oysters in a whiskey
cocktail. Drink the whiskey. Fish out
the oysters. Spread catsup,
Worcestershire sauce, and pepper over
the soused oysters.

In the saloons, dance halls, and bordellos, girls in striped stockings—or no stockings—served Oyster Pie, Oysters on the Half Shell, Oysters and Celery, Champagne and Oysters.

Saloons were the first institutions in the frontier West. The first ones often were dugouts and tents. Next were shabby one-story buildings, often with huge false fronts—part of the carnival frontier masquerade. "The false fronts," as author Richard Erdoes explained it, "were pasted like sheets of cardboard to one-story log cabins or board shacks to give the impression of splendid two-story saloons."[15] The terms "false front" and "saloon" became almost interchangeable, according to Erdoes.

As the gold came in, so did more places of entertainment. Notorious Blair Street in Silverton, Colorado, boasted at one time "forty saloons and dance halls, twenty-seven gambling saloons, and eighteen houses of ill fame . . .."

These places were there for the sole purpose of selling liquor, the main commodity on the carnival frontier. Thirteen-year-old Harriet Hitchcock, who traveled with her family to mining camps of Colorado in 1864, observed, "Bread is considered the staff of life. Whiskey the life itself."

Flashy women sold a lot of liquor as waiter girls, bar girls, dance hall girls, and prostitutes. Whatever their occupation, their main job was to sell liquor, most often by getting men to buy them drinks, which typically were watered down.

From the grimy to the opulent, a saloon's center-piece was the bar, with the foot rails and spittoons in front, and the huge mirror, the obligatory picture of the nekkid lady, and the bottles of booze and stacks of glasses behind.

Saloons were the meeting places, the getting-warm places, and often the eating places in town. As a child in St. Elmo, Colorado, Charlotte Merrifield would fetch her father from the Pat Hurley Saloon.

> **Schooners of beer were served for five cents and a free lunch was put out on the bar consisting of roast beef, baked ham, pickled tripe, and pigs feet, pretzels, crackers and hard boiled eggs. The idea of the free lunch was to keep the men there instead of going home to eat. Pat was afraid they wouldn't return to spend their money gambling. . . .**
>
> **The beer was drawn from a keg, placed behind the bar. The miners used to take a bucket full when they went home, this was called a growler. If you greased the inside of the bucket it made the beer foam less so you got more beer for your money; a ten pound pail full was twenty-five cents.[16]**

It was a big day in Durango when the first batch of whiskey arrived on a wagon train in 1876. After the train came through, the liquor would arrive quite regularly in barrels.

Oldtimers would tell the story about the two

drunks unsteadily observing a delivery down at the depot: keg after keg of booze was deposited. And finally, a bag of flour was delivered. Says one drunk to the other, "What the hell are they gonna do with all that flour?"

Whiskey and beer were the most popular saloon drinks. But in the Southwest, many saloons were known as pulquerias.

> **Know ye what pulque is?**
> **Liquor divine!**
> **Angels in heaven**
> **Prefer it to wine.**[17]

Anglos learned from Hispanos and Indians about pulque (pronounced POOL-kay), a drink distilled from the agave, or maguey (MAH-gay), a Southwestern cactus.

Some of the most colorful gamblers and dealers were women. An observer of French women gambling in California shuddered to "see the forms of angels in the employ of Hell; to witness the anxious and angry glare of disappointment when they lose; the feverish and eager glance of triumph when they win . . . . Oh! it is terrible! and enough to make a gambler forswear his unholy trade."[18]

In Durango, "where wine flowed more freely than water," a single mom made her living dealing faro, a game in which players bet on the order of cards the dealer turns over. The lady faro dealer sometimes could be seen riding one of those newfangled bicycles with the huge front wheels—all three-hundred pounds of her.

Somewhat smaller women danced for a living—

either on stage or with the men on the main floor.
They'd get paid by the dance, plus extra for the expensive drinks they'd charm the men into buying for
them.

> **Bonnie are the hurdies O!**
> **The German hurdy-gurdies O!**
> **The daftest hour that e'er I spent**
> **Was dancing with the hurdies O!**[19]

Dance halls often were known as hurdy-gurdy
houses, hurdy-gurdies, or plain hurdies, from the old
German hand organ played by street musicians. The
girls, often German or Scandinavian, were hurdy-
gurdy girls, pretty waiter girls, and sometimes beer-
jerkers or box rustlers, depending on their activity.

In Silver City, Nevada, two saloon owners sailed to
Germany and came back with girls to dance for fifty
cents a turn. Known as the Silver City Hurdy Gurdy
girls, they "learned to speak English and as soon as
they could pay their passage money back to the promoters, they were free to marry."[20] And some of them
did.

By the 1870s, troupes of hurdies roamed from town
to town, bringing tinny music and gaudy women.
Some hurdy girls dressed quite modestly and made
their living entirely by dancing and selling liquor.
Others supplemented their earnings in the back or
upstairs rooms. Some circles drew a distinction
between dance hall girls and prostitutes; the chippies
were the dance hall girls.

The girls "would waltz drunken miners dizzy,
being certain that the miners stopped now and then to
purchase more drinks at the bar. If the men had any
money left at the end of the evening, the prostitutes
would lead them away to private rooms."[21]

On the carnival frontier, ladies of the day and
ladies of the night were more likely to socialize at the
same places, especially the masked balls of carnival
San Francisco. There, "respectable ladies often mixed

with their sinning sisters, sometimes each parading as the other behind silk masks."

"All the women in town appear . . . and one often sees beautiful costumes richly adorned with lace," reported a Frenchman. "A masked ball naturally permits a certain freedom, but here the feverish atmosphere of the city produces an abandon I have never seen elsewhere."[22]

Behind the mask of merriment was the sinister face of violence. Before the carnival ends and the masks come off and you have to account for your actions, violence and vengeance became as seductive as any painted lady.

The violence went with the carnival frontier. Isabella Bird, an English woman who rode her horse throughout the Rocky Mountains, observed one form of violence. "[T]hat talent deified here under the name of 'smartness' has taken advantage of Dr. H. in all bargains, leaving him with little except food for his children."

"Smartness"—swindling and getting away with it—was "the quality thought most of."[23]

Gun violence was part of protecting property (including women) and proving manhood. Isabella related this story.

These women had a boarder, only fifteen, who thought he could not be anything till he had shot somebody, and they gave an absurd account of the lad dodging about with a revolver, and not getting up courage enough to insult any

**one, till at last he hid himself in the
stable and shot the first Chinaman who
entered. Things up there are just in that
initial state which desperadoes love. A
man accidentally shoves another in a
saloon, or says a rough word at meals,
and the challenge, 'first finger on the
trigger,' warrants either in shooting the
other at any subsequent time without
the formality of a duel.**[24]

"In Colorado," wrote Isabella, "whisky is significant of all evil and violence and is the cause of most
of the shooting affrays in the mining camps. There are
few moderate drinkers; it is seldom taken except to
excess."[25]

On the carnival frontier, the liquor flowed, so they
drank. Guns were there, so they used them. There may
have been food shortages, but seldom was there a
shortage of liquor, and nobody ran out of guns and
ammo.

Anne Ellis remembered the priorities in her family.

**Here the gun-rack was kept, and I
hated it, because it seemed to me that
we never needed anything but there
was a shotgun or Winchester, twenty-
two or double-barreled shotgun,
cartridges or reloading outfit to come
first.**[26]

It was the Code of the West. This set of rules, part
of the Cult of Individualism, "demanded personal
courage and pride, reckless disregard of life, and
instant redress of insult, real or fancied—all traits
with great appeal to the young adventurers who
flocked to the frontier," according to author Robert
Utley.

One Texas preacher shook his head over the whole

thing. "They say it is very healthy here. None, scarcely, die a natural death," he said, "because they do not
get an opportunity. There is too much lead in the air."

In 1879, during the rush to Leadville, "it was nothing to see dead men lying all along the road. Shooting
on the streets and hold-ups were daily entertainment."[27]

The myth persists that even with the liquor flowing and the guns exploding, men protected women on
the frontier. "[A]ll men," it was said, "even vicious
and depraved men, always respect a true woman, who
respects herself."[28]

It's true that men tended to "respect" and protect
women who appeared to be True Women, or
Respectable Ladies, especially if they had a hus-
band/protector. But women who were not Respectable
Ladies—those who worked in the dance halls and bordellos—were not safe from rape, stabbings, beatings,
or shootings.

Women who appeared "loose" or
"free" were vulnerable to attack. So
how could you tell a Lady from a
loose woman? Check out her costume. Does she wear a divided skirt?
Bright colors? Can you see any part
of her limbs (legs)? Her arms? Her
throat? Does her hair fly free? Does
she speak in slang?

Any of these infractions could
"invite" trouble. To be mistaken for
anything but a lady could be down-
right dangerous.

The justification for attacking a woman who
appeared to be "less" than a Lady was that she was, of
course, ASKING FOR IT by the way she dressed or
acted. That's one reason women were so careful to
dress like Ladies. They knew the unspoken rules for
being relatively safe in public.

Some women, however, were still vulnerable to
male violence, no matter how they dressed. Women

and children were not always safe from violence at home.

Dark-skinned women, Mexican, Spanish, Indian and black women were not always "protected." Songs were part of the mythology that dark-skinned women were sexually available and could be treated as such.

> **Spanish is the loving tongue**
> **Soft as music, light as spray**
> **'Twas a girl I learnt it from,**
> **Livin' Down Sonora way.**
>
> —traditional

A much higher proportion of dark-skinned women than light-skinned women were jailed, often for minor crimes. And if a dark-skinned woman killed someone, even in self defence, there may be no one to protect her.

In Downieville, a Hispanic woman named Josepha fought back after a spurned lover called her a whore during an argument. At her trial, she testified, "I told deceased that was no place to call me bad names, come in and call me so and as he was coming I stabbed him." With a loud and hungry mob outside, Josepha was found guilty and sentenced to hang. As the executioner carried out the sentence, the mob cheered.

Sarah Winnemucca wrote about white men coming into her people's camp and telling her mother to give Sarah's sister to them. "My uncles and brothers would not dare to say a word, for fear they would be shot down," Sarah remembered. "So we used to go away every night after dark and hide, and come back to our camp every morning."

At the notorious military brothels called "hog ranches," often the prostitutes were Indian women. Rape of Indian women often triggered reprisal Indian attacks on Anglo settlements.

Between the hard work of mining and the saloon life, men longed for women who would relieve them of some of their most onerous chores.

**Whoora! for a live woman in the mines.
What'll the boys say? They'll peel out o'
their skins for joy. A live female
woman in the mines! . . . Wheat bread
and chicken fixins now—hoe cakes and
slapjacks . . . whoora![29]**

On the California mining frontier, men were so desperate for someone to wash their clothes that some actually would send their laundry all the way to the Sandwich Islands (Hawaii) or even China. Now if they had only two changes of clothes—well, you figure it out.

At Washerwomen's Bay in San Francisco, a disparate collection of people gathered to apply suds to the miners' grimy duds. Mexican women, Indian women, Irish women made good money there—so good that men soon joined them, enduring jibes from the other men. Competition began to force prices downward, especially when Chinese men arrived on the scene with their efficient and excellent operations.

Then there was trouble. By 1869, the washerwomen formed a Woman's Cooperative Anti-Chinese Laundry to force out the Chinese. Laundry women in other places in the West, including Montana and Colorado, moved against Chinese launderers. The washerwomen's rebellion was part of growing anti-Chinese sentiment that led to violence and purges of Chinese people throughout the West, including the Chinese Exclusion Act of 1882, barring further Chinese immigration.

Enterprising women on the carnival frontier found an open market for designated women's work, and many, like Luzena Stanley Wilson, made wild profits cooking, sewing, ironing, and boarding. Most of the women worked harder than they ever had imagined, and many made money beyond their wildest dreams. And many lost it just as fast as Luzena Wilson did.

Death, violence, destruction, disease. There was a

reason for all this chaos. "I attribute so much gambling and drinking to the fact there is no women in the country," one miner wrote home. With so few women to provide amusements and refinements, what did anyone expect? Women—Ladies, that is—were responsible for morality, not men. So obviously they needed more ladies to tame this carnival that had gotten out of hand.

But the carnival frontier was no place for a lady.

Think how a lady was supposed to dress. Yards of skirts reaching to the ground, and underneath that, several petticoats, also reaching the ground.

You open your door to step outside, and before you is a sea of mud, an institution on the carnival frontier.

Dearest Cousin

I should have written long before
But trouble entered at my door
And with it I am quite bowed o'er,
The mud.

I strove to visit you last week
But went no farther than the street
Ere I was buried up complete
The mud.

Indoors all things with blackness
    spread
E'en to our butter and our bread
And out door nigh up to your head
The mud.

Afflictions not from ground arise
If that is so, I have no eyes
You'll not see me until it dries,
The mud.[30]

     —by a frontier lady

It wasn't clean mud either. The streets were also the sewers and garbage dumps. In the rainy season the mud was way past ankle-deep.

There's a story about a head sticking out of the mud in front of a saloon. Pretty soon the head asks for a slug of whiskey. Some kind soul obliges, brings the whiskey, and asks if there's any more he can do to help.

"No thanks," replies the head. "I've got my horse under me."

A newspaper editor eloquently described the contents of San Francisco mud.

> **Its ingredients are dust and water, egg shells, cabbage leaves, potato parings, onion tops, fish bones, and other articles too numerous to mention. . . . It is utterly impossible to do anything without thinking of mud, to go anywhere without stirring the subject, for, sober or muddled, a man is sure to put his foot in it.**[31]

A woman is sure to put her foot in it too, if she ventures out at all. Jennie Megquier wailed, "O the mud, it is dreadful, man and beast get stuck in the slush and cannot move. It is like glue and takes their boots off their feet. It is a foot deep."

So what's a lady to do?

It is indeed a dreadful situation. Imagine dragging your skirts and petticoats in such filth. Wash day is bad enough without adding all those muddy skirts, not to mention cleaning up your shoes. If you wear bloomers, you'll be laughed at, maybe even pelted with eggs, because only brazen women wear those immodest things. High-topped boots are so unladylike, and only harlots wear short skirts.

But tonight there's a circus and then a dance in town!

On the carnival frontier if there's a dance, you go.

Even through the mud. So grab your man, put on your unladylike high-topped boots and slog through the mud.

You can always carry your dainty dancing shoes with you.

> **O yes, pretty boys, we're comin' out**
> **tonight,**
> **We're comin' out tonight, we're comin'**
> **out tonight,**
> **O yes, pretty boys, we're comin' out**
> **tonight,**
> **And dance by the light of the moon.**
> —from "Buffalo Gals" (traditional)

CHAPTER SEVEN

Sporting Women

I'm not too young, not too old,
Not too timid, not too bold,
Just the kind you'd like to hold,
Just the kind for sport, I'm told[1]

Josie loved to dance.

She came one day to Buckskin Joe, a mining town near Fairplay, high in the Colorado Rockies. Here, after cool green and blue summers and shimmering autumns, the snows would come, so deep that miners would cut stair steps in the banks of snow so they could get in and out of their cabins.

By 1861, gold fever had dug away at the mountain side and plunked down a settlement with a post office, stores, hotels, a bank, and the county courthouse. Accompanying the static drumming and scraping of the mine operations on the edge of town, a brass band led the parade of gamblers, miners and merchants to the fun spots: the saloons, pool halls, and dance halls.

The men, seeking warm refuge from cold loneliness, loved to watch Josie dance. She would dance an Irish jig or a Spanish fandango or a highland fling—always wearing her shimmering silver-heeled shoes. And they began to call her Silver Heels.

One day smallpox invaded Buckskin Joe and the dance halls closed. Silver Heels nursed the sick, including her lover. Some say he died and Silver

Heels herself caught the disease, then disappeared as quickly as she had come. But another legend says that Silver Heels' lover didn't die in the epidemic, that pretty Josie married her love, and the two left town to seek their fortune together.

I hope the second version of her story is true—the one with the happy ending. I hope the young Josie danced away with her lover and lived happily ever after. But I doubt it. Happily ever after was for fairy tales. And the mining frontier was no fairy tale. Most stories of pretty young girls drawn to the glamour and excitement of the dance halls and parlor houses did not end with them dancing away with mild-mannered lovers.

Home! home! sweet, sweet home!
There's no place like home!
There's no place like home!

That's one of the songs Josie sang. No one knows where her own home was. But in the frontier West, home was an elusive thing. And so was respectability.

There's another legend about Silver Heels, probably closer to the truth. Some years after Josie disappeared from Buckskin Joe, a woman showed up in Salida, Colorado who nursed some local people through an epidemic. She said she lived in one of the cribs (a row of cheap rooms). And they called her Silver Heels.

If that was Josie, the girl who loved to dance, she probably never intended to be a prostitute. Most of the fifty thousand prostitutes on the western frontier probably didn't either. But on the carnival frontier a woman who danced in front of men was no lady. And if you weren't a lady, you were treated like a prostitute. And if you were treated like one, chances are you'd become one.

The prostitutes and those who would become them came from every direction and faraway places, and their voices were many. In the red light districts all over the frontier, invitations could be heard in many variations of English and many foreign languages.

The women followed the miners from strike to strike, seeking their own gold mine. The towns, like their inhabitants, could be rich and raucous one day and poor and empty the next. Sporting women followed the railroads, the army, the cattle drives, the lumber camps, the shipping ports. And they often migrated between the growing cities.

Like everyone else who came to the western frontier, they hoped for something better than what they had, for greener pastures, gleaming gold. The reasons for getting into the sporting life were as varied as the landscapes in which they plied their trade.

Some were prostitutes before they came to the frontier, like the ones kicked out of France by Louis Napoleon. In 1850 he conducted a lottery to raise money to pay passage for prostitutes on ships bound for the Pacific coast.

Poverty, desperation, bad marriages, boredom, youth, naiveté—all propelled women into prostitution. As author and historian Anne Butler wrote, prostitutes nearly always were poor and they were young.

Maybe Josie, the girl who loved to dance, was one who was running away from marriage. It was easier for women to divorce in the West, but hard to come out of it with any money. Procurers prowled streets in cities to the east and abroad, looking for vulnerable girls and women.

"Agencies" would advertise for domestic workers, promising high pay and travel expenses. Poor and eager young girls would get on boats to seek their fortune on the West Coast, and find themselves inside brothels or on the streets with no way to work off their debts other than through prostitution.

Perhaps, like Colorado madam Lillian Powers, Josie hoped to escape a harsh home life. Lillian told an interviewer:

> **Well my father had this farm, you see, and nobody to work it but him and us two girls. I was fourteen, two years older than my sister, and he forgot most of the time that we wasn't horses. Got so I couldn't take it anymore. It was drudgery, day after day, and I'm telling you they was long days from sunup to sundown. One morning, I decided that instead of going into the field to plow, I would run away . . .. I swore to God that I'd never return and I never did. Never wanted to see my father again or anybody else in my family.[2]**

So, you may say, go out and get a respectable job!

Lillian Powers tried that. She fled to St. Louis, where she got a job in a laundry

> **and if you think that was easy, my God! It was almost as bad as the farm and my pay was one dollar a week. A room cost fifty cents a week—there wasn't much left for all the fancy folderols I thought I could buy when I went to the big city.[3]**

Lil asked around, wondering how other young women made it on "such a piddling wage."

"I don't," said one. "None of us girls do on what they pay us. Every last one of us has had to get ourselves a pimp. The quicker you do this the better off you'll be."

Lillian Powers moved westward, worked in Cripple Creek, and eventually settled in Florence, Colorado, where she quietly ran a small crib operation for many years.

So what else could a woman like Josie or Lil have done to make a life for herself? In the frontier service economy, "women's work" was in high demand. A woman could sew or make hats, clean houses, wash clothes, or cook or take in boarders. All were options that paid poorly or erratically, or required start-up money or property. She could teach if she had enough education, and didn't mind living with her students' families, and getting half the salary given a man. She could marry if she didn't mind playing by the rules of marriage and True Womanhood, and giving up many of her rights as a single woman.

Or she could go where the action was—and the gold. The best opportunities in prostitution were as an entrepreneur—having your. own house and getting other women to work for you and share their earnings. Big money could be made, especially selling liquor along with the entertainment.

> **She was only a convict's daughter,**
> **but she knew all the bars.**[4]
>
> —Western proverb

Madam Bessie Rivers made her living from the most popular sport on the frontier in the wild southwestern Colorado town of Durango. Bessie became one of the town's most successful entrepreneurs, building an elegant place of entertainment and buying up prime real estate with the profits.

All the while, madams like Bessie were paying taxes, supporting local merchants, and paying fines for what officially was an illegal business nearly everywhere on the frontier. "It was a quasi-legal status," says author Anne Butler. "They paid property taxes and were allowed to operate, depending on the financial and political needs of the community."

Bessie Rivers was one of the well-known "prostitutes with a heart of gold." According to local legends, she and her employees gave money to local charities and she put kids through college, often from the sale of diamonds and gold left in her safe. That was the deal—do good works in the community and the community will let the operation run in relative peace.

It was all part of the masquerade on the carnival frontier, where prostitution flourished. Prostitution played a major economic role in building frontier towns, yet it was illegal. Prostitutes were seen as bad women but expected to do good.

In the masquerade of the carnival frontier, prostitutes were to put on the mask of free living so ladies could preserve their masks of propriety. Hookers were free to paint their faces and wear flouncy clothes. Ladies covered their bodies and wore proper faces. Courtesans shaved their legs and underarms. Ladies wouldn't dare. Shady ladies knew about birth control and abortion. Respectable ladies were not supposed to. Harlots could ride horses astride. Ladies rode sidesaddle. Soiled doves openly drank alcohol. Ladies drank Lydia Pinkham's compound and whiskey at home. Women who looked like floozies were fair game for attack. Ladies were safer.

As more women came into the frontier who could wear the mask of True Womanhood, the more the contrast grew between the hookers and the ladies, and the less tolerance for prostitutes.

"The streets are crowded with people laughing, singing, swearing, running foot races, betting, etc.," wrote Louisa Cook in a letter from Boise, Idaho in 1863. She was having a hard time finding any "Lady acquaintances."

> *Ladies* are not plenty. There are a great many in all the mining towns who wear the form of woman, but o so fallen and vile, a living, burning shame to the sex they have so disgraced. As soon as the miners began to flock to this country these women began to come out of Portland, The Dales, Walla Walla, and other places, sometimes a dozen in a

**drove, astride an Indian pony dressed
in mens clothes, rude boisterous and
more obscene than the male bipeds who
accompany them. Once here they dress
very richly and in gay colors and go by
the name of fancy women. . . .**[5]

A rich lore and language grew around frontier
prostitution and its various forms. Much of the lore
had ancient and historical roots. Prostitution districts
came to be known as red light districts from the custom of railroad men hanging their red lighted lanterns
outside a hooker's door to let others know the place
was occupied. It was the Row, the Tenderloin, or the
Demimonde, French for half-world.

The line, or crib row, was a row of cribs (shacks),
often with common walls. Women worked cheaper on
the line than in the fancy houses, known also as bordellos, hook-shops, pleasure houses, parlor houses,
cat houses, brothels, cow yards, bawdy houses, and
sometimes boarding houses or pest houses.

It is said that a Union army general named Hooker,
who had a legendary sexual appetite, popularized the
term hooker for prostitutes. But the term goes back
farther than that. A hooker was a nautical term for a
harlot who had seen better days, after hoeker, "an
awkward Dutch fishing boat."[6]

Hookers also were known as inmates, hustlers,
nymphs, chippies, painted cats, calico queens, fairy
belles, broads, kimono girls, *filles de joie,* scarlet
ladies, bawds, birds, heifers, fillies, whores, and

strange women. Some of the fancier names for fancy women were Cyprians, after ancient sexual rites to Aphrodite and Astarte on the Mediterranean island of Cyprus; and harpies, after ancient mythical female death-spirits with bird bodies and women's heads and breasts. Harlots were ancient temple prostitutes whose patroness was the Babylonian goddess Ishtar, or the Great Goddess Har.

Prostitution took place in a variety of settings: in hotels and boarding houses, near military posts on "hog ranches," on cattle ranches, barges, houseboats (gunboats), and bedrooms on wheels called cat wagons.

The Laundry

In the high mountain mining town of Silverton, Colorado was a place called The Laundry. There, "if you went in with any money, you came out clean." A fancy house outside Durango caused confusion when it came to be known as the Convent. Near Port Townsend, Washington, Madam Fannie Cardwell rented small houseboats known as "Fannie's Flotilla."

The famous Creek Street in Ketchikan, Alaska, was a line of cribs along a boardwalk built over the water on pilings. A fisherman could steer his boat right under Creek Street and climb a ladder to his favorite crib.

Western frontier lore is full of gaudy, romantic stories starring beautiful women who sold their bodies and ran fancy houses. We usually hear the first part, the glamour part of the story, not the rest.

Maybe Silver Heels, the girl who loved to dance, heard stories of Red Stockings, who hit California Gulch (later Leadville), just over the mountain from Buckskin Joe, on the crest of a gold strike. In less than a year, the courtesan with the red ribbons in her hair and the red stockings on her legs, mined the miners for one hundred thousand dollars and promptly left town for Nevada, where she lived happily ever after. So they say.

Peg Leg Annie Morrow got her nickname after she froze both legs in an Idaho blizzard. She had set out on snowshoes with a sister Cyprian for a spring dance on the other side of Bald Mountain. The friend died, but Annie walked again after the community took up a collection to buy her artificial legs. Her story should have a happy ending but it doesn't. The saloon keeper who started the fund set up a rooming house and housekeeping with her. He lived with her for twenty-two years, and then took off with her savings.

Mary Ann Pleasant, known not as madam but as "Mammy," came to San Francisco and made millions with her investments. Her boarding house catered to a wealthy and fashionable male clientele, whom she introduced to beautiful and classy women. Mystery and wealth surround the story of the former slave who earlier had helped thousands of slaves escape to freedom in Canada. Known as the "mother of civil rights in California," she sued the street-car company for discrimination and fought for the rights of blacks in California.

Julia Bulette was said to have collected up to one thousand dollars a night at the peak of her career in Virginia City, Nevada, site of the Comstock Lode, in the 1860s. She quickly made a lot of money and then built Julia's Palace, the first grand building in town. Her house featured imported wines along with imported girls. Julia endeared herself to the town firemen, raised funds for the Sanitary Commission for Civil War soldiers, and nursed the miners after they drank

arsenic-tainted water. Julia lost status as more
respectable women arrived, and met a violent end
when three robbers entered her palace and strangled
her. The respectable women shuttered their windows
to avoid the sight as a procession of miners and firemen accompanied Julia's body for burial. The militia
band played

> **It's drinking I throw over,**
> **card-playing I resign,**
> **For the only girl that I ever loved**
> **was the girl I left behind.**
> —from "The Girl I Left Behind"
> (traditional)

Julia Bulette's memory is not left behind. The
Virginia & Truckee Railroad named a club coach in
her honor and her portrait still may be found in
Virginia City saloons.

Colorado madam Laura Evans once drove a horse-
powered sleigh straight into Leadville's famous two
hundred thousand dollar ice palace, a magnificent
structure built entirely of ice. Laura told author
Caroline Bancroft that her horse got scared, kicked
one of the pillars, and tore down the exhibits before
he finally found his way out of the fabulous structure.

Laura was one of a relative few who made a life-
long vocation of prostitution. She ran brothels and
cribs in Salida, Colorado until 1950 and died three
years later at age ninety-one.

Then there's Kitty Le Roy, who began jig dancing
when she was ten. She went on to win fame in the
Black Hills, where she dealt faro, and had "five husbands, seven revolvers, a dozen Bowie knives, and
always went around armed like a gunfighter." Not surprisingly, she met her end when her last husband beat
her to the draw and shot her dead, then killed himself.

Pearl DeVere would ride her sleek horse through
the streets of Cripple Creek, perched sidesaddle on
her steed, and dressed in full riding habit. When busi-

ness boomed, she had her own horse-drawn carriage with spinning red wheels as bright as her dyed hair. By 1896, she parlayed her riches into an enchanting two-story brick parlor house quaintly called The Old Homestead. This fabulous place sported unbelievable luxuries like recorded music, electric lights, and live orchestras within its Parisian-papered walls.

BEST HOUSE IN TOWN!

Come all you boys who've been around,
Chambermaids you'll find at hand!
Best damn girlies in the land!
Press the annunciator and you get
All you want, and more, you bet![7]

—ad from the Strater Hotel
and Saloon, Durango, Colorado

In the finest places, the set was lavish. On the early frontier, saloons, dance halls, and parlor houses were about the only places where men could get good food, music, and female companionship. The finest ones were social centers, offering lavish quantities of fine liquor and cuisine, dancing, gambling, and conversation.

At Bessie Rivers' place in Durango, Colorado, thirsty customers could belly up to the long, ornately carved bar and feast on a free lunch with an order of beer. The more beer, the more free lunch.

Bessie's Horseshoe Saloon
Lunch Menu
with purchase of one beer
Pickled beets with hard boiled eggs
Pickled fish
Boiled ham and salami on sour dough
with purchase of two beers add
Potato salad
with purchase of three beers add
Oysters on the half shell
Spanish stew[8]

Liquor and prostitution went together like a cowboy and his horse. Box seats in a dance hall or a lower-class theatre were not for intense play-going. They were for behind-the-curtain drinking and carrying on. Some dance hall/theatres actually were called box houses, and in Skagway the female performers developed the art of "box-rushing." After the performance they would rush the boxes, ring for the waiter and order expensive wine. And, we assume, pull the curtain.

> **But oh, of the wiles**
> **And the gold-tooth smiles**
> **Of a dance hall wench beware.**
> > —Robert W. Service

Dance hall girls—some with names like The Waddling Duck, Dancing Heifer, Galloping Cow—could make good money, especially if they were pretty, clever, and devious. Martha Black wrote that in Dawson, girls made a commission of twenty-five or even fifty percent on drinks. "It was said, that some girls made as high as two hundred and fifty dollars a night, but this could only be done by 'rolling,' which meant getting a man drunk and stealing his poke."

> **And when we parted in the rain**
> **She said, 'We'll never meet again.'**
> **And so she hooked my watch and**
> > **chain,**
> **The girl with the striped stockings**
> > **on.**
> > —from "The Girl with the Striped
> > Stockings" (traditional)

The object was to get as many men to part with their money as possible. In San Francisco, Souvenir Sporting Guides pointed the way to fine pleasure palaces.

In the saloons and parlor houses, young boys might

catch their first glimpse of the female flesh that they could actually buy when they had enough money to pay the price.

> **Drinkin' pink lemonade**
> **In the shade of Lavinia's Parlour**
> **Rockin' the rockin' chair,**
> **Feet almost touchin' the floor**
> **Drinkin' pink lemonade**
> **In the shade of Lavinia's parlour,**
> **As the angel Lavinia murmured**
> **Like perfume of more.**[9]

—Lyrics from "Lavinia's Parlour" ©1976
Travis Edmonson, reprinted with permission from
Katie Lee's book, *Ten Thousand Goddam Cattle*,
©1976 by Katie Lee

Let's climb the richly-carpeted staircase leading to the elegant boudoirs above and take a look. A first glance inside the carpet-covered, lace-curtained room takes in a clean-sheeted bed, a table with a basin and pitcher and a "pleasure towel." Beside the table is a spittoon. A clock and pictures adorn the flashy wall-paper. The room smells of cheap perfume and hair oil, mixed with smoke from the wood stove. A pet magpie peeks out of his cage and voices a greeting: "Come in, Boys. Come in."[10]

The eye rests on a large, locked trunk. The imagination pictures secret pieces of a woman's life: photographs of family far away, a child's toy, a letter from a long ago love, perhaps a quilt made by a sister, French silk scarves, lacy corsets, and fancy gowns.

On the dressing table is a velvet-lined perfume box and a lidded jar. Beside the table is an ornate wooden chair, too narrow to sit on.

It's time for the lady of the evening to put on her costume. She clings to the back of the elegant narrow chair while a colleague cinches up her corset tight, narrowing her waist and pushing her breasts upwards. From the jar she takes belladonna to relieve the pain from the encasing corset. Before she leaves the room to glide down the stairs in her flashing gown, she checks her image in the mirror. Time to put on her smile.

To the outside world, the painted ladies put on a raucous, colorful show, parading their feathers and furs, satins and laces, for the men to admire and the proper ladies to envy. Like their wearers, the fancy finery invited touches and enjoyment but were easily wrinkled, used up, and discarded. The gaudy clothes were more than a costume. They were a way of thumbing their noses at a world that used them while treating them with contempt.

With awe mixed with envy, little girls and their Respectable mothers would peek out their windows to see the parades of harlots in their feathers and velvets and satin. Young Anne Ellis watched wide-eyed as the fancy ladies on horseback flounced past her one-room house in Bonanza, Colorado.

> **[T]he women are on side saddles and are dressed in long wide skirts, tight basques [laced bodices], and stiff hats with veils floating behind them. The dress I remember best was double-breasted with gilt ball buttons running up and down either side of it. When they galloped, the little tails on the basques went flippy-flop in a very graceful manner, or at least I thought so. The 'fancy girls' all had their favorite horses and rode each day.[11]**

The fancy girls in Denver took to wearing yellow after the town fathers ordered all prostitutes to wear yellow ribbons to identify themselves. Soon the downtown streets bloomed with fancy women dressed in yellow, from their satiny shoes to their flowery parasols. The yellow caught on and became a code color for hookers far and wide. No proper lady would be seen in yellow, or walking a French poodle, the pooch of choice for parlor girls.

Proper ladies watched in fascination as fancy ladies used ingenious tricks to enhance their appeal. Some accented their gowns with boas and sashes, and enhanced their curves with "gay deceivers," false bosoms with little springs for added bounce and cleavage. "Plumpers" were devices fastened to the teeth to add an appealing, plump look to the face.

Some daring proper ladies began to use some of these tricks, along with hoop skirts. These were shocking fashions, for, when the lady bent over, the skirt would swoop up, "accidentally" revealing her limbs (the proper term for legs). Especially bold ladies took to wearing "false calves" to make the sight even more interesting. It was all "harlot-mocking," huffed a Montana newspaper editor.[12]

The color and excitement and splendor must have caught the imagination of countless bored or impoverished girls and housewives. One woman wistfully noted that the courtesans had "a man servant to clean their house, and they eat in a restaurant," while "I am cleaning all the time."

They heard the stories of wealthy madams. They saw the beautiful clothes, the lovely surroundings. And Josie wore her beautiful silver heels.

They probably heard of Pearl DeVere, the Cripple Creek madam, and her charmed life in her lavish Old Homestead. But I wonder if they heard of her death. This is the part of the story that often isn't told. About how, on Christmas day, after an extravagant party where she danced to the music of two orchestras from Denver, the rich madam, still dressed in her eight hundred dollar pink chiffon ball gown, ended her life with an overdose of morphine.

Mounted police and the Elks Club band escorted Pearl's body, still dressed in her pink gown, outside of town for burial. Behind the lavender casket draped with red and white roses, sleek black horses led the empty carriage with the shiny red wheels that once matched Pearl's flaming hair. On the way home, the band played Cripple Creek's song, "There'll Be a Hot Time in the Old Town Tonight."

Pearl DeVere got out of prostitution with a drug overdose. Drugs were part of a prostitute's life. And often, her death.

A dance in the Butte, Montana red light district inspired this bit of doggerel about the popularity of drugs on the sporting scene:

> [B]efore they play the grand march
> Let each dancer have a shot;
> It will act as stimulation,

And should make the dancin' hot.
So from scores of hiding places
Guests brought forth their hypo gats;
From sleeves, brassieres and bustles,
Some even hid them in their rats.[13]

In the chaos of the nineteenth century, many drugs were legal and common all over the country. Even high-class ladies routinely took remedies high in alcohol, codeine, morphine, and opium. Being sickly and taking potent medicines fit the image of Victorian ladylike frailty, and the remedies made the ladies even more sickly.

Prostitutes had access to all kinds of drugs, beginning with alcohol. Morphine, opium, and arsenic were dependable and comforting, not like anything else you knew in a throwaway life where the only friends and family you have could turn on you or be gone tomorrow.

Here lies Charlotte,
She was a harlot.
For fifteen years she
    preserved her virginity,
A damn good record for this vicinity.[14]

Author Marion Jarvis wrote of the death of a Durango, Colorado prostitute known as "Girlie." "When her owner found her dead one morning, she merely turned to the doctor and remarked, 'Oh well, she was getting to the place where she couldn't earn an honest dollar.'"

They could mix mercury with tobacco for venereal disease, opium and carbolic acid to prevent and abort pregnancies. Arsenic, morphine, and strychnine, and carbolic with opium deadened physical and emotional pain. Taken in large quantities, they could take off their masks forever.

**The miners came in '49,
The whores in '51,
They rolled around the bar room
    floor
And made a native son.**
           —popular western ditty

One of the hidden means of birth control for respectable ladies of the nineteenth century was prostitution. It was an outlet for husbands whose wives feared more pregnancies.

"The higher sense of mankind says that the family is the essential unit of the state," said Dr. Emily Blackwell. "Our practice says that the family plus prostitution is the essential unit."[15]

Birth control, abortion, and venereal disease were realities in women's lives, but things only prostitutes were supposed to know.

Some prostitutes bore children. Some grew up in the brothels, some with relatives. Bessie Rivers could afford to send her son away to a boarding school and, as the story goes, he never knew where his mother got all her money.

On the frontier, people were as status- and power-conscious as they were anywhere else, even in the Red Light District. In some brothels, the higher the floor, the more expensive the entertainment. French women were likely to be on the top floors.

For most prostitutes, the kind of place they worked determined how much money they made, the working conditions, and how they were treated. A young prostitute could perhaps start out in the cribs, work up to a parlor house, and, as age and hard living caught up with her, fall back down to the line again. Boarding houses, saloons, and dance halls often rented second-story and back rooms to prostitutes of all levels of status.

> **First you ring the bell and then you ask
>   for Anna;**
> **then you put a nickel in the 'Bell'
>   pi-a-na,**
> **down comes Anna in a silk kimona,**
> **all dressed up in pa-her-fume and
>   co-lo-na**
> **then you pay two dollars for the music
>   that you hear,**
> **then you pay two dollars for a lousy
>   bottle o' beer**
> **then you pay two dollars for a couple
>   o' weeks o' fear down the line.**[16]
>
> —"First You Ring the Bell," words and music
> assumed to be in the public domain, arrangement
> ©1976 by Katie Lee, reprinted with permission
> from Katie Lee's book, Ten Thousand Goddam
> Cattle, ©1976 by Katie Lee.

The courtesans with the highest status were those you didn't see. They were the concealed mistresses of the very wealthy men, the women whose discretion and secrecy were valued almost as highly as their sex appeal.

Parlor houses like Pearl DeVere's Homestead were at the top of the ladder in the Tenderloin heirarchy. Courtesans there could spend more time talking, drinking, eating, and gambling than working.

Next down the ladder were the brothels or cottage operations. Lillian Powers preferred this smaller operation, and prided herself in having "a nice spread and clean linen on the bed, clean towels . . . on the washstand, and frilly curtains at the window."

Next step down could be a dance hall, or the

Cribs, St. Elmo, Colorado.

Photo by author.

lower-class hurdy-gurdy. From there it was usually downhill, a step at a time, or a free-fall, in one boom town after another, in a variety of brothels, dance halls, and saloons.

No matter how she started, a prostitute's path usually ended in the cribs. Hookers would stand at the windows or doorways, soliciting quick tricks that didn't last long or pay much.

A standard feature in a crib was a strip of oil cloth across the foot of the bed so the customer wouldn't have to take off his boots. A girl has to keep the merchandise moving. As one man described it, "I'd say the whole thing, from the time you got in the room until the time you came didn't take three minutes."[17]

After the cribs came the streets for women who had no home at all. As author and historian Anne Butler says, "For every madam in Denver, there were two thousand prostitutes living in the cribs or on the streets, in extreme economic conditions and exposed to violence and drug addiction."

Some of the saddest stories of crib life are of the Chinese women who were bought and sold in China, then shipped to the U.S.—Gum San, Land of the Gold Mountain.

Chinese culture valued girl children far less than boy children, as in the Chinese proverb: "Eighteen gifted daughters are not equal to one lame son." Lameness in a daughter, in fact, was a sign of gentility. "[F]eet were tightly wrapped until the arches were broken and the toes permanently bent under," according to author Judy Yung. "The ideal size of a bound foot was said to measure no more than three inches. Bound feet . . . also served to prevent women from 'wandering.'"[18]

Like their sisters in the U.S., Chinese women were valued for the Four Virtues: "chastity and obedience, reticence, pleasing manner, and domestic skills." If a girl wasn't "virtuous" enough or if she wasn't crippled from foot binding, she risked not finding a husband and then being sold or kidnapped as a slave. Or parents could unknowingly "sell" her as an indentured servant.

Most Chinese prostitutes were brought to San Francisco beginning in the early 1850s, then Vancouver, B.C. and Portland after 1875. In San Francisco, the women, some as young as twelve, were taken to the barracoon or "auction block," also known as the "Queen's Room," which could house up to one hundred women. Here, they were stripped and displayed for sale "like livestock," for maybe two hundred to five hundred dollars. As one writer pointed out, this was in the late 1860s, after African-American slaves were legally free.[19]

For the journey to Gum San, girls were made to memorize phony stories to tell customs agents. One later told a Congressional committee how she memorized her story during the long journey by steamer from Shanghai:

> **As I was told my landing depended upon my remembering my story, I went over it every day from the day we started, at times singing it as we would a song, though often weeping as I sang, whenever I thought of mother and of home.**[20]

I weep as I record all I know of this woman's story,

and the words on a sign advertising the going rates in the cribs. More than anything, the sign tells of the dehumanization of all prostitutes, no matter their color, no matter their station. The sign read:

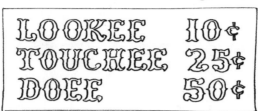

LOOKEE   10¢
TOUCHEE   25¢
DOEE   50¢

Among the most notorious cribs were the "hog ranches" near military posts like Fort Laramie. These places, with names like "My Lady's Bower" and "Dew Drop Inn," specialized in "watered whiskey and wayward women."

Of the fifty thousand women who paid enormous prices for putting a price on themselves, each had a name. Each had a story.

There's a postlude to the story of Josie, known as Silver Heels, the girl who loved to dance.

Back in Buckskin Joe, Colorado, where Silver Heels used to dance, they said that for many years, a heavily veiled woman could be seen at the cemetery, watching over a lone tombstone. They said it was Silver Heels herself, the girl who loved to dance. Her deep scars hidden under the veil, she was visiting her lover.

Maybe she comes there yet, this mysterious woman, one of thousands whose stories, dreams, and tears remain veiled and faded in the frontier past.

Today, a fir-clothed Colorado mountain stands watch over the place where Josie entertained the miners. It's named Mt. Silverheels, after the girl who loved to dance.

CHAPTER EIGHT

Over There: The Search for Home

My home over there, now I remember
it!
And when I see that mountain far
away,
Why, then I weep. Alas! what can I do?
What can I do? Alas! What can I do?
My home over there, now I remember
it.[1]

—Tewa song

The women who were there dreamed of returning. The women who came had many dreams, and most of those dreams were of making a new home. For many women on the western frontier, at least in the early years, a permanent home turned out to be a misty dream, just there around the corner with the next move. So they spent their lives making a new home where they were, for however long it was.

My husband was considered a visionary
by his friends. He always thought that
the farthest fields were greenest. On
our 14th wedding anniversary we
figured that we certainly must be
rolling stones, for we had made 21
moves in 14 years.[2]

—Elizabeth Paschal Gay,
Oregon pioneer of 1862

As women moved into the new frontier, most came with families and lived on the farming frontiers. Most came overland from east of the Mississippi, particularly on the early frontier. Later, as trails became roads, and rails brought iron horses westward, fences went up and plows broke the land, and more families came from other lands across the seas.

In the 1840s, families already were crossing the plains in hopes of claiming new lands for themselves. Some were Mormons bound for Utah, some were fortune seekers bound for California, and most were families headed for Oregon Country.

> **I've reached the land of corn and wine**
> **And all its riches now are mine;**
> **Here shines undimmed one blissful day,**
> **For all my night has passed away.**
>
> **Oh Beulah Land, sweet Beulah Land**
> **As on thy highest mount I stand:**
> **I look away across the sea**
> **Where mansions are prepared for me,**
> **And view the shining glory shore —**
> **My heaven, my home, forevermore.**
> —"Beulah Land," a hymn sung by
> westward-bound emigrants

The 1850 Oregon Donation Land Law encouraged single family settlement of what is now Oregon. But while immigrants were moving onto the land, it was still in dispute with England, and still occupied by Indian people. Those who passed the law hoped that the very presence of American settlers would help to claim the land for the U.S., and it did.

By 1853, the law extended into present-day Washington state. Until 1855, qualified settlers could claim up to 640 acres—320 each for husbands and wives, or 320 acres to a single man, but not a single woman, unless she inherited her claim from her husband. By 1855, most of western Oregon had been claimed, and settlers could claim only 320 acres.[3]

Families east of the Mississippi began to look hungrily at present-day Kansas and Nebraska, considered until then part of the Great American Desert—fit only, in their eyes, for Indian people. With growing scarcity of claims in Oregon, plus development of the Weston plow, which could cut under the thick roots of the tall grass prairies, the Great American Desert began to look more like a promising Great American Farmland.

The Homestead Act of 1862 granted 160 acres to a homesteader who would live on the land seven months out of the year for five years. Single women could claim homesteads, and many did. Many, in fact, delayed marriage to claim their land, refused to marry, or lied about their married state. Some couples claimed not to be married, and claimed homesteads side by side.

Married women could not claim land under the Homestead Act. Often, however, the women and children stayed on the land to prove up the claim, while the men were away working, marketing their products in town, hunting for gold, or, in the case of Mormons, on overseas missions.

People continued homesteading across the West into the twentieth century. Meanwhile, the U.S. government continued making and breaking treaties with Indian people, pushing them onto smaller and smaller pieces of land, "freeing" their former lands for settlement.

No matter where the newcomers landed, most found themselves face to face with extremes of weather and climate they hadn't counted on and didn't know how to live with. Parodies of the hopeful "Beulah Land" grew out of more realistic views of the "heaven" they found themselves in:

**We've reached the land of rain and
     mud,**

Where flowers and trees so early bud;
Where it rains and rains both night and
**   day**
For in Oregon it rains always.

Desperate for shelter—any shelter—on the early frontier, settlers used their imaginations to fashion places to live. Mud, sticks, canvas, whole trees, cactus, and wood gave shelter.

One family in Washington Territory cleaned out two huge tree stumps and moved in—all eight of them. They "found them to be very comfortable, indeed. [Mother] used the burned out roots for cupboards and closets and so we lived in them until fall; during this time father had built a log house, his work was very slow as he had few tools and little help."[4]

This is a land of dusty roads
Of rattlesnakes and horny toads;
It never rains, it never snows,
The doggone wind just blows and
**   blows.**
New Mexico so fertile and rich
We think you are a—honey.[5]
                    —Parody of "Beulah Land"

Maria Duran Apodaca, who moved in the 1880s with her family from Mexico to land in New Mexico Territory, remembered her family's house "of only two rooms. It was not adobe; it was made out of sticks. We called them *jacals.*"[6]

An Arizona family in the 1880s "had one room made of saguaros (giant cactus) and covered with dirt. In it were one six-paned window, and a door. The house had a brush shed on three sides where they cooked and ate."[7]

Tents—often torn, ragged, and "leeky"—frequently served as temporary homes while on the move, or while more substantial shelter was being built. One woman described a good day as one when her tent didn't blow down.

Some couldn't afford even the luxury of a tent.

We were not rich enough to indulge in the luxury of a canvas home; so a few pine boughs and branches of the undergrowth were cut and thrown into a rude shelter for the present, and my husband hurried away up the mountain to begin to split out 'shakes' for a house. . . . Our bedding was placed inside the little brush house, my cook stove set up near it under the shade of a great pine tree, and I was established, without further preparation, in my new home.[8]
—Luzena Stanley Wilson, Nevada City, California, 1849

Elsewhere, on the lonely plains, without much wood in sight, men would dig caves out of hillsides for their families' first homes. Sod houses were a step up from dugouts. Sod was cut from the prairie with special oxen-drawn plows or sod cutters, weighed

Rebecca Jane Brooks Tatum, 1880s, along Salt Creek near Bernard, Kansas.

From the collection of Molly Wullstein Van Austen.

fifty pounds, and measured one foot by two feet by four inches thick. Laid grass-side down, they formed two-feet thick walls, with wood-framed holes for windows and doors. Frames of poles and willow brush, topped with sod, formed the roofs. Sod for one house, according to author Joanna Stratton, weighed nearly ninety tons.

> **I am looking rather seedy now while**
> **holding down my claim**
> **And my victuals are not always of the**
> **best**
> **And the mice play shyly round me as I**
> **nestle down to rest**
> **In my little old sod shanty in the West.**
> **—from "The Little Old Sod Shanty**
> **on the Plain" (traditional)**

Sometimes an entire hill would be the home, with holes left for door and windows, with a front wall and a roof of "prairie marble" (sod bricks). You could even grow flowers up there.

Dugouts and soddies were good for insulation, but lousy for keeping out rain and snakes. One woman told this story.

> **[W]hen it rained, the water came**
> **through the roof and ran in the door.**
> **After the storms, we carried the water**
> **out with buckets, then waded around in**
> **the mud until it dried up. Then to keep**
> **us nerved up, sometimes the bull**
> **snakes would get in the roof and now**
> **and then one would lose his hold and**
> **fall down on the bed, then off on the**
> **floor. Mother would grab the hoe and**
> **there was something doing, and after**
> **the fight was over Mr. Bull Snake was**
> **dragged outside. Of course there had to**
> **be something to keep us from getting**
> **discouraged.[9]**

Imagine a woman used to living in a two-story frame house in the east, arriving at the end of a journey through dust and downpours, perhaps sickness and birth and death. And she stares at a little hill that will soon be her home.

A Kansas woman remembered:

> **When our covered wagon drew up beside the door of the one-roomed sod house that father had provided, he helped mother down and I remember how her face looked as she gazed about that barren farm, then threw her arms about his neck and gave way to the only fit of weeping I ever remember seeing her indulge in.**[10]

Some women crumpled and never recovered. Prairie women, they were called. Most "fell into line" and made the best of it, and a few even enjoyed the challenge of making a home out of next to nothing. A gaily colored quilt from home, a precious china pitcher that survived the journey, a freshly-ironed table cloth, red yarn trimming on gunny bag curtains, a rug braided of rags—a precious gift from a neighbor—all brought touches of color and love and home to give a woman something pretty to look at.

Board floors were a luxury. First floors usually were packed-down dirt. Mrs. Robert Smith, who settled in Washington Territory in the 1880s, remembered:

> **Gravel was spread over the dirt. The women wore moccasins and their sweeping was done with a rake. They would ask each other, 'Have you done your house raking today?' When they prospered and could afford a floor, Mr. Johnson threw down his hammer and danced a jig on it. The women put on**

**shoes again. They stepped high and had
to become accustomed to walking in
them.**[11]

Once they moved into the log cabin, Mrs. Smith
finished the inside of the cabin with "fifteen dollars
worth of good muslin." Lining tent canvas and rough,
drafty cabin walls with fabric or newspaper was a
common way of perking up a cabin and keeping out
drafts and crawling critters.

Fabric stretched overhead formed "skating ceil-
ings," which looked better but often gathered dirt and
other unsavory things. Anne Ellis remembered a dis-
gusting scene in her family's Colorado cabin:

**The ceiling of our cabin was usually
covered with canvas—in this dirt would
collect, making it sag in places . . ..
Mountain rats also made their nests
just on top of the canvas and this would
make a big sag. Once a rat ran along
the canvas and Mama saw the shape of
his body and stuck a fork into him. The
blood dripped through, and I cried, not
because I was sorry for the rat, but just
at the sordidness of it all. Then I go out
on the hillside,
throw myself down
flat on my back,
and stare straight
up at the sky, with
such a feeling of
relief, knowing
that nothing dirty
will drop into my
eyes.**[12]

**The hinges are of leather and the
    windows have no glass
While the board roof lets the howling
    blizzards in**

**And I hear the hungry coyote as he
slinks up through the grass
Round my little old sod shanty on my
claim.**
—from "The Little Old Sod Shanty
on the Plains"

Windows, like floors, were a luxury. With a window, you could let in the light and see outside without letting in bugs or cold. Until the arrival of a glass window, you hang a quilt or animal skin over the hole. But a *window* . . .

"I have a *window* in my house," wrote Susanna Townsend in 1852 from California. "It is a fine thing to have a tight roof and a floor but you have no idea how delightful it is to have a window. . . . All the passers by stare and gaze at the wonderful phenomenon, a glass window! in a log cabin! I don't think there is another in all the county round."[13]

Some laws required homesteaders to have at least one window. If they didn't have the money for it, they would pool resources with neighbors and buy one window. Then, when they were ready to "prove up," they'd borrow the window, invite the inspector to come take a look, then save the window for the next family that needed it.

Windows were a luxury. A safe place to live was a necessity.

A woman named Laura moved westward to a place where she hoped she and her small daughters would be safe.

Laura Bangston Finley was the grandmother of Kathryn Hall Bogle, who told me Laura's story, although she knows only pieces of it. It's hard to trace black family history, Kathryn explained, because slavery broke up so many of the families.

Laura's mother and grandmother had been slaves. "Laura's family was broken because of slavery," Kathryn told me. She continued:

> Laura's mother, Priscilla Bangston, was
> the mother of three daughters. All of
> them were light. Laura, my
> grandmother, was light, yet the darkest
> of the three. Their father was the white
> slave owner. The two lightest girls were
> raised by white families.

Fair Laura never saw her lighter-skinned sisters
again. Here, Kathryn Bogle paused. Then she said,
"We black people often laugh at the idea that whites
don't always know who they are."

> My mother's father was Creek Indian,
> very strong and alert. [White] people
> didn't know another word for him but
> nigger, but they respected him for his
> strength. He was not black, and he
> lived with fair Laura. He loved his
> family that he made with Laura. He
> taught my mother, Lillian, some dance
> steps. The little family lived in the
> Mississippi Bottoms, where the river
> came in. Houses there were built on
> stilts.
> They lived near a swamp. My
> grandfather drove a team of oxen and
> went into the woods and cut down logs
> of mahogany. The teams were his own,
> and he brought logs from the swamps.
> Someone where they lived
> threatened him. They were white men.
> They said they would get him because
> of his "arrogance." My mother said he
> was proud. You might say he walked
> with his head unbent. He carried his
> head high no matter what. It was the
> pride that was the focal point of the
> men's anger.
> In the evening the family would sit

on the porch of the house that was on
stilts. One night the white men on
horseback rode round and around the
house. Laura and her children, my
mother and her sister, were inside. My
grandfather was out on the porch with
his rifle across his knees while they
rode around. No shots were fired. They
called him nigger.

After that Laura told my mother
they were leaving Mississippi to go to
the homestead of her mother, Priscilla,
in Oklahoma. At the railroad station
my grandfather was pacing up and
down the platform. Some white men
had come there and challenged and
taunted him. He didn't have a gun.

On that platform he fought with at
least one of the men, and killed him
with his head—just rammed him in the
stomach.

That won for him a place in jail. No
one ever heard any more about him.

That was the story my mother,
Lillian Finley Hall, told me.

And so fair Laura and her little daughters got on
that train bound for Oklahoma. Laura never again saw
the Indian man who loved the family he made with
her and taught their little girl how to dance.

Many other women never again would see the families they had left behind. How many women gazed
out their windows—if they had them—toward the
east, memories rushing through their heads in a language strange and foreign to their neighbors?

Then as now, events far away triggered migrations
that tore communities apart and brought people
together in strange ways. Beginning in the eighteenth
century with Catherine the Great, a series of Russian
czars invited European peasants to settle areas to the

Corn-husking bee, Bessarabian village, now in Ukraine, c. 1930s.

Courtesy Erhardt Hehn.

north of the Black Sea, largely to spur the farming economy and keep the lands out of the hands of Asiatic and Turkish tribes.

The czars promised economic help, religious freedom, and exemption from military service. For more than 100 years, tens of thousands of farmers from German states streamed into the Ukraine, fleeing wars and religious and economic oppression. Then, in the 1870s, Czar Alexander II changed the rules. Settlers would be required to speak Russian and, most important, subject to compulsory service in the Russian army.

Thousands of families fled the new policies, to migrate yet again, this time westward across the sea to the United States—most to the western states. Among those German-Russian immigrants were my great grandparents, Andreas Reimann and Katharina Höhn Reimann.

A family history, including a letter from Andreas Reimann, sketches their story. How I wish I knew

Andreas and Katharina Höhn Reimann.

Courtesy Erhardt Hehn.

more, had some words from Katharina. This I know. Katharina, born in Russia to German-Polish immigrants, migrated to Parkston, South Dakota, in 1878 with her husband, their three children, and a child from Andreas' previous marriage.

It had to be a wrenching journey over thousands of miles by wagon, train, ship, and another train. They tear themselves away from family in Russia, never to see them again. Then they face punishing weather, sickness, seasickness, crowded into suffocating quarters with strange languages all around, perhaps rats, bed bugs, rancid food, and fear of being turned away by immigration officials.

They carry with them a precious piece of paper. On it is the name of the town where they are to get off the train: Yankton. The train stops. It is December, "in a cold, northwest-wind driven snow storm." The brother who came before is there to meet them. They fall into his wagon, pile in their few belongings from the old country, and set out for the brother's farm thirty miles away. But they can't stay. There's barely room for one family, let alone two. They leave after two weeks to stay with another family.

Katharina would have been twenty-five. All this time, one of the children has been sick. She herself is in the early months of pregnancy. The day after their arrival in a strange, crowded house in a strange, cold land, her child dies.

How Katharina must have longed for home, for her mother's care, for a familiar room where she could cry. Perhaps she drew some comfort from a familiar hymn sung in her family's Lutheran church back home.

Ein' feste Burg is unser Gott
Ein' gute Wehr and Waffen.
Er hilft uns frei aus aller Noth
Die uns hat jetzt betroffen.

A mighty fortress is our God,
A bulwark never failing.
Our helper He, amid the flood
Of mortal ills prevailing.
    —Hymn by Martin Luther, 1535

Andreas wasted no time claiming land and building a house. By spring, through the biting cold of a South Dakota late winter and early spring, he had "built myself a cottage and a summer kitchen out of pieces of sod" *(rasenstucken).*

Having a summer kitchen meant that cooking could be done away from the main house, keeping it cleaner and free of flies.

"The beginning was hard," wrote Andreas. The first autumn, "a prairie fire swept across the land, not leaving enough hay to start a fire in the stove. Hay and straw [for the horses he had bought] had to be hauled from ten to fifteen miles away and wood was found only along the Missouri River. Construction lumber and food had to be brought from Yankton, forty-five miles away."[14]

We've reached the land of dying wheat
Where nothing grows for man to eat,

**Where the wind it blows the fiery heat
Across the plains so hard to beat.**

**Dakota Land, South Dakota Land,
As on thy burning soil I stand;
I look away across the plains
And wonder why it never rains.**
                    —Parody of "Beulah Land"

Katharina would bear fourteen children, one of them my grandmother. Fourteen live births in twenty-three years. Two were born in the same year, one in January, the second the following December. I wonder if Katharina had a choice, or the means, to limit the births. One German Russian immigrant to North Dakota wrote that "men were unwilling to practice birth control, which, in rural areas, typically meant abstinence. . . . Scriptural injunctions to 'multiply' too often were the excuse to ignore common sense in birth control."[15]

Katharina Höhn Reimann.

Courtesy Erhardt Hehn.

This attitude was not at all limited to immigrants from foreign lands. American preachers and medical men regularly reminded women that controlling births was only for prostitutes.

Martin Luther, founder of Katharina's church, was himself no help to the German-Russian women, having once written, "[W]omen . . . have but small and narrow [chests] and broad hips, to the end they should remain at home, sit still, keep house, and bear and bring up children."[18]

Katharina must have taken comfort from the presence of the families of relatives who migrated to South

Dakota within a few years of her own journey, bringing with them a traditional folksong.

**O may I go a-wandering until the day
I die
And may I always laugh and sing
beneath God's clear blue sky.**

Katharina Höhn
Reimann with
grandchildren
Erna and Vesta
Reimann in
front of the sod
house originally
built in 1879,
near Parkston,
South Dakota.
In this
photograph, the
sod house has
been expanded.

Courtesy Erhardt
Hehn.

After the family's wanderings across the sea, Katharina's family was able to settle down safely on their own land. For forty-four years, Katharina lived on that land in the solid sod house Andreas built.

Katharina Höhn Reimann was one who came to the new land, found her home, and stayed there. Perhaps here she found what was reflected in a proverb on a plaque over the desk of her grandson, my father, Ruben J. Greffenius.

My peace I give you.

From the collection of Ruth
Hendricks Greffenius.
Photo by Mike Griswold.

CHAPTER NINE

Stories Entwined:
Weaving and Quilting the
Fabric of Home

My grandmother's hands
   wove the cedar and
   bear grass
Into this fine basket I hold
   in my hands.
To hold bitter root,
   camas, fern, tiger lily
Blackberries, cranberries—
   gifts from the land.

My grandmother's hands
   worked with bright
   colored fabrics
Taken from dresses I
   wore long ago
With strong cotton thread
   and the finest of needles
Weaving my memories in
   patterns she'd sew.

       —from
"Weaving and Quilting"
  by Linda Allen ©1991

Left: **Nina Bright, Neah Bay, Washington, weaver of many baskets.**
From the collection of the Jefferson County Historical Society, Port Townsend,
Washington #11.815.
Right: **"The Patchwork Quilt" by Joseph Patrick McMeekin.**
Courtesy of Idaho Historical Society 83–2.29/d (undated).

Think of the hands of the grandmothers who knew
the fibers of earth and with them shaped the containers and covers that sustained the journeys of their
children and grandchildren, husbands and lovers and
neighbors, through time and distance. With the fibers,
they wove the rhythm of the seasons of their lives—
the cycles of moon and stars, days and weeks, months
and years.

The grandmother knows where to find the finest
grasses and fibers to weave into baskets. Tiny baskets
to hold treasures and secrets. Tall, handsome baskets,
finely woven, and perhaps decorated with quill
designs or feathers, to decorate her head. Smooth baskets to cradle infants. Baskets loosely woven and big
enough to carry on a woman's back, suspended from
her forehead, to carry the life-sustaining gifts of the
earth, food, and fuel for her people. Huge baskets to
store the grains and dried berry cakes for winter,
when the earth sleeps. Baskets woven so tightly that
water cannot escape them, baskets to hold cool water
or water heated from rocks, hot enough to cook deer
meat, salmon, soup, and mush.

Her old eyes are clouded from many seasons of
cooking over a smoking fire. But there's no need for
her to see her work. She's known the feel and rhythm
of weaving the strands for as long as she can remember. As she weaves the fibers, warp and woof, she
sings. She sings her hopes and dreams, and incanta-
tions to the spirits of the plants and animals whose
bodies and fibers sustain the lives of her people.

She sings to Grandmother Earth, who ultimately
will receive her own body again, and her spirit, to
guide those who come after. As she sings, she weaves
into her baskets ancient symbols of woman's power,
and spirits of the plants and animals of the earth,
endowing them with the power of her song. She sings,
too, the people's stories that became their history.

My great-grandma Towsalee passed on her knowledge

**To her daughter Sally—she was only
    six then.
Our tribe's own designs such as Salmon
    Gill, Trail of Eel,
Flowers for women and
deer
    for the men.[1]**

Twined root bag, salmon gill pattern.

Photo by Mary Dodds Schlick.

The young girl watches her grandmother's dark,
life-hardened hands guiding the fibers into form,
while her own smooth hands memorize the patterns.
As she weaves, she listens to the stories in the songs,
learning the wisdom handed down, grandmother to
mother to daughter, from ancient times.

**My grandmother's hands worked with
    bright colored fabrics
Taken from dresses I wore long ago
With strong cotton thread and the finest
    of needles
Weaving my memories in patterns she'd
    sew.[2]**

The grandmother bends over the quilt stretched
out on the frame suspended from the ceiling. Some
afternoons, she can lower the ropes that hold the
frame to have perhaps a precious hour to record the
seasons of her life. As her expert hands weave the
treasured needle through the fabric, she remembers
laughing children now grown, and the home she left
behind.

**Now this quilt, honey, I made out of the
pieces of my children's clothes, their
little dresses and waists and aprons.**

Some of them's dead, and some of
them's grown and married and a long
way off from me, further off than the
ones that's dead, I sometimes think. But
when I sit down and look at this quilt
and think over the pieces, it seems like
they all come back, and I can see them
playing around the floors and going in
and out, and hear them crying and
laughing and calling me just like they
used to do before they grew up to men
and women . . ..[3]

—Aunt Jane of
Kentucky

The girl tosses her long pigtails out of the way and
watches the gentle, veined hands as they follow the
pattern penciled on the fabric, sewing the layers
together. As she listens to the stories, she tries to
imagine her own mother young enough to wear pigtails and just learning to quilt.

My great grandma Eleanor passed on
    her knowledge
To her daughter Susan when she was
    just nine
Lone Star, Log Cabin, the sweet Rose of
    Sharon
Basket, Medallion—her favorite
    designs.

Salmon Gill, Trail of Eel, Flowers and
    Deer
Bringing the lives of our ancestors near
Lone Star, Log Cabin, Basket design
Weaving and Quilting, our stories
    entwine.[4]

As the migrations flowed, first from the south, then from the east, and then from all directions, the stories entwined, sometimes peacefully and sometimes violently, as seekers and settlers displaced the ones who were there first—the Indian peoples, followed by the Spanish and then mixed-race mestizo and metis.

As the stories entwined, so did the dreams.

When I think of the grandmothers, I often think of them in their aprons.

> **They were made of strong dark**
> **gingham**
> **If used for every day wear—**
> **White muslin, lace on the pocket and**
> **hem**
> **For Sunday, or when Grandma went**
> **anywhere.**
>
> **. . .**
>
> **They helped with a million chores**
> **Saved Grandmother oodles of trips,**
> **From the garden they brought in the**
> **food**
> **From the woodpile they carried the**
> **chips.**[5]

—from "Grandma's Apron"

Apron crocheted by Amalia Reimann Greffenius.

Photo by author.

I have a small, dainty red and cream colored apron crocheted by my grandmother, Amalia Reimann Greffenius. I don't use the apron in the kitchen, ever. It is much too dainty. I have wondered why an apron would be so beautiful.

Kathryn Hall Bogle, who has studied and pioneered black history in the Northwest, told me that her great-grandmother, Priscilla Bangston, on her homestead in Oklahoma, "wore multiple aprons—at least five," one on top of the next. As she changed jobs, she would change aprons.

"The top one was the big one," Kathryn tells me. "It could be several pieces patched together. That was the working one. It covered a cleaner one underneath. Now each one was smaller than the one on top. The third was nicer and smaller than the second, the fourth nicer and smaller still.

"When company came, off came the aprons that were objectionable," Kathryn explains. "The last would be the dainty one. So Priscilla always was ready to meet people. It really wasn't unique to have many aprons on at once."

So that explains my grandmother's dainty red and cream crocheted apron.

I think of the pioneer farm women in their work aprons, often made of gunny bags. They felt they were moving up in the world if they had several aprons to wash and iron each week to cover ragged, faded dresses.

An outside apron would be a necessity for the woman's jobs of tending the chickens and milking the cows. Women's butter, cheese, and egg money kept many families going.

A Kansas woman recalled the year "cinch bugs took the corn. . . . Such years as that it was that dairying and poultry saved the day. Butter and eggs, what would people have done without them?"[6]

Many farm women developed mini-industries marketing eggs and the butter they made, proudly trading them for needed items or cold cash. Butter and egg money paid for many a pair of shoes, many a wind mill to bring water from the earth, and many stores of food.

Keturah Belknap, who traveled the Oregon Trail to Oregon Country with her family in 1848, worked with other women to provide for their families during 1849 while the men were away for seven months searching for gold in California.

> **Some men were coming home and the company sent us a letter and a little bunch of gold dust and said they would be home late in the fall. . . . [Mrs. Gilbert] had four cows and I had four, and grass of the best quality. So we made butter and cheese and the demands was such that we could sell every pound for cash. Cheese was 25 cents a pound and butter from 40 to 50 cents. So instead of my having to use the gold dust money, I had money laid by for winter. . . . We went down on Marys River and bought two good Durham cows, paid a hundred dollars for each one.[7]**

Butter and eggs were so identified with women that one Englishman figured girls didn't need to learn about much else. "All the heducation a girl needs," he declared, "is to know enough to go into the 'ay and gather heggs and all the figgering she needs is to know enough to weigh butter."[8]

Tending the milking cows and chickens, gathering

the eggs and making the butter and cheese—those were almost invariably the women's jobs and many males refused to do them. Author and historian Julie Roy Jeffrey recorded the story of a woman still weak from childbirth whose sons helped their mother to the milking stool and held her up while she milked the cow because "milking a cow was 'woman's work' so they would not do it."

> **Churned ten pounds, cleaned windows and floor, cleaned up the front room, made cake, done up all my work and had my bath. Five o'clock I went to town to take tithing. Took one dozen eggs, ten pound of butter, forty pound of cheese. The Primary Fair came off today. I forgot it with all my cares and labor. I got a sack of sugar this evening. The first whole sack I ever had.[9]**
> **—Lucy Hannah White Flake,**
> **Arizona, 1898**

> **Mother and I took pleasure and pride in our chickens. We had a number of hens and had them all named. Some of them developed almost human qualities and we made great pets of them. One of them—a black one, we named 'Molly', was unusual. She would sneak into the living room . . . and we used to watch her tip-toe across the room and go way back under the bed in the bedroom to lay her egg, then tiptoe out again, before she commenced to cackle.[10]**
> **—Sadie Martin, Arizona, 1888**

Elinore Pruitt Stewart, who homesteaded her own
place in Wyoming, accepted a Dutch neighbor's invitation for a breakfast of "cackle-berries und antelope
steak."

"Never having seen a cackle-berry, my imagination
pictured them as some very luscious wild fruit," she
wrote. Her host piled her tin plate high with breakfast—steak, an egg, and two delicious biscuits. Elinore
dug in, finished what was on her plate, and
announced that she was ready for her cackle-berries.

"How many cackle-berries does you want?" asked
her Dutch host. "You haf had so many as I haf cooked
for you."

"'Why, Herman, I haven't had a single berry," she
said. Then, "such a roar of laughter" as she was
informed that "eggs and cackle-berries were one and
the same."[11]

Kate Robbins journeyed to the gold fields of northern California from Massachusetts in the late 1850s
with her husband, who had returned from the mining
fields to bring Kate with him. Soon they were off for
central Oregon to raise cattle.

In letters home, Kate wrote of the everyday details
that made up the tedious drama of farm living.
Planting her own garden of familiar flowers and vegetables was like planting seeds of home.

Dear Brother,
      . . . Abner and I have each a garden
by ourselves, that is he planted one and
I the other, with Tommy's [her son's]
help; and there is quite a competition to
see whose will do best, it is about an

even thing so far, but he has the
advantage by having the wettest spot.
Peas, onions, lettuce, radish, turnips &
cabbage are all up and doing fine.
Beans and corn do not do well but
Tommy and I are going to try some also
squash and watermelon also
cucumbers . . .. I have a flower garden
and lots of the seeds are coming up. . . .
—Kate Robbins, May 24, 1871

Kate Robbins' letters speak of the loneliness and
the overwork that made up the ordinariness of many
pioneer women's lives.

In an August 1874 letter to her mother, Kate went
on to describe her confusion at having so much to do.

. . . and so I have a great deal of out-
doors work, I always attend to the hogs
and hens, help milk and of course take
care of the milk and the butter, Eunice
[her daughter] has gone to Albany and
Portland on a visit and that leaves me
more to do just now as she is a great
deal of help about the house . . ..

I have a man here at work on the
grain now and he and Tommy [her son]
must have their regular meals, and out
here it is so different from home there
are so many who go to a place just to
get their victuals that one never knows
who or how many they are cooking for
as they generally come in about dinner
time. I very seldom go any where but it
dont seem to make any difference
whole <u>tribes</u> come here just the same.
There is no formaility, but the first
thing you know in comes a whole
family to stay till after dinner, and the
women folks who will all start out into

**the kitchen to 'help' but I cant get used
to it entirely it confuses me and I had
rather have the kitchen to myself.**

**Sunday Baked Beans
Soak beans over Friday night and
boil them on Saturday morning until
when you take some in a spoon and
blow on them the shells split. Then put
them into the big pot in layers with salt
pork. Pour molasses all over it and
bake the rest of Saturday and until
noon Sunday.**[12]

Part of the Code of the West was welcoming
friends and strangers alike to the table. Sunday was
the regular visiting day and women often didn't know
how many people might be at the table. Most pioneer
women welcomed the visits, especially if women were
among the guests. Often the company would stay for
several days.

But for some, like Kate Robbins, unexpected company just added to the work load. Oregon Trail pioneer Abigail Scott Duniway wasn't thrilled with the
hungry men who showed up around dinner time after
her hard day's work. Seeds for her later work as the
Northwest's leading suffragist already were being
planted.

**We had eaten lunch and I had washed
the dishes and started work at the
quilting frames, when four men came to
the cabin. They sat around the fireplace
and talked. I replenished the fire and
then went ahead with my quilting. After
an hour's stay I noticed they were
becoming restless. Finally one of them
said, 'Well, I guess we might as well go;
I don't see any indications of dinner.' I
was shortly to become a mother. I had**

**been working hard; it was after the
dinner hour when they arrived, so I
said: 'If you had told me what you were
waiting for you could have gone home
an hour ago.' I will never forget how
troubled and shocked my husband was
when I told him about my lack of
hospitality.**[13]

For the pioneer women who had come by covered
wagon and cooked over campfires for months, a
indoor stove would have been a wondrous luxury.

Mary Stewart, after her arrival in Oregon country,
built her own clay fireplace where she did her cooking for several years. In 1851 she had one of the two
stoves brought to Oregon City. "You have no idea,
after you have stooped over a fireplace doing your
cooking, for years, what a comfort it is to be able to
stand up and do your cooking over a stove," she
remembered. "During the early years of my married
life, I had two ambitions—one was to have a stove to
cook on and the other was to have bread made of
wheat flour."[14]

In 1886, my great-grandfather, Richard Jones, left
his wife, Mary Isen Jones, and their three children in

**Richard and Mary
Isen Jones, c. 1880s.**

From the collection of
Ruth Hendricks
Greffenius.

depression-torn England for the greener pastures of Colorado's coal fields. According to family legend, Great-grandpa Jones didn't even tell anyone he was leaving. Just up and took off. Great-grandma Jones didn't hear anything from him, the story goes, until one day she received a message and traveling money to come to America.

Richard, perhaps to make amends for leaving like he did, had a wonderful surprise waiting for Mary in their Canon City, Colorado home. It was a new indoor stove. It must have been the envy of all the other ladies.

Well. When Mary arrived, she refused to cook on that newfangled thing. She didn't know how to use it and wasn't going to learn. So Richard built her an outdoor oven just like the one at home in England. As the story goes, Mary cooked in that oven for a while, and then quietly switched to the indoor stove.

Apparently, Mary's dislike of the new stove wasn't unusual. Until the end of the 1800s, stoves were complicated, with all sorts of flues and ventilators. Few women liked these stoves, especially European immigrants, whose receipts weren't suited to them.

Receipts and cookbooks were important links to home for frontier women, but some things were even more important, as one well-meaning husband found out in this incident reported by Washington Territory pioneer Phoebe Judson.

Our family was subsisting on bran, and were all sick, when my husband had the good fortune to find employment. I naturally expected that with his first day's wages he would bring home some nourishing food, but, what was my indignant disappointment, when in the place of food, he handed me a cook book.[15]

A cook book!

Imagine her sitting down, trying to ignore her own empty stomach rumbles and the hungry gaze of her children as she leafs through the clean, crisp pages . . . Chicken Pie with Oysters . . . Rice Croquettes . . . Apple Compote . . . Eggs sur le Plat . . . Blackberry Jam Cake . . . Tea Cookies . . .

Claribel Rathbone Dahlen, a teacher in Washington's Puget Sound, related a similar incident told by a friend.

> **The worst time of all, [Husband] took
> the money the land agent sent us from
> Minnesota, went to town expressly for
> salt, flour, nails, and feed. And what
> did he come home with? He met a man
> who bought him a drink for past favors.
> He came home with no staples. Instead,
> he held in his hands a silver thimble
> for me and a gun for the boys.[16]**

With little access to stores, pioneering women needed to know how to preserve and store foods.

> **Preserving Eggs for Winter
> Pack in a clean vessel with small end
> down, strewing bran between each
> layer. Then place one or two
> thicknesses of brown paper on top and
> cover about one inch thick with salt.
> Cover close or keep in a cool place.[17]**

Cool storage space was important for pioneer women. Dugout or potato cellars dug into the cool earth, wells, springs, and supplies of ice provided cool places to store food supplies.

Kathryn Hall Bogle remembers her great-grandmother Priscilla's cellar dug into the Oklahoma earth with two doors on top that swung up to rest on the roof of the cellar. Kathryn would go down the steps and be surrounded by shelves laden with jars of pickles, fruits and vegetables. Hanging from the ceiling were smoked ham and bacon and other meats. The cellar was also used as a storm shelter.

"Great-grandmother Priscilla was self-sufficient on her farm," remembers Kathryn Bogle. "She hardly ever went to the grocery store. About the only foods she ever bought were salt and pepper."

Army wife Elizabeth Burt, stationed in Arizona for a time, marveled at the blocks of ice delivered weekly in the summer from Phoenix, twenty-five miles away.

One of these blocks of ice lasted four days and during that period made our menus somewhat tempting. Four days of each week were thus enjoyed, but in the other three, as far as the table was concerned, the butter was oil, the cheese already melted for a rarebit; the quail of which the hunters brought in great numbers, were delicious on ice days but at other times had to be eaten as soon as killed.[18]

Spanish and Indian women of the Southwest had some of the most colorful preserving techniques in all the West. Preserving bright red chile peppers for the winter was a task requiring much skill and many hands, ending with *ristras,* strings of crimson peppers drying in the sun.

All the strings of peppers hung
On the 'dobes in the sun,
Blazin' red as some young puncher's
    new bandana,
And the scented smoke that came
From the piñon wood aflame
Smelt like incense to Our Lady of
    Mañana.[19]

—"The Town of Old Dolores,"
by James Grafton Rogers, reprinted with
permission from Katie Lee's book, *Ten Thousand
Goddam Cattle*, ©1976 by Katie Lee.

Indian women from New Mexico to California braided roasted or boiled caterpillars into long ropes called *pilgi*. Anna Moore Shaw, a Pima woman of Arizona, described her mother's preparation of *pilgi*:

When caterpillars were plentiful, Molly
would gather them in large quantities,
cut off their heads, and squeeze out
their insides. Then she boiled them in
salted water, and when they were
cooked, she salted them again before
braiding them into long strands for
storage.[20]

Pioneer women judged themselves and each other by the lightness of their bread, the flakiness of their pie paste, by how they kept their houses, how their clean clothes lined up on the clothesline, how clean they could get their floors, how smooth they could spin their yarn.

Many pioneer women, like their rural sisters to the east, had the huge job of manufacturing clothing, beginning with fiber from flax or cotton, or wool from sheep or goats. The arrival of a spinning wheel was a big event.

For my thirteenth birthday I was given
a spinning wheel. This was in 1854.
Mother was a good hand at carding
wool. People used to bring in their
wool, and we washed, carded, spun and
wove it on shares, so we soon had
plenty of clothes. Mother used alder
bark to dye the cloth brown and oak
bark to dye it butternut color.[21]
                    —Kate Morris, Oregon pioneer

Courtesy Hood River County Museum, Hood River, Oregon.

"[M]any a long winter evening was cheerfully
passed picking, carding, spinning and knitting before
the open fire," wrote Phoebe Judson. She continued:

> We found that, with so many feet to
> clothe, that making our own stockings
> and socks was a great saving.
>
> Besides providing stockings for my
> own family, I knit many a pair for the
> bachelor ranchers—they were much
> better than any they could buy. . . .
>
> My wheel was a great curiosity to
> the native women. . . . They had a
> unique way of making yarn from the
> wool of mountain goats. . . . They
> picked the wool, and without carding,
> rolled it on the bare leg, that had been
> well lubricated from the hip down with
> bear's oil; the left hand held a stock,
> which took the place of the spindle, on
> which they wound the yarn as they
> rolled it with the right hand.[22]

Mary Ann Hafen, a handcart pioneer to Utah in 1860, helped glean cotton from the fields planted in southern Utah.

> By the firelight in the evenings we
> shelled out the cotton. We dried it
> further in the sun. And then I traded
> mine to a peddler for calico. How well I
> remember that first new dress. I
> thought it very beautiful. It was yellow
> with little red and blue flowers. As we
> had no sewing machine, I made the
> dress by hand with my aunt's help. I
> was then twelve years old.[23]

On the early frontiers, women's clothing was practical and cheap.

> We wore calico for everyday dresses,
> and gingham for Sunday. The calico
> was only twenty-seven inches wide.

**Our dresses were made with full skirts
and long sleeves and were all lined.**[24]
—Frances J. Leonard,
Washington Territory

Clothing manufacture and cooking were just two of the time-laden jobs of many pioneer women.

America Rollins Butler, like Kate Robbins, trekked across the plains with her husband for California gold in 1852. But the promise of free Oregon land glittered brighter than the prospect of California gold, so the couple headed north to claim land in southern Oregon. On the trip by horseback, America wore men's clothes.

America wrote in her diary of everyday dramas of ague (malaria), aching teeth, "Indian troubles," summer heat, winter rains, financial problems, her husband's absences and sickness, and tedious housework.

**. . . as to my self I am maid of all traids
sweeping dusting churning ironing
baking bread and pies dishwashing &c.**

Amazingly, in her list of "traids," America doesn't list her most despised chore: "To day Oh! horrors how shall I express it; is the dreded washing day."[25]

**"Women dream many dreams and see many visions while bending over the washtub."
—Anne Ellis**

From the collection of the Jefferson County Museum, Port Townsend, Washington #28.245.

Think about facing a pile of shirts and pants and socks that probably weigh twice their clean weight with the mud and muck and manure of the fields and barn yard. Throw in a pile of rags used for diapers. Add shirts, pants, dresses, and petticoats of your ten other children after they've been playing and working in the fields. Add your own skirts and petticoats that have dragged around in the dirt and mud, and aprons that you've butchered the hog in.

Think about what you have to do to get this filthy pile ready to wear again, and you can understand why "thedrededwashday" became a single word for a lot of women.

Smart husbands would want to keep their distance on "thedrededwashday," as in this verse:

> Kate, she is a bonnie wife,
> There's none so free from evil
> Unless upon a washing day
> And then she is the devil!
> The very kittens on the earth,
> They dare not even play
> So away they jump with many a bump
> Upon a washing day!
>
> For 'tis thump, thump, scrub, scrub,
>   scold, scold away
> The devil a bit of comfort here
> Upon a washing day.[26]
>   —from "The Washing Day:
>   A Ballad for Wet Weather"

First, you have to have soap.

> **We made lye by making a "hop" of
> clapboards, and filling with ashes, then
> put water on the ashes and let it drop—
> the drippings were caught and made
> lye. Then the grease and suet and lye
> were put in a tub and soap was made.[27]**
>   **—Anna Knight, Oregon Territory**

Next, you have to have water. If you have a well, you can draw pail after pail of water from it and haul it to the wash tubs or kettles. If you don't have a well, you have to go to the creek or river perhaps a mile away and haul the water from there.

Homestead National Monument.

Photo by author.

One woman described her Kansas pioneer mother's experience hauling water. "A yoke was made to place across the shoulders, so as to carry at each end a bucket of water, and then water was brought a half mile from spring to house."[28]

If it's been raining, you'll have rain water you've collected in barrels. If it's winter and everything's frozen up, you'll have to haul snow for melting on the stove.

Once you have your water, here's what you do.

Grandma's Receet
(from Mrs. Bowman's scrap book)
For washing clothes—given many
years ago to a young bride by her
Kentucky mountain Grandmother. We

are passing it on, just as it was
originally written.
1. bild fire in back yard to heet kettle
   of rain water.
2. set tubs so smoke won't blow in eyes
   if wind is pert.
3. shave one hole cake lie soap in
   biling water.
4. sort things, making three piles
5. stur flour in cold water to smooth
   then thin down with bilin water.
6. rub dirty spots on board, scrub
   hard, then bile, rub cullored but
   don't bile, just rench and starch.
7. take white things out of kettle with
   broomstick handle then rench, blew
   and starch.
8. spred tee towels on grass.
9. hang old rags on fence.
10. pore rench water on flower bed.
11. scrub porch with hot soapy water.
12. turn tubs upside down.
13. go put on cleen dress—smooth hair
    with side combs—brew cup of tee—
    set and rest a spell and count
    blessins.[29]

The resting a spell with a cup of "tee" was a blessing right there. And if you could share that moment with a woman friend, that was a real blessing.

Apple Tea

Pare and slice thin three or four
pleasant sour apples, pour a pint of
boiling water on them, and boil them
six or eight minutes. Let them stand till
they are cold, then pour or strain off
the water, and sweeten it a little, unless
you prefer it without.[30]

If the baby cries as you're enjoying your tea, rock her and sing her a lullaby.

Across the frontier, mothers' voices in many tongues sing their babies asleep and awake.

The indian mother rocks her baby, but her method is different from that of her white sister. The top of a young tree, or sapling, is bent over, and to this the board on which the baby is bound is suspended. The mother holds a string that is attached to the board by which she keeps this Indian cradle in motion—a veritable illustration of the old song, 'Rock a by baby on the tree top.'[31]

—Phoebe Judson, Washington

Rockabye baby, in the tree top,
When the wind blows, the cradle will
**   rock.**
When the bough breaks, the cradle will
**   fall.**
Down will come baby, cradle and all.

Phoebe Judson was right about the song.

"We believe that lullabies are the oldest of all songs," says my friend from childhood Bonnie Jo Robbins Hunt, an operatic soprano whose heritage is half Lakota (Sioux). "A lullaby, like most of our songs, can be a prayer."

Bonnie Jo says that the lullaby "Rockabye Baby" came from Eastern Indian women who would place their babies' cradles in the tree branches, where they would gently sway. A pilgrim woman heard Indian women singing as the babies rocked in the boughs. The woman had the lullaby translated and the pilgrim women began singing it to their babies.

Lulliby Baby Bunting,
Your Father's gone a hunting,
To catch a Rabit for a Skin,
To wrap the Baby Bunting in.[32]

House made of dawn.
House made of evening light.
House made of the dark cloud.
House made of male rain.
House made of female rain. . . .
May it be beautiful before me.
May it be beautiful behind me.
May it be beautiful below me.
May it be beautiful above me.
May it be beautiful all around me.
In beauty it is finished.[33]
        —from "A Prayer of the Night Chant"
                        (Navajo)

Like the cedar and bear grass and bright colored fabrics, the voices entwine.

CHAPTER TEN

The Hush Was So Loud:
Frontier Dangers and Delights

**It was such a new world, reaching to
the far horizon without break of tree or
chimney stack; just sky and grass and
grass and sky. . . . The hush was so
loud.**[1]
—Lydia Murphy Toothaker, Kansas

The hush was so loud, especially the prairie farming frontier. Wind. Crickets. A baby's cry. Silence,
mostly.

A woman was supposed to "school in." If she were
to express the sadness or loneliness or rage welling
inside, she would risk being called a shrew or a scold.

It must have been that loud hush—the outside
hush and the inside hush—that stole women's sanity
more than anything. "Prairie women" would walk for
miles to stand and watch a train bump by, just so they
could see some human faces.

A woman who lived in Katharina Reimann's corner of South Dakota wrote:

> It was reported that the Insane Asylum at Yankton was filled with women who had been bereft of reason by the monotony and wretchedness of the hard and lonely life on the prairies. I have been taught from the pulpit all my life that God brought all the sorrows and griefs upon us for our own good. I have come to believe that the Lord has nothing to do with it. All things come about through natural causes and he has no supervision over the children of men. What possible good came to those women who filled the Insane Asylum. If I am skeptical I hope to be forgiven.[2]

One woman wrote about her mother, Susan's, South Dakota homesteading experience in the 1880s. Susan's husband had no intention of farming their claim. Instead, he walked three miles into town to work every day while "Mother's lot was to stay at home all day with a couple of small children, to hoe the garden, to wrestle with the fleetfooted Jersey cow."

> But it was the monotony, the loneliness, that was the worst. In all the five years we were on the Claim, she went to only one public entertainment, a dance at the 'Exchange' Hotel. She seldom got off the place for even part of a day. If we had had a horse and buggy, she could have found something different to look at once in awhile. If we had been building up a farm, getting stock about us, and making progress, she might have felt it worthwhile. As it was, it

**was like putting her, only twenty-eight
years of age, into prison for the five
best years of her life.**

Sickness, a family death, and a debilitating infection slowly took away the person that was Susan.

**She drifted into deep melancholia, long
spells of crying and talking to herself;
she kept saying that she wished she
were dead. Finally I became so
frightened that I told her she could not
do that, that she dared not leave us all
alone. She looked at me as if she had
forgotten who I was, and then said
bitterly, 'No, I guess I can't do even
that.'**

**Now, when people get in that
condition, they are said to be having a
nervous breakdown, and are sent away
for a complete change; but in pioneer
days they were said to be having the
'Blues,' and they had to fight it out by
themselves as best they could.**

**The five years were finally at an
end. The Claim was ours. And we
moved to town in time to save her
reason.**[3]

Susan paid five years of her life for that claim
before she moved to town. Many women, when given
the choice, moved from the isolation of the homestead
to town. There, they could savor company of other
people, especially other women, who could listen to
their troubles and offer warmth, advice, and help
when it was needed.

Over and over, the women's voices tell of their
loneliness—for home, for warmth from husbands, for
the company of other women, for meaning in their
lives.

constant rainy weather the last of this
month with sad and duzzled spirits
combining

—America Rollins Butler,
southern Oregon, 1853

Dear Mother:
    . . . I cannot write letters as I used
to, . . . I cannot seem to collect my
thoughts, I suppose it seems strange to
you that I have much to do, but Abner
goes off early in the spring and does
not get back till in the winter, and as
we live on a farm, whatever is done I
have got to attend to . . .

—Kate Robbins, Oregon,
August 18, 1874

This had truly been the longest and
most dreary week of my life, and the
first one without seeing and talking
with those of my sex. Just think of it
once; not one word from the late
fashions; no chance to indulge in a
little gossip, nor discuss the failings of
my neighbors.[4]
—Annie Green, Greeley, Colorado, 1871

Feel lonely to night. Wish husband
would converse about something. Fear
we are not that society for one another
which man & wife ought to be. Wish I
could find what it is prevents our
being.

—Mary Richardson Walker,
Oregon Country, 1839

**I think some days that I shall either go
crazy or run away.**
—Elizabeth Chester Fisk,
Helena, Montana, 1878

Scattered throughout the West are signs that read
"Crazy Woman Creek" and "Crazy Woman Mountain."
Behind each sign is a story, for on the frontier, the
percentage of women committed to institutions for the
insane was consistently higher than that of men.

Though the frontier held many dangers for pioneer
women, insanity was perhaps the greatest danger—
and perhaps one of their greatest fears.

Author Susan Glaspell's story "A Jury of Her
Peers" is a classic story of insanity and murder on a
lonely prairie. Two women accompany their husbands
who are investigating the murder of a farmer. His wife
has just been accused and arrested for his murder. As
the men search the home of the victim for evidence,
the two women unravel the story. They discover the
quilt the wife was working on, with "crazy sewing" in
it. They notice an empty bird cage with a broken door.
Then, in the bottom of her sewing basket, they find a
pretty little box. Inside is a dead canary with a broken
neck.

The women understand. When the men return,
they conceal the evidence.

The singing of a canary would break the loud hush.
It would be perhaps the only music in a woman's
world. If someone were to silence it, it would be like
cutting her only lifeline to sanity.

In the loneliness and silence, to lose a loved one who was a treasured companion would have left a hole in the heart. Oregon pioneer Kate Robbins mourned the loss of her twenty-year-old son, Tommy (whose name she sometimes spelled "Tommie"), to one of the many diseases that frequently swept the frontier. Here, she tells of her despair, and of the care and love that surrounded her son.

Ochoco Oregon
29th Jan. 1881.
Dear Mother,
    . . . [N]o one knows what he was to me, more to me than the others . . . I do not think he had an enemy in the world every one liked him and made a great deal of him, especially the old and the little children; during his sickness the elderly men took nearly all the care of him, . . . it took two all the time to wait upon him, . . . and for five weeks we were never without four men in the house, . . . they would come from along distance, some of them, and all wanted to be with him as much as they could, . . . he seemed to like to have them handle him best, and they would not leave him, two were old bachelors, the other a widower one of the kindest hearted men I ever saw, Tommie gave him his nice new rifle and equipments of which he always thought a great deal.

The frontier, with its loneliness, its wind and heat and dust, took its toll on women's health and beauty. The care of doctors and dentists was rare and expensive, and they often didn't know what they were doing anyway.

Before she traveled west to join her husband in Colorado in 1881, Maggie Brown of Virginia was known as "the beautiful Maggie Keller." She had "flashing violet eyes and long black hair—fifty-four inches—a real beauty." Three years later "the beautiful Maggie Keller" was "as much broken as an old woman and she is not middle aged and [her husband] cares nothing for her since she has broken so."[5] Maggie had lost two teeth, walked with a stoop from a difficult stillborn birth, and her skin was wrinkled from the assault of the wind, heat, and sun.

Women traded beauty secrets with one another to help fight the effects of age, weather, and hard work.

To soften and whiten skin: Use honey soap made by melting down two pounds of soap and stirring in half of a cup of honey.

For soft hands: Use honey.

To bleach freckles: Apply sour milk or buttermilk every night.

For soft hair: Use rain water and a hair wash of alcohol and castor oil, scented with lavender.

To hide grey hair: Touch it up with sage tea.

To invigorate hair: Bay rum, alcohol, castor oil, carbonate of ammonia, tincture of cantharides [a preparation of Spanish flies]. Mix them well. This mixture will promote the growth of the hair and prevent it from falling out.

Substitute for hair soap: Cut up the root of the yucca plant ("oose" or "soap

root") and leave in water to make fluffy
suds.

For offensive breath: Chew a few
grains of coffee.

For sun burn: The juice of one
lemon and one cup milk. Wash your
face in.[6]

Legions of pioneer women, used to tightly-built
houses with glass windows, found themselves in
unexpected battles with insects and animals they had
scarcely imagined.

Pioneer accounts are full of encounters with all
kinds of snakes, including rattlers. Yet few stories
exist of deaths, or even injuries, from snake bites.

"Rattlers were very numerous here in the early
days," a Kansas woman recalled. She remembered
how her mother rescued her when she climbed up on
the roof of their dugout to discover a "very large rattle
snake" coiled around a hole in the roof. "She came
running, catching me by the arm and ruthlessly
snatching me from my perilous position. By the time
she had finished killing this snake with the garden
hoe, she was ready to collapse."[7]

Young Martha Gay Masterson's family took up
land in Lane County, Oregon, in 1852.

We had only been in camp a short time
when we discovered we were in a
rattlesnake district. . . . We were trying
to like the place. I think we should
have but for the snakes. They were
everywhere. Mamie [Martha's sister]

**and I were walking one morning when
she spotted a rattler. I jumped back and
saw another. Just then she saw a whole
nest of them. We feared to move. We
had walked right to the mouth of a
snake den. We killed five and as many
more got away.[8]**

"Some of our neighbors collected the rattles of all
the snakes they killed, showing how numerous they
were," Martha wrote later. "A Mr. Maloney who had a
stock ranch near us had secured a string of rattles
eight feet long."

Sally Hester, a fourteen-year-old immigrant to
California in 1849, wrote about a winter flood that
brought snakes with it.

**As far as the eye can reach you see
nothing but water. It's horrible. Wish I
was back in Indiana. Snakes are plenty.
They come down the river, crawl under
our beds and everywhere.[9]**

Army wife Elizabeth Burt described a method of
protection from snakes when she was on the move and
living in tents in snake country.

**My husband took the precaution . . . to
purchase two buffalo hair ropes long
enough to lay on the ground around our
tents. Snakes would not cross the hairy
surface, we were told. Through several
years this proved to be true in our case
and we now rejoiced in their
protection.[10]**

Seña Martina, a *curandera* (Hispanic medicine
woman) of New Mexico, precribed the protective powers of the wild mountain parsnip:

> **You know, you should never let your children go out to the fields without a piece in their pockets. Its odor keeps poisonous snakes away.[11]**

Sadie Martin, who accompanied her irrigation engineer husband to Arizona in the 1880s, told about their "bedstead," built high to "elude" snakes, a trick that also worked for fleas and other jumping and crawling critters.

> **In order to prove up on our quarter section John and I had to sleep on our own land. I did not like the idea of sleeping outdoors on account of snakes, so John made a high bedstead of lumber and we sewed gunny sacks together for a mattress, which, when filled with straw, made a bed so high that I had to get on a chair to climb up to it. What fun John had watching me make the ascent! I told him I could almost hear the snakes 'gnashing their teeth' at my having eluded them![12]**

> **The June bug has a gaudy wing,**
> **The lightning bug has fame,**
> **The bedbug has no wings at all,**
> **But he gets there just the same.[13]**

Abby T. Mansur wrote letters to her sister in New England from the California mining camp of Horseshoe Bar in 1853. In this particular letter, she complained about how fleas and bed bugs may even

have threatened her own salvation by causing her to
swear so much.

> [Y]ou cannot take any comfort for the
> fleas are biting or the bedbugs or both
> and you might Just as well be in hell i
> never swore so much in my life i
> always swore bad enough but if i
> should die now god only knows [what]
> would become of me . . . there is hardly
> a night i go to bed but what i think of
> you how nice you can go to bed and
> sleep and here i am sometimes i have to
> get up a half dozen times in the night to
> hunt flease and besides bear the
> punishment they inflict on me i am sore
> the whole time from the effects of there
> bites i tell you there are not many that
> would bare it as i do . . .[14]

The women's voices amaze as they dismiss disas-
ters with a shrug of the pen.

One woman wrote about staying "in an old log cab-
bin where we go to bed on the flour" at St. Joseph
before leaving on the overland trip to Oregon. "[A]t
night the big norway rats run and caper over you so
you can not sleep the first night we was here one was
verry glad to se me he just came up and took me by the
hand but not so hard as to hurt much".[15]

Angie Mitchell Brown, a teacher living in a household of women and children in Arizona in the early
1880s, encountered a variety of scary critters.

> I furnished a good deal of amusement
> for my school today quite unexpectedly.
> I was hearing a Geography class &
> feeling something tugging at my dress
> as if there was a weight on it—shook it
> and went on with my class; presently
> feeling it again I looked down & there

> **lying on my dress skirt in a ray of
> sunlight was as hideous a reptile as I've
> ever seen. He was black & yellow &
> tawny & had a body like a monstrous
> lizard & a "spiky" looking tail & a head
> like a snake & was over a foot long—
> Lord! I gathered up dress & with a yell
> one could hear a mile jumped on the
> stool [where] I had been sitting . . ..**

The "Arizonans" laughed and explained to their teacher that the creature was a gila monster, poisonous, but it only bit when angry. The monsters could "blow themselves up" and "puff their breath in your face & make you awful sick."

The "hideous monster" took up residence in Angie's desk and periodically would come out and lie in the sun.

> **[He] sometimes snaps up an unwary fly
> & seems to enjoy himself greatly. I've
> ceased to fear him tho' it will be long
> before I shall consider him handsome. I
> stroke his scaly back with a pencil & he
> likes it apparently. Someday I'll try to
> make him mad, I want to know if it is
> true about their 'blowing.'**[16]

Angie Mitchell's lively narrative is full of encounters with wild animals. Cougars prowled the roof. One night Angie and her friends chased a rabid skunk out of the cabin and killed it. "No Arizonian attacks a 'hydrophobia cat' unless it is necessary," she observed, "for their bite is almost certain death." The skunk had attacked Angie's finger, but they "found it was not bitten, he had only lapped it—kitten fashion & wasn't I grateful!"

In another adventure, the women diverted stampeding cattle from their cabin with tin cans, horns, and a lot of yelling and apron waving.

Some critters Angie Mitchell didn't mention were grasshoppers and crickets. They suddenly could appear in a cloud, descend on the land, turn the sky black, and, in the time it would take to pick a bouquet of summer flowers, millions of tiny jaws could gobble up a summer's worth of crops and a lifetime of dreams.

In the notorious Grasshopper Year of 1874, Kansas pioneer Mary Lyon described grasshoppers four inches deep devouring "every green thing." People tried to cover their crops with blankets, quilts, winter coats, shawls—anything to try to stop them

Mary wrote:

> **I thought to save some of my garden ivy**
> **covering it with gunny sacks, but the**
> **hoppers regarded that as a huge joke,**
> **and enjoyed the awning thus provided,**
> **or if they could not get under, they ate**
> **their way through.**

One family started bonfires to shoo away the hoppers, but the green things swarmed down on the smoke and put out the fires. Trains skidded through scheduled stops on grasshopper-slickened tracks. The hoppers invaded houses, devouring food, and even furniture and walls. One pioneer remembered how they ate the green stripes off her Sunday dress.

Author Joanna L. Stratton, in *Pioneer Women: Voices from the Kansas Frontier,* described the aftermath of the grasshopper assault.

> **[E]verything reeked with the taste and**
> **odor of the insects. The water in the**
> **ponds, streams and open wells turned**
> **brown with their excrement and**
> **became totally unfit for drinking by**
> **either the pioneers or their livestock.**
> **Bloated from consuming the locusts, the**
> **barnyard chickens, turkeys and hogs**

**themselves tasted so strongly of
grasshoppers that they were completely
inedible.**[17]

On the army frontier in Kansas, Alice Grierson
wrote of a problem of the women who wore volumi-
nous skirts and petticoats, but no underwear as we
know it. Until the latter part of the nineteenth century many women wore no underwear, believing it to be
"tony" (high-toned), unnecessary, and even obscene.
Grasshoppers gave some women a practical reason for
wearing "solid drawers."

**They [the grasshoppers] were impolite
and unceremonious enough to hop up,
get up or in some way make their merry
way up under the hoops and skirts of
the ladies who were bold enough to
promenade among them . . . should the
grasshoppers remain here very long, I
have no doubt but what some Yankee
will invent some pattern for the relief
of the ladies in the way of *solid
drawers*.**[18]

Far to the west in the Columbia River Gorge, settlers faced armies of black crickets. Apparently they
weren't as overwhelming as the grasshoppers, because
settlers were able to trap them by the millions with
combinations of fences, fires, and trenches.

Many Indian women regarded crickets and
grasshoppers as food sources.

**Hiyu crickets shantie kunamokst
Clic atut, clic atut, clic atut**

**(Many crickets sing together
Clic atut, clic atut)**[19]
        —song of an Indian woman elder

On her 1851 Oregon Trail journey, Harriet Talcott Buckingham wrote about Indian women's use of crickets.

**The Crickets are large often an inch
and a half or two inches in length—
Black & shiney, the Indians make soup
of them—they catch them by driving
them into pits dug for this purpose—
they are dried for winter use . . ..**[20]

The pioneers blessed the rains and cursed the floods, gave thanks for the warmth of the sun and saw the droughts shrivel their crops.

In 1859 and 1860, no measurable rainfall came down on the plains of Kansas for sixteen months. Crops shriveled, streams shrank to wrinkled indentations, and the earth opened in huge, dry cracks. Food supplies vanished because the settlers hadn't had time to stockpile surpluses. "Distressed at the condition of their hungry children, pioneer mothers scoured the countryside for wild berries, acorns, nuts and grasses, while their husbands set off on distant hunting expeditions."[20]

More than thirty thousand people fled the state. Men trekked long distances to bring back supplies of food and water to share. Women in the state organized relief associations, and people and organizations from across the country sent seeds, clothing, boots, and food to "starving Kansas."

A parched land suddenly could become a sea of rushing water. In a 1903 flood in eastern Oregon, two hundred people died. Thirty-six bodies washed downstream to the farm where Gertrude E. O'Brien lived. Many were people she and her husband knew.

> **One day I found dresses of several of my women friends and two baby dresses of a child who, together with his parents, was lost in the flood. These little dresses I took up from the mud and washed them white, ironed them, and sent them to the child's grandmother who lived in San Francisco.**[22]

In Utah, the winter of 1848–49 was known as the "Starving Time," after thousands of immigrants arrived, with few provisions and inadequate food to provide for them. Many lived on "glue soup," ox hide boiled in water.

Winter could bring snow storms so sudden and intense that a comfortable jaunt in an open sleigh could turn into a battle with cold, unrelenting death. A man could go out to check the livestock and get lost in the swirling, howling, blinding snow.

"To be caught out in a blizzard is the frontier plainsman's great horror for its wind and snow bring piercing cold," wrote Army wife Elizabeth Burt from her post in Wyoming in 1866. "Hundreds of our frontier pioneers have perished miserably in these blinding storms which shut out all landmarks guiding to protection and shelter."[23]

Elizabeth herself became lost in a storm traveling in a mule-driven army ambulance (a common mode of frontier military travel). With no sense of where they were, she and her young son and their companions huddled under buffalo robes with their "blessed bulldog," who "proved a veritable stove, keeping our feet warm all night. If it had not been for him our feet might have been frozen." Although it was at least a four-dog night, the one bulldog was a blessing.

As it turned out, Elizabeth's party's mules had become disoriented in the storm and taken a wrong turn. The party had been stranded less than a quarter of a mile from home and were rescued.

Young Maggie Sherlock wasn't so lucky. On her way to boarding school by stage coach from South Pass City, Wyoming, she got caught in the blizzard of 1883, when temperatures reached more than thirty degrees below zero. In a letter to her son, also at boarding school, Maggie's mother wrote:

> **We got her home last Sunday. Her feet are frozen above her ankles and her hands above the wrists. They are very badly froze. She was very nearly gone when she was found. The people at Dry Sandy had to cut her clothing to get her out of the Sleigh. . . . [T]he two drivers are dead. . . .**

Maggie died four days later. Her devastated mother wrote to her son:

> **God knows best what is good for us. If I could only be reconciled to his will but it seems so hard. She was so much comfort to me. More like a companion than a child.**[24]

In 1887 and 1888, blizzards raged across the Great Plains, trapping and freezing whole families, and ruining the cattle industry. The "school children's storm" in January 1888, killed two hundred people, including many school children.

Minnie Freeman was a heroine of the Great Blizzard of 1888. The young Nebraska school teacher's clear thinking saved her thirteen charges. "The storm came up very suddenly and struck the school-house just about the time for closing." As she was getting the children "wrapped up," the door blew in, and then the windows. She knew she would have to evacuate with the children.

> Then I happened to think of a ball of twine I had taken away from a little fellow . . .. I began tying the children together . . .. Very soon the roof of the building blew off and I said, 'Come on, children,' and we started. The nearest house was three-quarters of a mile away, and in order to reach it we had to face the storm for about one third of the distance. I thought at one time we should be lost, and I came near losing hope, for I was nearly exhausted. You see, I was carrying the smallest child— a little girl—and my talking to the children and urging them to keep up their spirits, tired me very much.[25]

"Song of the Great Blizzard," honoring Minnie Freeman.

Courtesy Nebraska State Historical Society #B64–137.

But winter was also a time for playing in the friendly, fluffy snow. Charlotte Merrifield remembered frolic-filled winters as a child.

> **Happiness was an abundance of snow
> and much skiing, sledding, tobogganing,
> snow shoeing, and ice skating. We had
> sub-zero weather but winters were
> never long or lonely as many would
> imagine. We learned to cope with the
> snow and what most people would call
> severe winters. There is nothing more
> beautiful than sunshine glittering upon
> new fallen snow. The big snows were so
> quiet and peaceful.[26]**

Mrs. Austin Mires of Washington Territory remembered beef hide sleds.

> **A beef hide was tanned stiff and hard,
> handholds were cut in the sides. The
> horses were hitched to it and we had a
> sled. It was on a beef hide that I first
> rode to town. It was an old Montana
> invention. . . .[27]**

Some women enjoyed the freedom of riding horses to town, through the woods, or across the prairie. While the coming of the horse narrowed the lives of many Indian women, riding horses widened the horizons of many pioneer women and became a source of adventure and pleasure.

> **Indian Creek, [California]
> May 31st, 1859
> Dear Brother,
> . . . I have been out to ride this
> afternoon. had a first rate ride, they say
> Mrs. Robbins is a good rider, can you
> believe that poor skittish Kate would be**

seen going two up and two down
through the town? She really does do it.
but it is very different here from what it
is at home. All the women ride and the
horses are used to it, and they usualy
ride fast, they call it 'lopeing.' and
nobody thinks of trotting a horse all the
time. . . . I am going to have a riding
dress and hat bye and bye. If they
praise me so much about riding. I dont
know but I shall race with you when I
get home, wonder who would beat!
Depend upon the horses a good deal I
expect.
   Write often & tell all to write
    Kate.[28]

One woman remembered her mother riding out on
horseback in early morning to pick wild raspberries
for jam, jellies, and shortcakes to relieve their
Colorado mining camp diet of meat and potatoes. One

Berry picking.

Courtesy Washington County Museum, Portland, Oregon #LP72–32/27.

morning, though, she arrived home with an empty
pail after bolting away from a mountain lion perched
on the rocks above her.

Anne Ellis remembered the fun of picking berries
in the summer.

> The berry-picking season brings back
> some of the happiest times in my life. I
> loved to get them. Straight up the
> mountain-side in front of our house,
> was a small patch in the burned timber.
> I would take a five-pound lard pail and
> go after them . . . There is no finer sight
> than to see a wild raspberry bush from
> below, hanging full of ripe berries.
> Then the climbing over rocks and logs,
> squatting near each bush, the sun warm
> on your back, everything so still and
> peaceful—how you could dream and
> enjoy it! . . . Mama makes a cobbler of
> them, and, oh, the smell when the oven
> door is opened! The odor of raspberries
> cooking . . . can take me in a moment
> back forty years . . ..[29]

Raspberry Cobbler

Mix 1 1/2 cups of flour, 2 teaspoonfuls
of baking powder, 1/2 teaspoon of salt,
and 1/2 cup of sugar. Cut in 1/4 cup of
lard. Combine 1/3 cup of milk and 1
egg, beaten. Add the milk and egg to
dry ingredients, stirring just until all
the flour is dampened. Pour 2 cups of
sweetened raspberries into a baking
dish. Sprinkle over four large
tablespoonfuls of sugar, and dredge this
lightly with flour. Drop the batter in six
mounds on raspberries. Bake in a quick
oven for 30 minutes.

Women camping, c. 1890.

Courtesy Washington County Museum, Portland, Oregon
#LP72–176/273–24 #46.

Many army wives learned to ride horseback, and some learned to shoot, fish, and hunt.

Women turned anything they could into social events. They organized parties and feasts around quilting, sewing, berry picking, birthdays, christenings, revivals, house raisings, and holidays.

Angie Mitchell Brown, the teacher with the pet gila monster, delighted in learning about the Hispanic culture in New Mexico. Here she tells about being invited to a "Mexican evening party," where they were celebrating "some kind of a fete day—of the Senora's, birth, wedding, or something."

> We had music, singing also & dancing & games till we were all tired & then refreshments of all sorts of 'dulcies' (sweets of any kind) preserves, bread, 'chicken Tomales' & goodness knows what and some sort of Mexican liquor, coffee and chocolate. At last I said I must go and they came over & bade me 'good night' or 'buenos noches' one by

**one & wished me a pleasant journey
and a speedy return to Tonto I
certainly had a jolly time . . ..**[30]

Of course, they danced at the drop of an invitation.
Pioneers would go to great lengths to go to a dance.
Stories abound of men and women who would ride
horseback all night to get to a dance. One tale tells of
the birth of a healthy baby right there at the dance.

George Lamb recalled neighborhood dances in
Washington Territory.

**[G]allant husbands and beaus carried
the shoes and 'party gowns' of their
wives and sweethearts, while these
ladies accompanied them on foot or
horseback, dressed in old kitchen
clothes or even the men's overalls and
boots. . . . Not infrequently the strong
men of those days were compelled to
ford creeks and swampy places
carrying their ladies in their arms. The
dances were worth all the trouble it
took to reach them . . ..**[31]

Clara Smiley Gray of Washington Territory had to
thaw her dress for a dance.

**[T]he dress I wanted to wear was frozen
fast to the side of the house, and it took
me quite a while to thaw it loose with a
hot iron. In moving into the hotel I had
hung my spare clothing on nails against
the rough board sheeting and moisture
gathering on the boards had frozen
them tight to the side of the house. . . .
One of the soldiers asked me if I
would dance a waltz. . . . [T]his soldier
and I danced the first waltz ever
danced in Spokane.**[32]

Army wife Elizabeth Burt remembered one of the many dances she attended on military posts.

> **Colonel Reeve . . . called the figures for the young people in the square dances, in the merriest manner. 'Forward, four', 'A la main, left', 'ladies to the right', sound faintly in my ears now. The two-step was then unknown, but we waltzed with delight and danced the galop.**[33]

A great joy for Elizabeth Burt was getting acquainted with the wife of a new officer.

> **What an unexpected pleasure, to receive a lady just from the States, bringing the latest news, the new spring fashions, the most recent gossip. Gossip? Yes, indeed; we all needed such a tonic to our brains, stupefied by a winter of stagnation, spent out of the world. . . . Such pleasant chats we four ladies had!**[34]

"Shared Memories."

Courtesy Washington County Museum, Portland, Oregon.

After the horseback "lopeing," the berry picking, the parties, and the dances, there was warm pleasure in news from "the world." Often the highlight of the week, month, or year was a delivery of home—a letter, or perhaps photographs to treasure, seeds to plant, fabric to touch and smell.

A woman sits down to write of her own world, to reach out to the world she left behind.

> **I . . . seat myself at my little table with pen, ink and paper and commence scribbling.**
> —Kate Robbins, 1859 (May 31)

CHAPTER ELEVEN

Tea, True Womanhood, and Uppity Women

**In the territory of Wyoming
We've come to have some tea
And taste some tasty cookies
And listen to a plea[1]**
—from *The Wyoming Tea Party*,
an opera by Margaret Schumacher

A tea party. There, in a little Wyoming mining community, was the perfect place for something earth-shaking, even subversive, to happen. After all, a lot of radical things have begun at tea parties, where ladies gathered supposedly to drink tea and engage in lady-like conversation. Planning for the first women's rights convention in Seneca Falls, New York, where women and men first voiced their demand for the right of women to vote, began with a few women meeting over tea. Susan B. Anthony made her first speech for woman suffrage at a quilting bee, where, we assume, tea was served.

The setting for this tea party was the raucous mining community of South Pass City, Wyoming Territory. Population: less than a thousand. Number of liquor establishments: at least a dozen. South Pass City was one of the mining towns all over the West that boomed and busted during and after the first rush westward over the Oregon Trail, which passed through the Rocky Mountains just a few miles away.

The year was 1869. The stately Esther Morris, a

newcomer from Illinois, had invited leading candidates for the first territorial legislature to her cabin to get their promises, in front of forty guests, to support the vote for women as one of the new legislature's first acts.

That same year, 1869, the legislature passed a suffrage bill for women, making Wyoming the first territory or state ever to grant full voting rights for women.

Esther Morris' tea party became a legend, along with Esther Morris, who became known as the Mother of Woman Suffrage. Narratives, poems, even an opera, honored her. Statues of her now stand in front of Wyoming's state Capitol, and, representing the state of Wyoming, in the U.S. Capitol in Washington, D.C.

It's a great story.

**South Pass City
State Historic Site.**

Photo by author.

The story of Esther Morris and her famous tea party is on my mind as my mother, Ruth, and I walk the grounds of the restored village of South Pass City. While Mother stops at the general store, I head for the replica of Esther's five-room cabin down the street. I've been there before and I'm anxious to see it again.

Some distance from the cabin, a new sign catches my eye. I stop. It's about Esther Morris, and it starts out with "CONTROVERSY EXISTS CONCERNING ESTHER MORRIS AND WOMAN SUFFRAGE."

This is interesting. I've heard of some controversy over the tea party story. Maybe this will clear it up. I read on.

The sign tells of the legislature passing the 1869 woman suffrage bill, "authored by William Bright, a South Pass City resident," and Wyoming becoming the first state or territory where women could vote.

No mention of Esther Morris until:

"For eight months in 1870, Esther Morris served as South Pass City's justice of the peace, making her the nation's first woman judge."

Later on, it says that "recent studies indicate that Bright was the only author of the suffrage bill, although he may have received some urging from his wife, Julia . . .."

The sign concludes, "Today, Esther Morris is recognized as the nation's first woman justice of the peace. The . . . nearby 1870 period cabin honors Mrs. Morris, who exemplified the spirit of frontier women."

While I contemplate this new story, Ruth catches up with me.

"Mom, look at this. It looks like Esther Morris wasn't the one behind Wyoming suffrage after all. And it says nothing about a tea party. Maybe it never happened."

"What do you mean maybe the tea party never happened?"

"Well, read this."

After Ruth reads the final words, she declares, "Well, of course the tea party happened. I've given speeches on it and read poems about it. I've told lots of people about how this six-foot, two-hundred pound woman cajoled those Wyoming men into letting women vote. And I love the part about how the old justice of the peace gets so mad about women voting that he quits, and then Esther Morris gets his job!"

"Yes. I've given speeches about her too. Great stories."

"Well, somebody's going to have to prove it to me," says Ruth, undaunted.

We move on toward the cabin. As we step in the back door into the kitchen, the smell of baking cookies greets us. The ambience in the little kitchen is just right.

We walk through the wall-papered, curtained rooms, listening for the murmur of long-ago voices.

Ruth pauses.

"Something happened here. Something happened to set all those forces going so that women's voices could be heard."

Yes. Something happened here.

We do know something of the story of this uppity woman Esther Morris. Uppity as in a woman who defies the way things are.

Esther Morris was uppity, all right, from the time she was growing up in western New York state, a place they called the "burned-over district." That was because of the fires of religious and reform movements that quickly burned across the region.

Motherless at age eleven, Esther Hobart McQuigg learned early to make it on her own as a seamstress. She was bold enough at age twenty to confront anti-abolitionists who threatened to burn down a church where abolitionists met.

In Seneca Falls, not far from Esther's home, women and men in 1848 publicly demanded for the first time the right of women to vote, along with other human rights. By then Esther was a widow living in Illinois with her small son, struggling to win an inheritance that automatically would have been hers had she been a man. There, she remarried, lost a child in infancy, and bore twins to her second husband, John Morris.

By the time she traveled in 1869 by train and stage coach to Wyoming to join her miner husband in South Pass City, Esther Morris was in her mid-fifties with three grown sons. Wyoming Territory was a chance for the family to begin again, and for John Morris and the sons to make a satisfactory living. And here, in this rugged place of new beginnings, maybe John wouldn't drink so much.

Maybe Esther Morris' tea party happened, but probably not like the legend. Esther hardly had lived in South Pass City long enough to know forty people, let alone that many who supported woman suffrage. Besides, where would she crowd forty people into that little cabin?

Esther Morris did support women's rights, and some speculate that she may have helped to write the suffrage bill. But, as one historian wrote, her main claim to fame remains her appointment as the nation's first woman judge.

> **Considering her courage in accepting this position, opening herself to the ridicule of woman suffrage opponents in her town, and extricating herself from the social and political bonds of her time, she does not need a tea party to reserve her place in history.**[2]

On the heels of the 1869 Wyoming woman suffrage bill, the justice of the peace at South Pass City resigned—perhaps in protest. Poet Irene Arndt Huettl imagined the scene this way:

> **One man at least resigned**
> **as justice of the peace in anger. "Ask**
> **a woman!" Very well. She was not hard**
> **to find.**
> **Edward Slack [her son] would swear**
> **her in with pride,**
> **though Esther wished she were more**
> **'qualified.'**[3]
> > —from "Esther Morris of
> > Old South Pass"

Esther Morris wanted to prove women worthy of the right to vote, and that's one reason she asked for the job of justice of the peace. She accomplished her goal. In less than a year, she heard at least thirty cases, perhaps more, none of which was overturned by a higher court.

When her term of office expired less than a year later, she wrote in a letter to the Laramie *Daily Sentinel:*

> **Circumstances have transpired to make my position as justice of the peace a test of woman's ability to hold public office, and I feel that my work has been satisfactory, although I have often regretted I was not better qualified to fill the position. Like all pioneers, I have labored more in faith and hope.**[4]

Statue of Esther Morris, State Capitol, Cheyenne, Wyoming.

Photo by author.

Esther Morris became a larger-than-life figure. And she was. Large, I mean. At six feet tall and 180 pounds, she must have been a commanding presence.

I have photographed the imposing statues of her stately frame at the Capitols in Washington, D.C. and in Cheyenne. Studying her face and form, I saw in her that steely frontier woman toughness and determination—giantlike in form and manner.

According to one story, Esther Morris fined her husband for causing a scene in the court room. It seems John Morris didn't like his wife being so visible. And he didn't like his saloon customers calling him "Mr. Esther Morris." Other men confronted Judge Morris in the court room. "She was too mannish . . . to suit me," observed one detractor who nevertheless admired her stern manner.

Shortly after leaving the bench, Esther Morris was once again in court, this time to charge her husband with assault and battery. Apparently John was still a drinker and still didn't like what his wife was doing. Soon after that, the former judge left town. She eventually retired to Cheyenne, where she remained active in state and national politics.

The story of woman suffrage in Wyoming has many threads, but the main one has to do with what the men did, not the women. In the end, the notion of granting voting rights to women in Wyoming floated into the law books in the cracks between a new frontier yet being born and the more civilized, law-laden society it would become.

What probably happened is that when the twenty-one men gathered in Cheyenne for that first law-making session as a territory, they approved woman suffrage pretty much on their own. Esther Morris' role, if there was one, was more private than public.

That's mainly how women's rights and reform worked on the early frontier, especially suffrage. Early woman suffrage victories grew from the not-yet-settled carnival frontier, with its what-the-hell attitude. Later suffrage successes grew from—and often clashed with—other reform movements, especially temperance.

On the carnival frontier, where people made things up as they went along, and hadn't had the chance to choose up sides yet, creative things could happen. The press and special interests weren't paying a lot of attention, and in the vacuum, the men of that first Wyoming Territorial legislature approved this radical notion of women voting. They did it for various reasons, few having to do with pressure from women.

The first approval of woman suffrage emerged in Wyoming from a bundle of reasons and puzzles. Though it was widely reported as a joke played by roguish frontier legislators, it wasn't that simple. Wyoming's men needed women, and this was one way to get national attention and more women and stable families into the territory. Esther Morris said there was a political feud. Many in the Democratic legislature counted on the Republican governor to veto the bill. But he didn't. Colonel Bright, the Southern gentleman with strong anti-black sentiments who introduced the bill, saw no reason white women couldn't vote when black men could.

Since men outnumbered women six to one in Wyoming, there weren't enough women to make a lot of noise about temperance or suffrage or other reforms. The men didn't see them as a threat. Many of the saloon owners in the legislature wouldn't have taken kindly to handing power over to women if they thought they'd come after their businesses, which is exactly what happened as the frontier became settled. But at the time, *Harper's Weekly* suggested, "Wyoming gave women the right to vote in much the same spirit that New York or Pennsylvania might vote to enfranchise angels or Martians. . . ."[5]

One scholar summed up the carnival atmosphere this way:

> **The legislators of the youngest American territory, who convened the year iron rails linked the nation coast to coast, in fifty-one days created a functioning democracy. Wyoming rebels began in merriment, added woman to the roll call of American citizens, and ended in merriment at a ball.[6]**

For whatever reasons the men approved suffrage for women, many looked on it as an experiment, and one that could as easily be revoked as passed. In a territory, an issue like woman suffrage could become law with only a majority legislative vote and the governor's signature. Once a territory became a state, an issue like woman suffrage often required an amendment to the state constitution with two-thirds approval of both houses, the governor's approval, and approval by the citizens. So, laws were easier to pass on the carnival frontier, but they also were easy to take away.

Predictably, when women started making noise about liquor and crime, the legislature voted to rescind woman suffrage. The governor vetoed, and the legislature came within one vote of the two-thirds needed to over-ride the veto. From then on, voting rights for women in Wyoming were safe.

The voting women of Wyoming became a symbol for sister western states, and for eastern suffragists, whose movement had stalled during the Civil War, and split into factions about the time Wyoming women won the vote.

> **In Wyoming our sisters fair**
> **Can use the ballot well;**
> **Why can't we do so everywhere?**
> **Can anybody tell?**[7]
> —from "Song of Wyoming," words by
>   Julia Mills Dunn

When Wyoming statehood came before the U.S. Congress twenty years later in 1890, Congressmen debated whether or not they should admit as a state a place that allowed women to vote. Female suffrage was a "reform against nature," complained one. It was "unsexing and degrading the womanhood of America," griped another. One declared, "I like a woman who appreciates the sphere to which God and the Bible have assigned her."[8]

The men of the Wyoming legislative assembly telegraphed Washington:

We will remain out of the union a hundred years rather than go in without woman suffrage.

Wyoming came into the Union as the first state where women had full voting rights.

Wyoming State Seal.

Courtesy Wyoming State Museum, Cheyenne, Wyoming.

When those first legislators passed the woman suffrage bill, they passed other laws that most women hardly could comprehend—rights that women and men boldly had proposed at the 1848 Seneca Falls Convention and still not won. The laws passed by that first Wyoming legislature, some copied from Colorado Territory, were as important to women as the vote. They extended to women the right to own and retain property, guardianship of their own children, equal pay as teachers, and the right of married women to do business in their own name.

While they were at it, the men in Wyoming decided that voting rights for women included the right to sit on juries. In 1870, besides having the first women voters, Wyoming had the first all-woman jury and the first woman bailiff, as well as the first woman justice of the peace, Esther Morris.

The experiment of women serving on juries didn't last long. When women jurors went after saloons for not observing Sunday closings, lawyers and judges decided women would not be allowed on juries after all, and they didn't serve again in Wyoming until 1950.

Replica of Esther Morris cabin, South Pass City Historic Site.

Back in the cabin in South Pass City, Ruth and I pause before a desk like one Esther Morris may have used. "There is much lonelyness," Esther once wrote in a letter home.

The tough woman of legend and statue must have wept many soft tears because of the hardness she knew both within and outside her cabin walls. She was neither the fearless uppity woman many of us have imagined her to be, nor the obedient True Woman she was supposed to be. She was, after all, a woman like many others on the frontier, trying to build a life for herself, for her family, and for others to come after her.

Soon after Wyoming men granted suffrage to women, men in their neighboring territory to the west did the same thing, but largely for different reasons.

As in Wyoming, little public debate took place in Utah, the second territory to grant voting rights to women. Utah, as in Wyoming, the suffrage story contained many ironies.

In 1868 in Washington, D.C., some congressmen suggested that extending the vote to women in all territories would draw more women and stable families there. Another proposed letting women in Utah Territory vote. Prejudice against Mormons, and especially their practice of polygamy, fueled that idea. Surely, Utah women would vote to abolish polygamy. But Congress turned down any ideas of women voting anywhere.

Meanwhile, back in Utah, some men began to think allowing Utah women to vote wasn't such a bad idea. "Our ladies can prove to the world," wrote a Utah editor, "that in a society where men are worthy of the name, women can be enfranchised without running wild or becoming unsexed." Besides, Utah women surely would support their Mormon church and its "celestial law" of plural marriage.

Church leaders also saw that the new transcontinental railroad would be bringing gentiles into their territory. Having more Mormon voters would be good insurance. Voting women would help dispel popular notions that Mormon wives were subjugated. Just months after Wyoming women gained the ballot, Utah women went to the polls with full voting rights. Most supported plural marriage, just as the church leaders said they would.

Plural marriage, as the Mormon church called it, was only for men. Most Mormon men and women, however, were not in plural marriages. In the Mormon communal-based society, women often did most of the work while men were away on business and missions, and many lived in communities of women and children. Such arrangements offered women some economic, social, and personal security.

Some Mormon women, however, like Ann Eliza Webb Young, bitterly fought plural marriage. Ann Eliza made headlines when she defected as one of Brigham Young's wives and sued for divorce, demanding a large settlement plus legal fees. Soon she was a celebrity making good money from lectures and her exposé, "Wife No. 19, or The Story of a Life in Bondage." Her battle with Brigham Young and her sensational charges influenced passage of a federal law in 1887 banning polygamy. With that law, Utah women lost their voting rights.

Ann Eliza Webb Young then joined the battle to regain the vote, led by women's rights advocates including wives of several prominent church leaders. Utah statehood in 1896 restored woman suffrage.

Wyoming and Utah were the only territories to pass woman suffrage while still in the frontier improvising stage. After that, women began to go on the offensive to do their assigned job of "civilizing" the frontier, and men resisted. From then on, women had to organize and fight in every state to win the vote, and once they won, they could lose it again.

Colorado voted down woman suffrage in 1870, and several more times until 1893, when intensive organization, growing Populist support, and chaotic times combined to convince the voters themselves to approve woman suffrage.

In Washington Territory, the legislature had considered woman suffrage as early as 1854. By 1866, the men had passed a bill specifically banning woman suffrage.

After several battles, the Washington Territorial legislature finally approved votes for women in 1883. Then suffrage and temperance campaigns became closely tied, and women on juries challenged liquor interests as they had done earlier in Wyoming. Antisuffragists and antiprohibitionists got together, and through legal maneuvering, managed not only to take jury privileges from women, but also the right to vote. Washington women couldn't vote again, despite repeated efforts, until 1910.

Abigail Scott Duniway, through her newspaper, *The New Northwest,* and countless campaigns and speeches, fought for woman suffrage throughout the Northwest. In Oregon, her home, the struggle took forty-two years, due largely to opposition from Abigail's brother Harvey, who edited the influential newspaper *The Oregonian.* Despite Abigail's best efforts, suffrage became identified with temperance, which complicated and delayed voting rights for women.

Besides Wyoming, Utah, and Colorado, the only other western women with full voting privileges by the turn of the century were in Idaho, where voters approved woman suffrage in 1895. The suffrage debate continued across the West and the rest of the country until 1920, when ratification of the nineteenth amendment acknowledged the right of all women of the United States to vote. By then, all of the far western states plus Kansas had passed woman suffrage legislation. No eastern states had.

The strongest and most effective argument for woman suffrage was the most conservative one: that with the vote, [white] women in their role as civilizers of humanity would tame [male] society.

Colorado suffragist newspaper editor Carolyn Churchill wrote in 1880:

> **We are aware of the jealousies of many husbands in regard to any public work which the wife may become interested in, but women should remember that all the evils of society are caused by the bad management of men, and women are greatly to blame for folding their hands and permitting this state of things.**[9]

Until the militant early twentieth century national suffrage campaigns, rarely was it said that all citizens of all races and both sexes had that "inalienable right" to full citizenship declared in the Declaration of Independence. Rarely was it heard that no one should have to fight at all for the basic human right of participation in decisions affecting their own lives. The women and men of Seneca Falls, New York in 1848 had used the human rights argument, but in the West, the argument of the True Woman as Civilizer ultimately won out over the Woman as Citizen and Free Person.

Opponents to voting women consistently used the moral argument that voting women would be out of their proper sphere and destroy the home. They also claimed that women themselves didn't want the vote. The most powerful opposition, however, came increasingly from liquor interests as women's voices grew louder in facing down "demon rum," which destroyed many more homes than uppity women ever did.

Anne Ellis remembered as a child talking to a friend of the family about some uppity eastern women he'd seen campaigning for women's rights.

> **Once Slippery Joe told me: 'In the spring of 1876 I was workin' in Lake City; one day I saw all the boys gatherin' in front of a cabin. I figgered somebody had locked horns, so sauntered over, an' by gol! it was a woman talkin' politics, 'Wimmin's Rights,' she called it. She said she was a school teacher somewhere back East an' she only got nine dollars a month an' men got twenty-four an' it riled her an' she hit the trail a-talkin'—an', kid, it don't look like a square deal, does it?'**
>
> **'How was she dressed, Slippery?'**
>
> **'Nuthin' fancy, but good black silk, I guess, white collar and cuffs, a right purty breastpin on. She was a good talker an' we all took in what she said, but I bet it'll be a cold day before I ever vote for a woman.'**
>
> **'Was she married?'**
>
> **'She didn't look it. Her name was Susan B. Anthony. Another woman with her was called Elizabeth Cady Stanton. They was ridin' horseback from one camp to another.'[10]**

The fight for the right to vote was not the only—
nor even the central—social and political issue for
women on the western frontier. As more family
women settled the frontier, they knew that the drunkenness and pandemonium of the carnival frontier and
the isolation of much of the farming frontier was not
healthy for families.

Women looked around and saw men taking their
cherished frontier freedom to extremes. Women, the
appointed family nurturers and community "civilizers," saw the family destroyers of drunkenness, violence, prostitution, gambling, dirt, orphaned children,
child brides, and homelessness. They blamed the men
for what they saw. Taking to heart their role as the
civilizers of men and frontier, they began to demand
order and respect and more rights for themselves. In
spite of themselves, many became uppity women. The
Cult of True Womanhood, now the Cult of
Community, came head-to-head with the male Cult of
Individualism.

It was liquor that fueled what became perhaps the
most under-rated conflict on the western frontier, the
battle of the sexes. As author Richard Erdoes
observed, "the war of the sexes unfolded on the alco-
holic battlefield."

It came from women's own experiences, where epidemic drinking and drunkenness destroyed families.

"In Colorado whisky is significant of all evil and
violence and is the cause of most of the [shootings] in
the mining camps," wrote Isabella Bird, the intrepid
horseback explorer. "There are few moderate drinkers;
it is seldom taken except to excess."[11]

Anne Ellis remembered one well-oiled man in the
Colorado mining town where she lived.

**Si Dore . . . drank a good deal, and,
although I never saw him drunk, he
always smelled of it, as most of these
men did. They always kept a jug, and
would have an eye-opener on getting up**

**in the morning, an appetizer before
breakfast, a snifter before dinner, one
to settle the stomach after eating, a
friendly glass with any one who might
show up in the course of the day, and a
hot sling before going to bed.**[12]

The sale of liquor was the most lucrative enterprise on the carnival frontier. Saloons were hallowed ground, male sanctuaries for rites of manhood and bonding.

**Thirst
Comes first.
Drink till you burst!
Everything else can wait!**[13]

**A man because of the fact that he had
been drunk with another, felt that he
could and should be favored by his
companion. There seems to be a
peculiar and particular tie between
men who have been drunk together.**
                              —Anne Ellis

Drinking places became the enemies of "respectable" women, who saw them lure their husbands away from home and take money out of their pockets. As more women settled the frontier, men gave up some of their gambling and prostitution, or at least made them more discreet, but they refused to give up their drinking and their drinking holes.[14]

**I'll buy my own whiskey,
I'll drink my own dram,
And for them that don't like me
I don't give a damn!**[15]

Elizabeth Paschal Gay traveled the Oregon Trail from Virginia in 1862 with her husband and their little girl. Her husband, who was "a skillful surgeon and a good doctor when he was sober," set up a medical practice in eastern Oregon.

> **When he was not too drunk he had very good success. He spent all he made in the saloons. I took to washing to pay for our food. . . . I had to melt snow in a pan over an open fireplace to do the washing. We had no stove. I boiled the clothes in a brass kettle and strung lines from the rafters all over the house, so the clothes could dry. I had to walk through the deep snow to deliver the washing . . . .. My husband, though a skillful surgeon, was unable to leave liquor alone, so he did not earn enough money to feed our baby, Jessie, and myself.**
>
> **When my husband was sober he was not only a capable doctor but a kindly, considerate gentleman, but when he was drunk, which was most of the time, he would worry Jessie till she cried, and then he would beat her for crying.**[16]

To feed her family, Elizabeth earned money waiting table and nursing, besides washing. She finally divorced her husband and married another man.

Charlotte Vickerson Merrifield remembered the time her normally quiet mother attacked the town saloon in St. Elmo, Colorado. She had pleaded with her husband to stop gambling and drinking and bring his pay check home for the family. She even marched into the saloon and begged Pat Hurley to stop her husband. On pay day, Mrs. Vickerson watched through her lace curtains as her husband entered the saloon.

> **We lived just a little way up the hill from the saloon, Mama waited with**

tears in her eyes. . . . She waited two
hours but no Papa.

She was suddenly besieged by a
hatred for saloons, and drinking, and
gambling! . . . [S]he did not say a word
as she walked out the front door of our
home. She started for the saloon . . .. As
she walked down the hill, she picked
up the bottom of her apron and filled it
with rocks. She walked into the saloon
and saw Papa at the gambling table,
playing poker. Mother neared the bar
and began throwing rocks, shattering
the big diamond dust mirror of the back
bar and then breaking many of Pat's
whiskey bottles . . . sitting on the back
bar. . . .

From the day she wrecked the
saloon, Papa brought his pay check
home and her worries were less.[17]

There was a difference between temperance and
prohibition. Temperance was control of liquor; prohibition was the outright banning of it. Those differ-
ences flared in reform efforts, along with conflicts
between anti-liquor and suffrage campaigns.

Oregon Doctor Bethenia Owens Adair explained
why so many women took on men and their liquor.
"Liquor and lust are the two enemies of womanhood,
and when you attack womanhood, you attack childhood and our future citizens."

Arvazena Spillman Cooper made the Oregon Trail
trek in 1864 at the age of eighteen with her husband
and their child. She bore her second child on the journey and thirteen more in Oregon.

In her "Address to the People of the Year 2000,"
written in 1908, she created a dialogue between two
sisters living in the Year 2000, discussing conditions
for women one hundred years before. The sisters discuss racism, women's fashions, food, health, and

other issues, but their main topic is men's behavior
and the "rum demon."

> Its victims were disfigured till they
> were often very repulsive in appearence
> . . .. When they were under this baleful
> influence, to the extent of impairing
> their reason, they would commit all
> manner of crimes and follies.
>
> Dear Sister how was such a State of
> affairs ever changed So completely?
>
> There were many organizations in
> the land that had for their object the
> suppression of these evils.
>
> A notable one was the womans
> christion temperance union, or white
> riboners as they were often called, from
> the little knot of white ribons which
> was their badge.
>
> Their motto was 'Temperance in the
> use of all harmless things and
> prohibition for all hurtful things.'
>
> One of their main objects was the
> protection of the children, and through
> their influence many Salutory laws and
> regulations were Secured, but they were
> badly handicapped for the want of
> political power.
>
> Their arch enemy had full political
> power and all his agents were
> exceedingly cunning in all the ways to
> prevent the enforcement of these
> laws. . . .
>
> These white riboners were mostly
> made up from a middle class, between
> the fashionably rich and the extremely
> poor, and besides being powerless
> politically were discouraged by a
> mildly sarcastic indifferance of their
> fashionable sisters. . . .

It is a dreadful tale sister; but I am glad I heard it, for it makes me appreciate our advantages now, in this age when reason and religion unite to bless mankind.[18]
—Mrs. D. J. Cooper. The Dalles Oregon.
March 5 1908.

The battle between the Cult of Community and the Cult of Individualism led to showdowns over many issues besides suffrage and temperance. As the carnival frontier settled down and women initiated institutions that supported home and community, they demanded in ever louder voices reforms in many areas, including labor, prostitution, divorce law, property rights, education, child custody, use of natural resources, and even "expectorant control."

Like Abigail Scott Duniway, who began her work for woman suffrage in Oregon as a young woman, and finally cast her first vote in a wheel chair at the age of seventy-eight, uppity women would learn that their battles would be long, hard, and lonely.

They would learn the meaning of the words of Elizabeth Cady Stanton and Susan B. Anthony, written in 1881, after losing the campaign in Kansas, largely because the men who worked to free African-Americans refused to support women's struggle for the right to vote.

But standing alone we learned our power; we repudiated men's counsels forevermore; and solemnly vowed that there should never be another season of silence until woman had the same rights everywhere on this green earth, as man . . ..
But when at last woman stands on an even platform with man, his acknowledged equal everywhere, with the same freedom to express herself in

the religion and government of the
country, then, and not till then, can she
safely take counsel with him in regard
to her most sacred rights, privileges,
and immunities; for not till then will he
be able to legislate as wisely and
generously for her as for himself.

—Elizabeth Cady Stanton, with
Susan B. Anthony and Matilda Gage,
History of Woman Suffrage, II, 1882

CHAPTER TWELVE

Is Western Romance an Oxymoron?

O love is gentle, love is kind
And love's a jewel when first it's new

All day she's been on his mind, waiting there
inside the cabin door, her sinuous yellow hair falling
down in cascades over her creamy neck and shoulders. The thought of her makes him work faster to get
the last line of fence built. Then he can go to her, and
after slowly savoring the rich beef stew that's been
simmering on the stove all day, and the sweet apple
pie, now warm in the oven, he'll take her hand and . . .

Hold it.

Think about it. He's coming in from the fields all
sweaty and probably hasn't had a bath in weeks. His
clothes are crusted with dirt, and he's tracking globs
of mud on her clean puncheon floors.

She's just finished putting away the wash tubs
after scrubbing and rinsing and wringing huge piles of
muddy clothes and dirty rag-diapers. She doesn't
smell so good either. Her tightly fastened hair echoes
the tired tightness of her eyes as she watches him
come in the door and pile his dirty clothes on top of
his mud-covered boots. She greets him with the news
that all they have left to eat is a thin soup of bone and
flour. He recognizes her accusing glare as an
announcement that she's going to have another baby.

But love grows old and waxes cold
And fades away like morning dew
　　　—from "The Water is Wide"
　　　　　(traditional)

Romance on the frontier was like the frontier itself—a fast, intense, improvised two-step that could quickly turn into a dirge or propel its partners spinning in opposite directions. As one pioneer man put it, "[L]ove is hotter here than anywhere that I have seen when they love here they love with all thare mite & some times a little harder"[1]

Life on the frontier wore down people and romance. "[T]he inconveniences of our environment and the constant drudgery eventually took all the romance and poetry out of our farm life," wrote Washington pioneer Phoebe Judson.

Her work is done for another day. The bread is baked, the wash done. In the light of the fire, she focuses her tired eyes on the colors woven into the piece that will become part of the quilt for her granddaughter's wedding. In the sewing bag beside her are scraps of fabric and pieces of dresses and shirts and aprons, reminders of times and places and people.

Here is an old green shirt she made for Husband while he read to her in evenings. His persistent search for Some Place Else wore him out, and their love. She cuts more pieces into leaves, stems, buds, and flowers, and arranges them on the quilt top into the pattern she knows so well. Rose of Sharon.

As she works, she wonders. *What does the red rose really mean? The preacher always says the words tell of Christ's love for us. But every time I think of those words, I remember how sweet it was when Husband loved me . . .*

> **I am the rose of Sharon, and the lily of the valleys. As the lily among thorns, so is my love among the daughters. . . . His left hand is under my head, and his right hand doth embrace me. . . . Thy navel is like a round goblet, which wanteth not liquor; thy belly is like an heap of wheat set about with lilies. Thy two breasts are like the two young roses that are twins.**
> —from Song of Solomon 2:1,2,6. 7:2,3

She smiles as she dips her needle into the fabric, stitching the red rose. *The preacher seems to kinda skip over those last parts. But they are my favorite verses.*

> **The voice of my beloved! behold, he cometh leaping upon the mountains, skipping upon the hills.**
> —from Song of Solomon 2:8

My, but he was a handsome fella when he was young. Smiled at me so pretty. Hugged me so nice. But he changed. It started when he lost the first crop, that summer after we came all the way across that hard, sorrowful trail. He worked so hard, clearing the land, planting, and praying for rain. The rain didn't come. But sickness did, and then when we finally got a good crop, nobody had money to buy. Made him hard. Hard to talk to, hard to be with. Made him restless. But I remember how good it was when it was good. So long ago.

She stitches, smiling, the rose misting a little with the memories. She puts down her sewing, and her eyes rest softly on the quilt that covers the bed where she slept with Husband all those years.

It took me more than twenty years, nearly twenty-five, I reckon, in the evenings after supper when the children were all put to bed. My whole life is in that quilt. It scares me sometimes when I look at it. All my joys and all my sorrows are stitched into that quilt and all the thirty years we were married. Sometimes I loved him and sometimes I sat there hating him as I pieced the patches together. So they are all in that quilt, my hopes and fears, my joys and sorrows, my loves and hates. I tremble sometimes when I remember what that quilt knows about me.[2]

—Marguerite Ickis,
quoting her great-grandmother

Western romances in movies and books usually end with the part where the boy finally gets the girl and they live happily ever after. But for many, the "happily" didn't last for long "after." In a place and time where often a love died, or was left behind, or went away, romance was a fleeting thing. Love was far away, somewhere else, long ago. That's why most love songs were about a love that was either gone—or dead.

**Out in a western city, boys,
    a town we all know well.
Where everyone was friendly
    and to show me all around,
Where work and money was plentiful
    and the girls to me proved kind,
But the only object on my mind
    was the girl I left behind.[3]**

—from "The Girl I Left Behind"
(traditional)

Elinor Pruitt Stewart, who homesteaded in Wyoming, told the story of the lost love of her bachelor neighbor, Zeb Pike. One day he showed her a hand-made linen shirt made for him by the girl he left behind.

[H]e took from his trunk a long, flat box. Inside was the most wonderful shirt I have ever seen . . .. It was of homespun linen. The bosom was ruffled and tucked, all done by hand,—such tiny stitches, such patience and skill.[4]

It was a traditional sign of love for a woman to make a linen (cambric) shirt for her beau as a promise to marry.

You'll have for to make me a cambric shirt,
And every stitch must be finical work.
—from "Strawberry Lane" (traditional)

Pauline, the girl who made the linen shirt, came from a clan that had feuded with Zeb's family for many years. Their love could never be and Zeb had to leave because Pauline's brothers threatened to kill him. Zeb learned years later that Pauline died not long after he left. All he had of their love was the linen shirt and a faded photograph of a young woman with a "sweet, elusive smile."

In old age, when Zebbie spoke of Pauline, he spoke of her in poetry.

There is something in everything
that brings back Pauline:
the beauty of the morning,

the song of a bird
or the flash of its wings.
The flowers look like she did.
So I have not lost her,
she is mine more than ever.[5]

Anne Ellis' romance was Jim. She never married him. But Jim "was really my only love."

Had I the wings of the morning,
Would fly to you to-day.
But now can only whisper,
Soft whisper, hope and pray,
That in your heart for me,
There lies the same affection as in my
**   heart for thee.**[6]
                —poem inside a butterfly-shaped
                     booklet Jim gave Anne

At corn-shucking parties, young men and women got together and worked merrily until the corn was all shucked. The lucky finder of a red ear of corn got to kiss anyone he or she chose.

I'm a-goin' to the shuckin' of the corn
I'm a going' to the shuckin' of the corn
A shuckin' of the corn and a blowin' of
**   the horn**
I'm a goin' to the shuckin' of the corn.
                —traditional

Boys and girls, from the time they were tiny, were taught to be in separate and opposing worlds.

Women and men were to come together for the practical purpose of keeping order and being fruitful, and multiplying, and replenishing the earth, as the Bible says.

Although girls dreaded the scourge of spinster-hood, at the same time, they were warned about marriage.

Come all you fair and tender ladies
Be careful how you court young men
They're like the stars of a summer's
    morning
They'll first appear and then they're
    gone

       —traditional

And men saw marriage as a threat to their prized freedom.

When you are married
And living with your wife,
You've lost all the joys
And comforts of life.
Your wife she will scold you,
Your children will cry,
And that will make papa
Look withered and dry.[9]

And so, some vowed not to marry.

I never will marry,
Nor be no man's wife.
I expect to live single
All the days of my life.

     —from "I Never Will Marry"
       (traditional)

Marriage was the only accepted way for women and men to be together, so most of them did it.

Here stands a loving couple, joined
    heart and hand,
One of them wants a wife and the other
    wants a man.
They will soon get married, if they can
    agree,
So then it's all march down the river to
    hog and hominy.[7]

       —traditional

But, if the songs reflected people's feelings, a lot of wives and husbands wished they were single again.

> When I was single, went dressed all so
>   fine,
> Now I am married, Lord, go ragged all
>   the time.
> Lord, don't I wish I was a single girl
>   again.
> Dishes to wash, the spring to go to,
> When you are married, Lord, you've got
>   it all to do.
> Lord, don't I wish I was a single girl
>   again.
>   —from "Single Girl" (traditional)

> When I was single, o then, o then,
> when I was o then,
> when I was single my pockets did
>   jingle,
> and I wish I was single again again,
>   wish I was single again.
>
> I married a wife, o then, o then,
> I married a wife, o then,
> I married a wife, she's the curse of my
>   life,
> I wish I was single again, again, wish I
>   was single again.
>   —from "When I Was Single"
>   (traditional)

Romance was for the far away. Marriage was for the here and now. Men needed wives to raise a family and take care of the wash and cooking and housework and kids. Women needed a means of support, a shield against destitution.

Under the Oregon Donation Land Act, men needed wives for land because married couples could get twice the land a single man could. Since men outnumbered women, the rush was on, even for girls who still were children.

> **All the girls of Oregon marry by the time they are fifteen and the boys eighteen and in about a year they are parted. There is a law that will not give them a license until they are of age but the young people are too smart and run away and go three miles out at sea. There is no law there.**
>
> —Julia Holt, 1866

According to the Cult of True Womanhood, the True Woman would not have to dirty her pretty hands with work, but on the frontier, the ideal woman and wife was a work horse who often did both women's work and men's work.

The same strict rules in "The States" for married couples, especially wives, were supposed to apply on the frontier. Medical Experts explained the "natural" roles of men and women.

> **Man's physical development fits him especially to maintain the struggle for existence; woman's whole physique is designed for the preservation of her race. Man is essentially strong and selfish; woman, weak and generous. In man is embodied the individual; in woman, the race.**
>
> > **Love is of man's life a thing apart, 'Tis woman's whole existence.**[8]
>
> **Such is the fortune of all womankind, They are always controlled, they are always made mind, Controlled by their parents until they are wives,**

**Then slaves of their husbands the rest
of their lives.**
—from "The Red River Shore" or
"The Waggoner's Lad" (traditional)

The extremes of the Cult of True Womanhood and
the Cult of Individualism traveled the trails to the
frontier with the men and women who went west.
Women expected their husbands to stay put and build
a stable family, stay sober, consult them on decisions,
protect and provide for the family, and be good company. Men expected their wives to go wherever they
wanted to go, take charge of the household, do what
they were told, and not bother them.

**Wish I had a big, fine horse,
corn to feed him on
Pretty little girl stay at home,
feed him when I'm gone.**
—from "Shady Grove" (traditional)

Above all, a good wife was to be quiet.
A traditional song called "The Dumb Wife" tells of
a man who marries a woman who can't speak ("she
was dumb, dumb, dumb.") So he calls the doctor, who
fixes her tongue. She learns to speak but then the husband complains that she's become a scold. The doctor
replies:

**'Tis the easiest part belonging to my art
To make a woman speak
That is dumb, dumb, dumb.
But 'tis out the power of man;
let him do the best he can
To make a scolding woman hold her
      tongue, tongue, tongue;
Hold her tongue.**

Neither husbands nor wives obliged the other sex
to their satisfaction. The western showdown between

the sexes that erupted in the public arenas of temperance, suffrage, and other reforms, tore at marriages as
well.

Oregon and California poet Elizabeth Markham
wrote this unique poem to describe both sides of the
wedded state on the western frontier.

A Contrast on Matrimony
From the *Oregon Spectator*,
June 15, 1848.
To advocate the ladies' cause, you will
read the first and third, and second
and fourth lines together.

1 The man must lead a happy life,
2   Free from matrimonial chains,
3 Who is directed by a wife
4   Is sure to suffer for his pains.
1 Adam could find no solid peace,
2   When Eve was given for a mate,
3 Until he saw a woman's face
4   Adam was in a happy state.
1 In all the female face, appear
2   Hypocrisy, deceit and pride;
3 Truth, darling of a heart sincere,
4   Ne'er known in woman to reside.
1 What tongue is able to unfold
2   The falsehoods that in woman
            dwell;
3 The worth in woman we behold,
4   Is almost imperceptible.
1 Cursed by the foolish man, I say,
2   Who changes from his singleness;
3 Who will not yield to woman's sway
4   Is sure of perfect blessedness.[9]

A measure of the distance between wives and husbands was in what they called one another. Most
often, women called their husbands Mr. - - -, or
Husband. A delightful exception was America Rollins

Butler, who sometimes referred to her husband as honey or deary. Men commonly called their wives Woman, and in the Midwest, where many pioneers came from, a common name for wives was cook. Men and women alike referred to women as girls, and women often referred to men as boys.

Since men and women already lived in separate worlds, they probably expected a somewhat separate existence in marriage. But in the land of extremes on the frontier, the separateness went to extremes. The separate worlds of marriage often led to silence, absences, divorce, manipulation, violence, and even murder.

Anne Ellis as a child had witnessed terrible quarrels between her parents. "[S]eeing how useless it all was, I decided there would be no quarreling in my home." So Anne remained silent and learned to "manage [her husband] without his knowing it."

Men's erratic pursuit of Some Place Else took their families on what some women called "wild goose chases." Women's efforts to get their husbands to stay put even came through in their quilting. They considered the quilt pattern "Wandering Foot" to be bad luck and changed it to "Turkey Tracks."

"A man is soon ready for a journey," wrote Martha Gay Masterson. "Packs his grip, gets his ticket and is off before a woman can decide on the color of her traveling dress."

> **Will you wear white, my dear, O dear?**
> **Oh, will you wear white, Jennie**
> **Jenkins?**
> **No, I won't wear white 'cause it's too**
> **bright.**

Will you wear blue, my dear, O
   dear? . . .
black? . . . purple? . . .
Will you wear green, my dear, O dear?
Oh, will you wear green, Jennie
   Jenkins?
No, I won't wear green,
For it's a shame to be seen.[10]
   —from "Jennie Jenkins" (traditional)

Esther Morris wrote of "much lonelyness" in a marriage with a man who drank too much and couldn't tolerate a wife who had an important job. Loneliness was a common refrain, with men constantly away from home, leaving the wife in a lonely house, often far from neighbors.

In a letter to her husband, away mining for gold, Abigail Scott Duniway wrote of her despair after the death of her brother:

O, my dear husband! you have no idea
how lonely and desolate I feel. It seems
as if I hadn't a friend left in the world.
But the children, bless them! are
mother's own! and if papa is away,
he'll come home some day, if he lives,
and then we'll be happy again.[11]

Oregon pioneer Kate Robbins wrote to her mother about her loneliness and her husband's increasing absences after the death of their son.

Abner came home and stopped a week,
is almost constantly in the saddle, it
has become second nature to him, and
if he is worried or troubled in any way
when he is at home, it seems to be the
only way he can find relief, is to get on
his horse and ride in the hills, with no
one to speak to, they call him very odd,

but still he is very nervous, although he talks but very little.[12]

Carrie Williams, who lived in a Sierra mining town in the 1850s, recorded the deadening of her married life. She wrote of her husband's frequent absences, often practicing his "tuter" with the band.

Wallace's whole time and attention are directed here lately to practice music to play with the band. No persuits in common between us anymore, no more pleasant readings together, no more evenings spent talking and making plans as we used to. We go on day after day, without speaking a dozen of words to each other some days.[13]

Loneliness was not just a concern of women. The frontier was filled with men lonely for female company. Phoebe Judson invited bachelors into her family's home.

[A] number of men had taken up claims in the surrounding country. . . . I felt a deep sympathy for these bachelor boys in their loneliness, cut off, as they were, from home comforts and associations. My sympathy found expression in opening our family circle and giving them a real home dinner on Christmas day.[14]

Loneliness was not the only female complaint. Women resented the silences and what they perceived as Husband's indifference. "Tonight told husband how bad I was feeling," wrote Mary Richardson Walker, after he had criticized her for "some ingentilities." "He only laughed at me. Said I was mistaken in suspecting he did not love me, for he certainly did."

With no sure protection against pregnancy, and public silence toward birth control, many women feared sex. They feared dying in childbirth, permanent disabilities from too many pregnancies and births, and the exhausting work and worry of caring for and feeding yet another child. Abstinence was the most common way of spacing children.

South Dakota German-Russian immigrant Christina Neher sought refuge in a neighbor's shed from her husband's attentions while recuperating from her latest birth. A short while after returning home, she again was pregnant.

On her forty-second birthday, April 1, 1853, Mary Richardson Walker wrote:

> **Life seems to be a weary task & every year brings it nearer its completion. . . . To feed & clothe so large a family consumes all my time & energy. My mind seems left all in a tumble. I feel so much the need of time to pick out the snarls in my mind & put my thoughts in order.**

Men rebelled at wives they perceived to be nagging and ungrateful. A lot of men on the frontier must have been afraid—afraid of other men, trigger-happy from their own fear and too much whiskey. Afraid that the decisions they made alone may hurt their family. Afraid of the diseases that swept the countryside that they were helpless to do anything about. Afraid of losing crops, afraid of not finding any gold, afraid of destitution. Afraid that since they had all these fears, they weren't what a man was supposed to be.

Out of those fears, many escaped to the saloons and the company of men and the soothing taste and feel of whiskey. And out of those fears, some struck out at those closest to them.

The notion that there was no violence against women on the frontier is a myth. We've already seen

how women who appeared "slangy" or loose were
vulnerable to attack. The myth persists that women
were safe if they were Ladies and followed the rules.
Divorce records and personal accounts reveal they
were not. They were not safe from husbands worn
down by stress, or fear, or whiskey.

When Phoebe Judson arrived to tend a sick woman
one night,

> **We found the poor woman suffering
> much pain, and to add to her distress
> her insane husband paid several visits
> to her room during the night,
> threatening to kill her.**[15]

Elvira Apperson Fellows was ten years old when
her father died on the Oregon Trail, leaving nine children for her mother to feed. When the ragged family
arrived in Oregon country, the girl's mother took in
washing and then started a boarding house. Elvira, to
take the burden off her mother, married when she was
fourteen. Her husband was forty-four. She told an
interviewer:

> **Back in 1851 . . . we had slavery of
> Negroes in the South, and we had
> slavery of wives all over the United
> States, and saloons wherever there
> were enough people to make running
> one pay. What could a girl of 14 do to
> protect herself from a man of 44,
> particularly if he drank most of the
> time, as my husband did? I still
> shudder when I think of the years of
> my girlhood, when I had to live with
> that husband. When he was drunk he
> often wanted to kill me, and he used to
> beat me until I thought I couldn't stand
> it.**[16]

In her book *Old Jules,* Mari Sandoz wrote about scenes of abuse she regularly witnessed as a child on the Nebraska frontier.

> **When the young wife, Estelle, refused to build the morning fires, to run through the frosty grass to catch up his team, Jules closed her mouth with the flat of his long, muscular hand, dumped their supply of flour and sugar to the old sow and pigs, and loaded his belongings upon the wagon to leave her and Knox county behind him forever.**[17]

With abstinence the only way for most couples to avoid pregnancy, men's anger and frustration grew. Emma Plaisted left a successful career as a professional singer and music teacher to join her husband on a Dakota homestead. Her daughter, who watched her father's attacks on her mother, later wrote:

> **Years later I realized that it was the lonely prairie life, the deadly winter, the need for sex refused by my mother, unwilling to endure another pregnancy, that drove him.**[18]

Children did not escape violence from the adults in their lives. Matilda Jane Sager Delaney, a foster daughter of missionaries Narcissa and Marcus Whitman, survived the massacre of the Whitmans by the Cayuse Indians in Washington. A series of families took in Matilda Jane and her brothers and sisters. Matilda Jane told an interviewer about one home.

> **Her husband was an intensely religious man. Many of the religious people of that day were harsh, uncharitable and intolerant. . . . There was too much churchianity, too little Christianity. . . .**

The verse in the Bible he pinned his faith to was the one that says if you spare the rod you spoil the child. He did his full duty to me in that respect. For several years I was never without welts or black and blue marks from constant beatings.[19]

Family violence was neither discussed nor acknowledged. Women themselves often censured other women who revealed it. Most kept their secrets in silence.

In a German-Russian community of South Dakota, women and men came together for religious services to sing, discuss scripture, and give each other courage.

Women went to their knees and cried their woes out to God, but if a woman spoke of her husband's abuse, she was scolded then and there.[20]

Some women tried to obey. Others looked around at the surplus of men and decided that perhaps there was a Some Place Else for them. As one woman put it, "if he don't [please] there's plenty will." In a letter to her sister from Horseshoe Bar, California in 1852, Abby T. Mansur casually mentioned the opportunities for women she observed.

i tell you the woman are in great demand in this country no matter whether they are married or not you need not think strange if you see me coming home with some good looking man some of these times with a pocket full of rocks . . . it is all the go here for Ladys to leave there Husbands two out of three do it[21]

Louise Palmer reported from Virginia City, Nevada how she got to go to parties and dances.

> **John seldom finds time to go to balls and parties, and it used to trouble me at first, especially as I had an unnatural craving for such things . . ..
> But presently I found that the unmarried men were not so closely employed as their encumbered brethren, and that it was their allotted duty to become the escorts of the ladies, while their lawful knights remained in billiard halls and club rooms to battle on their behalf with the fickle goddess fortune.[22]**

If they could afford it, if they had the courage, if they had other options, and if they could close their eyes to a woman's stated duty to remain in a marriage no matter what, women left.

> **I couldn't stand Willie's laziness another day. I wanted to get away from him bad enough to do anything. . . . I hoped and expected to gather up the children later on. I didn't know how, but I'd find a way.[23]**
> —Malinda Jenkins, 1870

According to the editors of *Western Women: Their Lands, Their Lives,* the divorce rate increased in the U.S. fourfold from 1860 to 1900, and western states led the nation.

Most couples stayed together, and some experienced warmth and satisfaction—even romance. When there was romance, it was when they were confident enough, brave enough to break the rules and somehow bring their separate worlds together.

Perhaps the man listened to his wife, stayed in one place to build a home, asked her opinions, spent more time with her than with his drinking buddies, laughed and even cried with her. Perhaps the woman valued her own opinions and stood by them, accepted his participation in household chores, claimed her own property and time and money, allowed him to make mistakes, found a way to plan pregnancies so that she could freely love her husband.

Elinor Pruitt Stewart took a job as a housekeeper and hired hand for a Wyoming homesteader and filed a claim of her own on the land adjoining his. After she filed and began proving up her own claim, she married the man who had been her employer. In one of many letters to her former employer, Elinor confided some of her secrets of a life that to her was rich and good.

> I should not have married if Clyde had not promised I should meet all my land difficulties unaided. I wanted the fun and the experience. . . . Do you know?—I am a firm believer in laughter. I am real superstitious about it. I think if Bad Luck came along, he would take to his heels if some one laughed right loudly. . . .
>
> When you think of me, you must think of me as one who is truly happy. It is true, I want a great many things I haven't got, but I don't want them enough to be discontented and not enjoy the many blessings that are mine. I have my home among the blue mountains, my healthy, well-formed children, my clean, honest husband, my kind, gentle milk cows, my garden which I make myself. . . . I can load up the kiddies and go where I please any time. . . .
>
> I am as proud and happy to-day as I was the day I became his wife.[24]

John and Dora Huelsdonk.

From the collection of the Jefferson
County Museum, Port Townsend,
Washington #1.1.480.

I know where I'm going
And I know who's going with me.
I know who I love,
But my dear knows who I'll marry. . . .

Feather beds are soft,
And painted rooms are bonny,
But I would trade them all
For my handsome, winsome Johnny.
—from "I Know Where I'm Going"
(traditional)

Phoebe Judson, the Washington Territory pioneer, went through many moves into isolated places with her husband and growing family. The couple seemed to keep their sense of humor and appreciation of each other even in the most trying circumstances.

Phoebe had a hard time with directions, and was constantly getting lost in the woods. One day she couldn't find the place she was to meet her husband. He simply sat down and waited for her.

**Great was my relief when rounding a
clump of trees, I suddenly came upon**

**him; fatigue, fear and anxiety vanished
in a moment. Mr. Judson looked up
with a familiar twinkle in his eye and
coolly said, 'Where are you going,
Phoebe?' I answered by saying, 'How
long have you been sitting on that log,
Holden?' Mr. Judson enjoyed the joke,
and I profited by the lesson 'that to
progress through life, one should leave
the crooked paths and travel the
straight ones, that will carry us out of
the wilderness.' . . .**

**My experience in traveling 'the
circuit' was always a standing joke
with Mr. Judson; he never tired of
repeating it, and many a hearty laugh
we have both enjoyed, at my expense.**[25]

One of the most romantic frontier stories was that
of Lalu Nathoy, the Chinese girl sold into prostitution
and eventually brought to the gold mines of Idaho,
where she was won by a gambler in a poker game. The
only part of the story that probably isn't true is the
part about the poker game. Lalu, who became known
as Polly, was a dancer in Warrens, Idaho, where
Charles Bemis, a saloon keeper and gambler, was her
protector. Charles was shot in the eye by an unhappy
customer, and Polly nursed him back to health after
digging out the bullet with a crochet hook. A few
years later, when Polly was in her forties, the two
were married, and lived in a little cabin by the Salmon
River.

One of Polly's treasures was a blue silk dress with
rows of buttons Charles made for her from gold pieces.

We don't know much about the romance in the
lives of Polly and Charles, but it was a romantic story
that brought them together.

So yes, there was romance on the frontier.

Polly and Charles Bemis in front of their cabin.

Credit Idaho State Historical Society, Boise, Idaho #906.

**Romance is not nor ever will be dead,
not in the heart of a woman, anyway.**
—Anne Ellis

In a story called "The Paris Gown" by Estela Portillo Trambley, the heroine, through an outrageous act, escapes an impending traditional marriage that she knows would kill her spirit. Clotilde Romero de Traske leaves her home in Mexico and flees to Paris, where she leads a life of independence as an art dealer.

Looking back years later, she tells her granddaughter that she believes the walls that separate men and women can be broken.

I know that the instinct that respects
all life, the instinct that understands
equality, survives in all of us in spite of
overwhelming, unfair tradition. Men
know this instinct, too, although
thousands of years of conditioning
made them blind to the equality of all
life. The violence of man against
woman is a traditional blindness whose
wall can be broken. Isn't that the
objective of love . . . to break walls?[26]

Roses love sunshine
Violets love dew
Angels in heaven
Know I love you.
     —from "Red River Valley" (traditional)

CHAPTER THIRTEEN

To Everything There is a Season: Rituals and Celebrations

**To every thing there is a season
and a time to every
   purpose under the
   heaven:
A time to be born, and
   a time to die;
a time to plant, and a time to pluck up
that which is planted.**

                    —Ecclesiastes 3:1,2

Seasons and cycles measured frontier living: seasons of years and seasons of lives, cycles of moons, and cycles of the sun. The beginnings and the endings, the transitions. They watched the rounds of sun and moon and seasons, of birth, youth, old age, and death. They marked and honored the seasons of the earth so they would return, and the seasons of their lives so they would be remembered.

For all people living close to the land, spring was the time for planting, summer and fall for "plucking up that which was planted," and preparing for the coming winter, when the earth sleeps. Seasons of lives intertwined with the planting and harvesting, weaving a fabric of ritual and celebrations that directed and reflected who they were.

As families settled the land and brought with them customs from their homes far away, they saw the Indian people practicing "superstitions" they thought strange and called pagan. They didn't know—didn't want to know—that they shared with the Indian people many ancient roots of their own traditions.

Spring

As the earth warms and brings gifts of green clover and promising buds, life returns to a once-cold, seemingly-dead earth. Across the land, the people celebrate the earth's waking. Indian people give respect and thanks to the spirits of the animals and plants with ceremonies surrounding the gathering of the first food.

To the southwest, they call on the spirits of the dead living in the nether world. If they are respected, they will cause the clouds to send the rains and fertilize the earth, and the sacred corn will grow tall in the fields.

> **Thus in all the springs**
> **The rain makers say to one another.**
> **Aha ehe**
> **Aha ehe**
> **'The beautiful world germinates.**
> **The sun, the yellow dawn germinate.'**
> **Thus the corn plants say to one**
> **another.**
> **They are covered with dew.**
> **. . .**
> **They bring forth their young.**
> **Aha ehe**
> **Aha ehe!**[1]
> —from A Katcina Song (Zuni)

To the northwest, the women dig the abundant and versatile camas root, some for feasting, and some for drying, pounding, and storing for the winter that will surely return.

As spring wakes up the land along the Columbia River, seven women go out to dig the first roots, and seven men go out to catch the first salmon. The people thank and honor the first roots and the first salmon so they will return. Then, a feast and dance of thanksgiving for spring bounty.

Some believed the salmon to be ancestors who swam back to them from some magic place deep in the ocean. Washington pioneer Phoebe Judson described her neighbors' respect for the salmon.

The Indians carefully removed the spinal column, hanging them high in the dry house for safe keeping, as they have a superstition that the spirit of the fish dwells in the backbone and returns to the salt waters to lure other salmon to their traps. I have seen innumerable quantities of these backbones hanging in the dry houses, for they never destroy them.[2]

**Spring has now unwrapped the flowers, day is fast reviving
Life in all her growing powers toward the light is striving
Gone the iron touch of cold, winter time & frost time**

**Seedlings working through the mold
now make up for lost time**[3]
**—from "The Flower Carol,"
ancient Latin carol (sung to the tune of
"Good King Wenceslas")**

The Christian holy day of Easter celebrates Christ's death and rebirth, ending the forty-day period of fasting and reflection of Lent.

Ancestors of German immigrants celebrated the death of winter and rebirth of the sun with festivals to the goddess Eostre, or Eostara, whose name gave us the word for Easter. Eostre's sacred hare laid eggs, symbol of rebirth, for good children on Easter eve. The eggs would be colored, often red, the color of life.

European peasants celebrated the spring May Festival to Maj or Mai, the Maiden, with feasting, singing, revelry, and dancing around the May pole, symbol of male sexuality and the ancient tree of life. The Queen and King of the May symbolized Frey and Freya, the Lord and Lady "whose union made fertility magic each spring."[4]

Oregon pioneer Martha Gay Masterson wrote about welcoming the spring with the May Festival in Eugene, Oregon in 1864. The children gathered flowers and decorated the throne for the May Queen and her four attendants under a large oak tree.

There was music, a procession and winding of the Maypole. From base to top it was garlanded with flowers and the stars and stripes floated from its crown. Refreshment booths had been set up here and there. . . . The repast had barely concluded when a heavy shower drenched everything. A ball in the evening ended the festivities of that May Day.[5]

Sarah Winnemucca's Paiute people greeted the spring with feasts of thanksgiving, singing and dancing, and the joyful celebration of male and female.

> **Oh, how happy everybody was!**
> **Everybody was singing here and there,**
> **getting beautiful dresses made, and**
> **before we started we had a**
> **thanksgiving dance. . . . [W]e partook of**
> **the first gathering of food for that**
> **summer. So that morning everybody**
> **prayed, and sang songs, and danced,**
> **and ate before starting.**

For the spring Festival of Flowers, the young girls would celebrate the flowers honored by their names.

> **We would all go in company to see if**
> **the flowers we were named for were yet**
> **in bloom, for almost all the girls are**
> **named for flowers. . . . Oh, with what**
> **eagerness we girls used to watch every**
> **spring for the time when we could meet**
> **with our hearts' delight, the young men,**
> **whom in civilized life you call beaux.**

Girls dance together, and then each one "gathers the flower she is named for, and then all weave them into wreaths and crowns and scarfs, and dress up in them." The girls "all go marching along, each girl in turn singing of herself."

> **I, Sarah Winnemucca, am a shell-**
> **flower, such as I wear on my dress. My**
> **name is Thocmetony. I am so beautiful!**
> **Who will come and dance with me**
> **while I am so beautiful? . . . [C]ome, oh**
> **come, and dance and be happy with**
> **me!**[6]

And the young men would sing and dance with the girls.

> **Oh**
> **I am thinking**
> **Oh**
> **I am thinking**
> **I have found my lover**
> **Oh**
> **I think it is so!**[7]
> > —Love Song (Chippewa)

Spring was the time for love and for weddings for all their reasons and all their variety. Sarah Winnemucca described a wedding ceremony in her Paiute clan:

> **At the wedding feast, all the food is**
> **prepared in baskets. The young woman**
> **sits by the young man, and hands him a**
> **basket of food prepared for him with**
> **her own hands. He does not take it with**
> **his right hand; but seizes her wrist, and**
> **takes it with the left hand. This**
> **constitutes the marriage ceremony, and**
> **the father pronounces them man and**
> **wife.**[8]

In the community-based American Indian cultures, there were many ways of loving and marrying and celebrating the union of woman and man. Clans would exchange gifts of food and heirlooms. In some cultures, if one family objected to the marriage, they might give gifts of wormy food or blankets with holes.

On the wildly diverse frontiers of settlement, there were as many ways of marriage as there were reasons for doing it.

> **My beloved spake**
> **and said unto me,**

Rise up, my love, my fair one,
and come away.
For, lo, the winter is past,
the rain is over and gone;
The flowers appear on the earth;
the time of the singing of birds is come
and the voice of the turtle is heard in
our land.
The fig tree puttest forth her green figs,
and the vines with the tender grape
give a good smell.
arise, my love, my fair one
and come away.
—Song of Solomon 2: 10-13

Girls imagined and planned and dreamed of their wedding day from the time they learned it was to be their most important achievement. Many a girl had completed a dozen quilt tops by the time she was engaged. The thirteenth was to be the counterpart of the young man's Freedom Quilt, presented when he was eighteen and free to leave the family. A woman's Bridal Quilt was to be the most elegant her family could afford, often in the romantic Rose of Sharon design.

A girl dreamed of her special day, when she, enveloped in her virgin white gown, would dance away, feasted and toasted, with her handsome prince. But the dream rarely matched the reality on a frontier where marriage often was a way for women to survive and men to acquire land, where even food to live on sometimes was hard to come by, and where deaths, sickness, and separation stalked fragile family units.

Perhaps the shortest wedding ceremony was the one that went something like this:

"Ya want 'er?"
"Yeah."
"Ya want 'im?"
"Guess so."
"Done. That'll be one dollar."

Too often, a planned-for, longed-for wedding would coincide with a family death. But life and the wedding must go on. Oregon pioneer Kate Robbins wrote home (July 8, 1881) about the wedding of her daughter, Eunice, soon after the death of her adored twenty-year-old son. "It was Tommie's request that they should be married as soon as convenient," Kate wrote. Although the wedding "was very quiet and only seven invited guests present," still it was an elaborate affair.

The bride's gown was "a white princess dress made quite plain with a train veil, orange flowers, satin slippers and kid gloves." Kate made the wedding cake, and the wedding "lunch" menu prepared by the bride "was praised a great deal":

> **cold boiled tongue, boiled ham, roast**
> **chicken, salmon salad, tomatoes,**
> **pickles, bread and butter, wedding**
> **cake, gold & silver cake, marble cake,**
> **. . . drop cakes, jelly cake, float, blanc-**
> **mange, canned grapes, gooseberries,**
> **pears, and cherries, pear preserve,**
> **currant jelly and honey, nuts, raisins**
> **and candy, Tea and coffee and**
> **Lemonade, everything cold except the**
> **Tea & coffee.**

At a Kansas pioneer wedding, guests were escorted into a dugout to witness the marriage.

> **There was no floor, and a sheet had**
> **been stretched across one corner of the**
> **room. The bride and groom were**

**stationed behind this, evidently under
the impression it would not be proper
to appear until time for the ceremony,
but they were in such close quarters
and the sheet was so short it put one in
mind of an ostrich when it tries to hide
by sticking its head in the sand.**

At the wedding supper, the bride's mother served coffee made of dried carrots, seven kinds of wild plum sauce, bread and butter, and fried pork. After the supper, the bridegroom took the minister aside and arranged to pay him in potatoes for performing the ceremony.[9]

A shotgun wedding in Durango, Colorado was a different twist on the old story. A masked man with a gun rousted the Presbyterian preacher out of bed and took him a far piece to a lonely house where his prospective bride lived with her parents, who opposed the match. With some friends as guards, the still-masked man stormed the house with the preacher and ordered him to perform the wedding ceremony.

The flustered preacher, who wasn't yet ordained and had never performed a marriage, stammered something about God joining them together and no man putting them asunder. He concluded by advising the couple to "be careful that you do not both ever get mad at the same time—may you live long and die happy. Amen."

With the "Amen," the preacher and guards vamoosed, leaving behind the masked groom, blushing bride, and befuddled family.

Most weddings were planned a little farther ahead, and some lasted a lot longer.

An 1876 German-Russian wedding celebration in Kansas lasted five days.

**The guests took turns eating, drinking
and dancing the *hoch-zeit* [high time]
with an occasional nap at the home of**

**the near neighbors. Whiskey was
passed around after each dance and the
men smoked their longstem pipes even
while they were dancing. Every man
danced with the bride, and greenbacks
were pinned all over her dress by the
guests.**[10]

Fabiola de Baca Cabeza Gilbert described an elaborate wedding feast in her book *The Good Life,* based
on her childhood memories growing up on a New
Mexico farm with her Hispanic grandmother.

The elaborate wedding dinner consisted of decorated tables laden with bowls of *pozole* (lime
hominy), *carné con chilé,* macaroni with tomatoes,
mashed potatoes, roasted mutton, fried bread, and
bread baked in the mud oven piled a foot high in pans.
For dessert, they served *capirotada,* rice pudding,
pies, and canned fruit in deep bowls.[11]

Fiddlers and a guitar player provided music for the
grand march, followed by "old time dances," in which
dancing partners exchanged verses.

In this endearing verse from Alaska, rancher Frank
McGill swears his love to Aggie Dalton.

**I swear by my gee-pole*, under this
    tree,
A devoted husband to Aggie I always
    will be;
I'll love and protect her, this maiden so
    frail,
From those sour-dough bums, on the
    Koyukuk trail.**[12]

---

*stick used to direct animals pulling a wagon.

Summer

Summer is a time for hard work and celebration across the land. It is a time to pluck up that which was planted, to pluck up that which has returned with the warming of the earth.

In the summer camps of Indian people to the west, men catch summer salmon with their reef nets while the women roast fresh salmon and dry more salmon on racks for winter storage. The women gather abundant berries and roots, setting some aside to dry and make into cakes and flour for winter eating. Roots, cedar strips, and grasses are set aside for basket making during the long winter.

On trails westward, summer was a time of travel to the Land of Gold, the Land of Eden. In the summer dust and heat and storms and bugs, they needed to hold on to their traditions, so they could remember who they were, so they could know they were not like the "savages" whose lands they trod.

As long as they could, the women clung to their ironed table cloths, their clean dresses, their trunks filled with family dishes and silver, Bibles and cradles. As they slogged along, realizing they must lighten the animals' loads or they would never make it, and the dishes, the ball gowns, the trunks lay discarded along the littered trail beside the decaying carcasses of exhausted oxen. Sometimes even the Sabbath was thrown away as well. Birthdays, anniversaries,

births, even marriages came and went like any other
boring, terrifying day.

One tradition the westward pioneers often mentioned and usually celebrated was the Fourth of July,
the day marking the nation's independence. And was-
n't that what this whole long, wrenching journey was
about—freedom?

Early Oregon and California Trail pioneers who
had the most to celebrate were the ones who reached
Independence Rock in Wyoming by Independence
Day. That meant they were making good time.

Many emigrants, struggling with weather and sickness and breaking-down equipment, still managed to
save something special for this special day. One thing
they usually had plenty of was gun powder, so at least
they could have a noisy celebration. Music, dancing,
feasting, liquor, and sometimes orations made up
Independence Day celebrations on the trail.

> **To day has been the 4, Our company
> and another . . . fired guns and drank
> toasts and had a merry time.**
> —Amelia Hadley, 1851

> **The cattle had a stampede to day. The
> only thing nearly that was done in the
> way of celebrating the fourth.**
> —Eugenia Zieber, 1851

"The Doct . . . made *egg nog* for all of us," wrote
one delighted woman. "[H]e has kept very quiet about
those eggs he had been saving up for this occa-
sion . . ."

Phoebe Judson remembered her first Fourth of July
in Washington Territory. After everyone feasted and
sang patriotic songs, her father delivered the
Independence Day oration. In it, he noted:

> **Through a kind Providence we were
> safely guided to this goodly land, and**

**we have found what so many before
sought but never found, the 'Far West,'
we can truly say that our lives have
fallen in pleasant places.**[13]

In late summer across the land, the harvest continues and women dry and preserve the food and store it
for winter eating.

In the Southwest, the giant saguaro cactus grows
ripe and it is time for cactus camp, a time for family
work and play, and singing and dancing to bring the
rains. Maria Chona of the Papago people remembered
harvesting the cactus fruit with *ku'ipad,* poles of
saguaro cactus.

**At last the giant cactus grew ripe on all
the hills. It made us laugh to see the
fruit on top of all the stalks, so many,
and the men would point to it and say:
'See the liquor growing.' We went to
pick it, to the same place where we had
always camped, and every day my
mother and all the women went out
with baskets. They knocked the fruit
down with cactus poles. It fell on the
ground and all the red pulp came out.
Then I picked it up and dug it out of
the shell with my fingers, and put it in**

my mother's basket. She told me always
to throw down the skins with the red
inside uppermost, because that would
bring the rain.

It was good at cactus camp. When
my father lay down to sleep at night he
would sing a song about the cactus
liquor. And we could hear songs in my
uncle's camp across the hill. Everybody
sang. We felt as if a beautiful thing was
coming. Because the rain was coming
and the dancing and the songs.

> Where on Quijota Mountain a cloud
> stands
> There my heart stands with it.
> Where the mountain trembles with
> the thunder
> My heart trembles with it.

That was what they sang. When I
sing that song yet it makes me dance.

Then the little rains began to come.
We had jugs of the juice my mother had
boiled, and all the women carried them
in their nets as we came running down
the mountain back to our village. Much,
much liquor we made, and we drank it
to pull down the clouds, for that is
what we call it. . . .[14]

"Ours is good liquor," said Maria Chona. "It does
not make you fight and think unhappy thoughts. It
only makes you sing."

In the warm summer, Indian people and pioneers
concocted potions from berries, roots, bark, leaves,
and twigs. They made healing teas, sociable coffee,
spirit-lifting and ceremonial wines and beers, as well
as life-destroying liquors.

Southwest Indian people fermented several kinds

of cactus juice for wine and beer, *mescal* and *pulque* (also known as virgin's milk). From ground corn, they made *tiswin* (tis-WEEN), or *tulapai* in its fermented form. For ceremonies, liquors like *tulapai* transported participants to a place where they could sense the spirit world.

From fermented grape pulp, Christians made wine to represent the drinking of Christ's blood in the sacrament of Holy Communion.

Autumn

> They that sow in tears
> shall reap in joy.
> He that goeth forth and weeping,
> bearing precious seed,
> shall doubtless come again with
> rejoicing,
> bringing his sheaves with him.
>
> —Psalms 126:5,6

> Sowing in the morning, sowing seeds of
> kindness
> Sowing in the noontide and the dewy
> eves
> Waiting for the harvest and the time of
> reaping
> We shall come rejoicing, bringing in the
> sheaves.
>
> —from "Bringing in the Sheaves,"
> old hymn based on Psalms 126

In the northwest, as autumn approaches, the Indian people move to the shores of the sea, the women digging clams and the men hunting small deer and south-bound ducks. Winter storage begins in earnest, smoking and drying fish and meat, and filling baskets and boxes for the approaching cold and wet winter. Then begins the slow migration back to winter houses, laden with filled containers of preserved food.

> *Hi-iya naiho-o!* **The earth is rumbling**
> **From the beating of our basket**
> **drums.**[15]
> —from "Rain Song" (Pima)

In the southwest, Hopi women dance their prayers invoking the ancestral cloud spirits to give rain for the fertility of the earth and her people. Women's flat, disc-shaped baskets symbolically hold first the corn seed, then the fruits of the seed, then the thin *piki* bread made of corn in ceremonial colors.

> **From where you stay quietly,**
> **Your little wind-blown clouds, Your**
> **fine wisps of clouds,**
> **Your massed clouds you will send forth**
> **to sit down with us;**
> **With your fine rain caressing the**
> **earth . . .**[16]
> —from "Prayer to the Ancients After
> Harvesting" (Zuni)

With the last harvests and preparations for winter, there is a sense of life's passage into death. All Saints Day followed by All Souls Day are the ancient Feasts of the Dead; Halloween is observed on the eve of All Saints Day. The ancients believed that at this time the spirits of the dead could cross through the "crack between the worlds" and visit the living. The ancestor spirits would bring gifts and candy to the children during their visit.

Mary L. Stright was a Presbyterian missionary schoolteacher in New Mexico. On November 1, 1882, she wrote in her journal from Santa Fe:

Tomorrow is the Catholic feast of the dead. The Indians will lay on the graves tonight offerings of corn and other things for the dead. The priest will take them away of course for his own use.[17]

The Catholic religion teaches that the bread and wine of Holy Communion actually become (transubstantiate into) the body and blood of Christ. In most ancient Indian traditions, wearing the mask of a spirit or diety enables a person actually to become that spirit. The sacrament of Holy Communion and the wearing of masks at Halloween or Carnival or masquerade or an Indian ceremony share roots in human longings for spiritual transcendence.

I'm just a poor wayfaring stranger
Travelin' through this world of woe
And there's no sickness, no toil, no
**   trouble**
In that fair land to which I go.
> —from "Wayfaring Stranger"
> (traditional)

Death was no stranger to pioneers on the western frontier, nor to the people who were already there. Sickness, plagues, wars, and famine were world travelers.

On the frontier, the Indian people knew death better than anyone, as first disease, then racism, indifference, and savagery struck them down. They experienced in the world around them the cycle of death and rebirth in the seasons of the earth, in the moon, and in sleep. And so it is with the spirits of the people. They simply move on to the place we cannot see but know. The Hopi called it Shipap. The Anglos called it heaven.

When a child died, the Mother in Shipap told the grieving parents:

> **The child is dead. If your people did
> not die, the world would fill up and
> there would be no place for you to live.
> When you die, you will come back to
> Shipap to live with me. Keep on
> traveling and do not be troubled when
> your people die.**[18]

> **When a cloud comes this way, you will
>   say,
> 'That is he!'
> When I get to the place of the spirits,
> I will hear everything you ask.
> You must always remember me.**[19]
>   —from "Song of a Child's Spirit"
>   (Santo Domingo)

As the immigrants came into the western lands, they saw a dying people. There were thousands, perhaps millions, to mourn, and many ways of mourning. One of the signs of mourning among Indian people was cutting of their long hair, believed to contain power and a part of one's soul.

Sarah Winnemucca's people mourned when the men her grandfather had called his white brothers shot ten men of her clan while they were fishing. Six died, one her uncle, the son of her grandfather, who urged his people through tears not to harm his white brothers.

The people wept.

The widow of Sarah's uncle, and her own mother and father cut off their long hair and cut gashes in their arms.

When the woman's husband dies, she is first to cut off her hair, and then she braids it and puts it across his breast; then his mother and sisters, his father and brothers and all his kinsfolk cut their hair. The widow is to remain unmarried until her hair is the same length as before, and her face is not to be washed all that time, and she is to use no kind of paint, nor to make any merriment with other women until the day is set for her to do so by her father-in-law, or if she is at liberty to go where she pleases. The widower is at liberty when his wife dies; but he mourns for her in the same way, by cutting his hair off.[20]

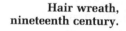

Hair wreath, nineteenth century.

From the family of Mary Granger Morgan, in the possession of her granddaughter in Oregon.

The sense of the sanctity of hair is an ancient one, one that remained in nineteenth-century Euroamerican culture. Women would give locks of hair to beaus, save curls of their babies' hair, and make mourning pictures of the hair of deceased loved ones.

Oregon pioneer Martha Gay Masterson's "dear little Freddie" died after a brief illness, leaving his mother to mourn. She wrote how a few days before he had gotten sick, she had cut off his curls. He looked at the hair and told her, "You take one curl, Mama, then I will put the others out by the big tree and the birds can have them to build their nests." And he ran outside.

The next fall, after little Freddie died and the leaves had fallen from the trees,

> the children were out playing near the big tree and Bess found a bird's nest in a bush. She got it and soon saw it was lined with hair. She ran to show it to me. I recognized Freddie's curls woven into the little nest and told Bess we would keep it. I remembered then what the dear little boy had said. I have the nest yet.[21]

It is the women who are to weep, to keen, to wail, for the children, for the husbands, the lovers, the kin.

Anne Ellis, in the sleep of dreams one night, woke to the sounds of miners bringing her husband home. He had been killed in a mine accident. Later, an Irish woman came to comfort her and her small child.

> 'Here, dear, make a petticoat for the wee wan. Me man was kilt, too, about wan month gone. Oh, the throuble, the throuble'—and she begins to cry. I, too, at this, open up and we cry together, for ourselves, for each other, and for all sorrowing womankind.[22]

They embraced and wept and shared food. They sang of finding strength in a power greater than they, and of a better life beyond. Women embroidered mourning pictures and mourning quilts, and saved photographs of their dead babies.

In some Indian cultures, the dead one's belongings were buried with the body or immediately destroyed. In others, belongings were kept for a year, and then given away as remembrances.

An Ojibway woman, Betty Laverdure, told author Steve Wall about the old Wiping of the Tears ceremony.

> **Long time ago they used to completely dress you. People wearing mourning clothes used to wear ragged clothes, never have the new clothes while mourning. So they'd come and they'd dress you in new clothes, in the old ceremony, wash your face—that was the wiping of the tears—comb your hair. Somebody'd comb your hair. Just combed your hair and wiped your tears and gave you this water signifying the taking away the grief, the grave, and the death. All the mourning.[23]**

Life goes on, and they give thanks.

In the Willamette Valley of what is now Oregon, the Calapooia Indians hunted the last animals and harvested the last food before the long, rainy winter. And when the work was done, they gave thanks and feasted on deer, elk, or bear, pit-roasted camas, hazel nuts, and perhaps smoked wasp nests.

> **Come, ye thankful people come,**
> **Raise a song of harvest home**
> **All is safely gathered in,**
> **E're the winter storms begin.**
>
> > —from "Come Ye Thankful People
> > Come," traditional hymn by
> > Henry Alford

On Thanksgiving Day, pioneers continued the Pilgrims' and Indians' tradition of giving thanks for their lives and their families, for their harvests and their homes, and celebrated their bounty with feasts from the land.

Eliza Frances Cook traveled the Oregon Trail when she was five and settled with her family in Washington Territory. She remembered well her family's first Thanksgiving in their new home.

Thanksgiving of 1870 on Put-chem-mee creek was a frost-tanged day, filled with the gay tinkling laughter of eight children. I was eight years old and instead of helping mother, I climbed trees and slid from amazing heights on wild clematis vines.

That seemed to be one of my happiest Thanksgivings. . . . We knew mother would use her best linens and silver and the marvelous caster [turntable] would occupy the center of the table.

My, I remember how much salt and pepper we used to take just to turn that caster around. And such a dinner! By one o'clock we were considered prim enough to sit at the table. Our hair was combed straight back over our ears and we had on our short white aprons. I almost forgot—we wore home-made shoes. Father made them . . ..

That Thanksgiving dinner was grand, though. We had three deliciously stuffed wild prairie chickens, baked a golden brown; mashed potatoes and lots of gravy, dried corn, for we had a very good garden that summer, and winter radishes. But the prize dish was mother's apple dumplings. . . . Mother made those delicious dumplings from dried apples father brought from The Dalles in the spring. Mother's jelly cake put the finishing touches to a wonderful Thanksgiving.

I remember that evening as I lay in my bed thinking of the happy times we had that day, I quietly drifted into sleep to a lullaby of low weird howls of the many coyotes.[24]

Winter

The earth sleeps. In the dugouts, cabins, tipis, hogans, pueblos, and winter houses, it is time to share the fruits of the harvest that will last until the earth awakes. It is time for weaving and quilting, for making and mending clothing and tools and fish net, time for story telling, singing, dancing, and gift-giving.

From Heaven she descended,
Triumphant and glorious
To favor us —
La Guadalupana.

Farewell, Guadalupe!
Queen of the Indians!
Our life is Thine,
This kingdom is Thine.[25]

This is the song they sang to honor the Virgin of Guadalupe, whose feast day is December 12. According to tradition, the Virgin of Guadalupe appeared to Juan Diego in Mexico in 1531, soon after the first Spanish arrived. The Virgin asked that a shrine be built to her, the Virgin of Guadalupe, the Dark Virgin, the mestiza (mixed race) *Virgin Morena.* On the hill where the Virgin's shrine stands, Indians danced and chanted rituals to the Aztec corn goddess Tonantziu. Some say the Virgin of Guadalupe *was* the dark Aztecan Tonantzin.

"The Mestiza virgin was a mediating figure between the old and new cultures and religions."[26] Her veneration blended the ancient Aztecan Indian tradition and the Spanish Catholic tradition of the Virgin Mary. The Virgin of Guadalupe tradition quickly permeated Mexican tradition and spread throughout Mexico and into the Southwest and West with the Mexican American community, where it continues today.

The Virgin's feast day combined solemn religious ceremonies with ritual circle dances, masks, story dances, story songs, feasting, and drinking the popular *pulque,* the "drunken sauce," made of the fruit of the maguey cactus. According to the Christian-Indian myth, Tonantzin is said to have fed *pulque,* Virgin's milk, or "honey water," to her children who survived God's flood sent to destroy evil people. "God destroys, the Virgin protects," they say.[27]

Mary L. Stright wrote from the Jemez pueblo mission in New Mexico, where she taught school:

Tuesday, Dec. 12, 1882. This is a great feast day for the Catholics. It is the feast of Guadalupe . . .. Mexicans from

**all around and lots of Indians went
there today and I suppose with whiskey
and dancing had a jolly time. It was all
religion too. . . .**[28]

**The flesh of our earth mother
Will crack with cold.
Then in the spring when she is replete
 with
 living waters
All different kinds of corn
In our earth mother
We shall lay to rest.**[29]
 —from "The Growth of the Corn: Prayer
   of the Fire Keeper at the Winter
       Solstice" (Zuni)

In the darkness of winter, the lights of Chanukah are lit, one each night until on the eighth night, the entire menorah glows with light to honor the Jewish struggle for freedom.

**Oh Chanukah!
 Oh Chanukah!
The sweet celebration
Around the feast we gather
In complete jubilation!**

     —traditional

In the darkness, when the earth seems dead, the light of the sun begins to grow once more on the day of winter solstice. In the century before the birth of Christ on the Julian calendar of Julius Caesar, winter solstice was on the twenty-fifth of December. It was called the Nativity of the Sun. At midnight the celebrants cried out, "The Virgin has brought forth! The light is waxing!" The Sun was Mithra or Attis, Dionysus, Osiris, or Baal. The Virgin was Astarte or the heavenly Virgin or the Heavenly Goddess.[30] (In ancient times, a virgin was simply an independent woman.)

The holly bears a berry
as red as any blood
And Mary bore sweet
    Jesus Christ
to do poor sinner good.

—from "The Holly and the Ivy"
(traditional)

Ancestors of the European immigrants celebrated with processions and singing and dancing. They lit the fire of the Yule log and feasted on the Yule Boar, an ancient symbol of the corn-spirit and fertility. They made crowns of holly with their red blood-of-life berries, symbol of female power and fertility. They made merry under the golden bough of the mistletoe with its death-white berries, symbol of male power and fertility. They carried sacred decorated pines into the temple, and greeted the new Sun with the light of candles. Green boughs of female holly and male ivy decorated doorways.[31]

By the fourth century A.D., the Christian church declared the Nativity of the Sun as the Nativity of Christ the Son, born of the Virgin Mary. Church fathers tried to suppress many of the "heathen" symbols and rituals, but the people kept them alive.

In a strange land far from all they had known, especially at Christmas, immigrants from across the sea remembered family celebrations in the old country. They remembered the weeks of preparation for the feast, the smells of pastries baking and meat roasting, the familiar decorations, the visits with friends. In their new country, they recreated old traditions and made new ones.

Dagmar Thomsen immigrated with her Danish parents and nine brothers and sisters to Nebraska in 1890. She remembered the preparations for the family's first Christmas in their new home.

[Father and Mother] bought some little
gifts for each of us, also Christmas

**candles and tissue paper for trim, and a
goose and a leg of lamb. . . . We made
cookies, peppernuts, tree decorations,
the usual Danish baskets, cornucopias
and Danish flags. We added two
American trimmings;
popcorn strings and
cranberries strung into
long garlands. Mother
had bought some
gumdrop dolls with
picture faces. We made
candle holders from
wire. . . .**[32]

Whole frontier communities celebrated Christmas together in the community hall, which often was the school house, a church, or any building big enough to hold a crowd.

In 1881, in the little community of Hermosa, outside Durango, Colorado, women organized their first community Christmas, held in a big log house with no floor and smoke-blackened walls. The women solicited lumber and labor for the floor, and papered the walls. They brought in a spruce tree, decorated it with popcorn, cranberries, and candles, and tucked presents underneath.

THE STORY
**I remember my grandfather
rocking in his chair
in his house
on Christmas Eve.
Read the story, he says
to his son, my father.
And my father reads**

**And the angel said unto them,
Fear not: for, behold, I bring you good
    tidings of great joy,**

which shall be to all people.
For unto you is born this day in the city
    of David a Saviour,
which is Christ the Lord.
And this shall be a sign unto you;
Ye shall find the babe wrapped in
    swaddling clothes,
lying in a manger.
And suddenly there was with the angel
a multitude of the heavenly host
    praising God, and saying,
Glory to God in the highest, and on
    earth peace, good will toward men.

My grandfather rocks
in his chair.

Again, he says.
Read it . . .

    again.
          —Susan G. Butruille, ©1994

Anne Ellis remembered a glowing Christmas in Colorado.

Henry [fixed] us a tree, . . . making tiny candles by dipping string in hot grease, letting it cool and dipping again, till a dear little candle was the result. When these and our candy were hung on the tree, how filled the cabin was with light and gladness![33]

Christmas was not always a happy family time on the frontier. Many were lonely, many poor in a strange and chaotic land. Sometimes neighbors could help make a Christmas a little warmer.

Wyoming homesteader Elinore Pruitt Stewart had just met a German woman who lived alone on a neighboring ranch. Both women, lonely at Christmas time, decided to take Christmas to "the poor exiles, the sheepherders." The two women set out with a horse-drawn sled piled with baskets of Christmas to deliver to twelve camps and twenty-four lonely men. In the baskets were roast goose, ham, chicken, meat loaf, sausage, bread, doughnuts, fruit cake, and "little cakes with seeds, nuts, and fruit in them,—so pretty to look at and so good to taste."

> **It would have done your heart good to see the sheep-men. They were all delighted, and when you consider that they live solely on canned corn and tomatoes, beans, salt pork, and coffee, you can fancy what they thought of their treat.**[34]

Sometimes the pioneers had to face a bare, poor Christmas with no one to help. Young Anne Ellis recalled learning about Santa Claus, how he brought toys and candy to children. Visions of an enchanting doll and a full stocking danced in her head.

> **Christmas night our stockings are hung up, and we go to bed with high hopes; but morning finds these stockings as lank and raggy-looking as the night before. . . . Mama saw how hurt we were and said, 'Never mind, he will come to our house New Year's.' It seems we did not have a payday till the first, and then Santa Claus did come, and leave shoes and stockings, but the thrill was gone; also my belief in Santa Claus.**[35]

KR 95

For Indian people, winter was the time for telling stories, retelling histories, and for ceremonies. In many cultures, winter also was a time of gift-giving, an important part of communal living and redistribution of wealth. In the Northwest, a chief who had accumulated a lot of possessions could have a potlatch, where, with great ceremony, feasting, and dancing, he would give away what he had and gain great prestige. The U.S. government outlawed the potlatch, but many Indian people continued with the ceremonies in secret, or they would simply tell government officials they were celebrating Christmas.

With the coming of the Sun and nativity of the Son, comes rebirth and the New Year. Ancient Romans greeted the new year with revelry.

For Japanese immigrants, the New Year celebration was one of the biggest of the year. It was a time to "cast away evil influences and [greet] the birth of a new year with its fresh promise and good fortune." It was a time to complete unfinished business, pay debts, clean homes, and visit shrines to pray for good health and happiness in the new year. Some New Year celebrations would last a week, with men making the rounds to feast and socialize with friends and relatives. "Women did not go with the men, for they were busy cooking," recalled an Issei (first generation) woman.[36]

On New Year's Eve, Danish immigrants might light Christmas tree candles for the last time and dine on boiled cod with mustard sauce. Games and perhaps fireworks would follow, sometimes with a carnival air, complete with masks and practical jokes.

Then, in the quietness of the coming light, they read, or sewed, or told stories by the light of the lamp or fire.

Many, like Anne Ellis' neighbors, "lived on the hope of 'things opening up in the spring.'"

Much like the Yana people close to the fire in their earth-covered houses far to the west, their dreams "turned to a time, not far off, when the earth would be covered with new clover."

And so the seasons and the cycles continue in their round.

> **I add my breath to your breath**
> **That our days may be long on the Earth**
> **That the days of our people may be**
> **   long**
> **That we may be one person**
> **That we may finish our roads together**
> **May our mother bless you with life**
> **May our Life Paths be fulfilled.**[37]
>
> —Old Keres song

ENDNOTES

Prelude:
1. Dewhurst et al, p. 100.
2. Axelrod, p. 12.

Chapter One:
1. Astrov, p. 195.
2. Axelrod, p. 11.
3. Kimball, p. 67.
4. Bertha Anderson, p. 40.
5. Della Holt, May 13, 1866.

Chapter Two:
1. Quoted in Green, p. 22.
2. Author's note: The Yakama Indian people have reclaimed the original spelling of Yakama, but "Yakima" is still found on most maps and literature.
3. Astrov, p. 195.
4. Astrov, p. 27.
5. Norwood, p. 167.
6. Quoted in Green, p. 56.
7. Coronado State Monument.
8. Wiegle, p. 337.
9. Coronado State Monument.
10. Wiegle, p. 340.
11. Paula Gunn Allen, p. 14.
12. Quoted in Jensen, p. 20–21.
13. Quoted in Green, 65.
14. Astrov, p. 281.
15. Turney-High, p. 127.
16. Quoted in Jensen, p. 27.
17. Beckham, No. 2, p. 79.
18. Turney-High, p. 111, 128.
19. Holmes III, p. 49.
20. Quoted in Green, p. 49.

Chapter Three:
1. Quoted in Niethammer, p. 48.
2. Niethammer, p. 46.
3. Underhill, p. 33.
4. Estes, p. 293
5. Claypool, III, p. 16.
6. Quoted in Niethammer, p. 12.
7. Cameron, p. 147.

8. Sarah Winnemucca Hopkins, p. 53. Author's note: Although Sarah Winnemucca used "Piutes," the contemporary spelling is "Paiutes."
9. Astrov, p. 102.
10. Liberty, p. 18.
11. Ewers, p. 13.
12. Quoted in Mathes, p. 45.
13. Wall, p. 105.
14. Weigle, p. 346.
15. Means, Boulder Public Library, Boulder, Colorado.
16. Astrov, 221.
17. Coronado State Monument.
18. Underhill, p. 44.
19. Williams, 1986, p. 138–139.
20. Williams, 1986, p. 23.
21. Astrov, p. 143.
22. Quoted in Dee Brown, *Bury My Heart at Wounded Knee*, p. 419.
23. Quoted in Time-Life, *The Wild West*, p. 247.
24. Sara M. Evans, p. 16.
25. Judson, p. 188.
26. Astrov, p. 227.
27. Ferrero et al, p. 68.
28. Masterson, p. 119.
29. Lockley, 1981, p. 221.
30. Judson, p. 220.
31. Sarah Winnemucca Hopkins, p. 34.
32. Judson, p. 262.
33. Sarah Winnemucca Hopkins, p. 207.
34. Cameron, p. 149–150.

Chapter Four:
1. Quoted in Levy, p. 108.
2. Holmes V, p. 210.
3. Quotations by Mary Richardson Walker are from four sources: Horner; Karr; Luchetti and Olwell; and papers, Oregon Historical Society.

4. Lockley, 1981, p. 255.
5. Quoted in Ehrenreich and English, 1973, p. 29.
6. Quoted in Bank, p. 70.
7. Quoted in Welter, p. 89.
8. Quoted in Welter, p. 105.
9. Quoted in Welter, p. 112.
10. Quoted in Jeffrey, p. 8.
11. Quoted in Erdoes, p. 202.
12. Talmage, p. 14.
13. Lockley, 1981, p. 134.
14. Lyman et al, p. 982–983.
15. Moynihan et al, p. 105.
16. Butler, p. 357.
17. Stewart, p. 25.
18. Ashmore, p. 20.
19. Ellis, p. 191.
20. Lyman et al, p. 876–878.
21. Lyman et al, p. 882.
22. Quoted in Bank, p. 94.

Chapter Five:
1. Quoted in Sherr and Kazickas, p. 505.
2. Hickok, n.p.
3. Quoted in Sheafer, p. 69.
4. Moynihan et al, p. 178.
5. Wertheimer, p. 249
6. Stewart, p. 215.
7. Kaufman, p. 18.
8. Rebolledo, p. 9.
9. Sherr and Kazickas, p. 432.
10. Moynihan et al, p. 242.
11. Quoted in Lucia, p. 41.
12. Rebolledo and Rivero, p. 194–195.
13. Rebolledo, p. 123.
14. Gilbert, p. 13, 14.
15. Adair, papers.
16. Quoted in Luchetti and Olwell, p. 84.
17. All passages by Julia Archibald Holmes are quoted from Holmes VII, p. 194+.
18. Lockley, 1981, p. 270.
19. "Some Colorado Journalists," The Southwest.
20. Quoted in Reiter, p. 180.
21. Western Star, June 18, 1880, quoted in Applegate.

Chapter Six:
1. Ellis, p. 18.
2. Hickok, n.p.
3. Linda Allen, October Roses.
4. Fischer, p. 46.
5. Schlissel, Gibbens, and Hampsten, p. 115.
6. Quoted in Jeffrey, p. 113
7. Schlissel, Gibbens, and Hampsten, p. 29.
8. Fischer, p. 154.
9. Fischer, p. 157.
10. Fischer, p. 158.
11. Jeffrey, p. 109.
12. Royce, p. 80.

13. Adapted from Erdoes, p. 113.
14. Erdoes, p. 37.
15. Merrifield and Kelly, p. 30.
16. Erdoes, p. 98.
17. Quoted in Levy, p. 164.
18. Quoted in Fisher and Holmes, p. 181.
19. Simmons, p. 80.
20. McGrath, p. 114.
21. Quoted in Levy, p. 159.
22. Bird, p. 62.
23. Bird, p. 166.
24. Bird, p. 69.
25. Ellis, p. 82.
26. Pioneers of the San Juan Country, I, 122.
27. Quoted in Levy, p. 116.
28. Quoted in Armitage and Jameson, p. 181.
29. Quoted in Erdoes, p. 42.
30. Quoted in Levy, 179.

Chapter Seven:
1. Lucia 1962, p. 90.
2. West, 1982, p. 23.
3. Ibid, p. 24.
4. Erdoes, p. 182
5. Moynihan et al, p. 167–168.
6. De Pauw, p. 4.
7. Erdoes, p. 199.
8. Adapted from Jarvis, p. 26.
9. Lee, p. 163.
10. Bancroft, p. 61.
11. Ellis, p. 26.
12. Brier, p. 58.
13. Armitage and Jameson, p. 200.
14. Erdoes, p. 130.
15. Quoted in Sochen, p. 116.
16. Lee, p. 199.
17. Quoted in Murphy, p. 202.
18. Yung, p. 20.
19. Nation, p. 5.
20. Quoted in Simmons, p. 17.

Chapter Eight:
1. Astrov, p. 222
2. Lockley, 1981, p. 198.
3. Moynihan, p. 28.
4. WPA, I, p. 168.
5. Toelken, p. 37.
6. Quoted in Jensen, p. 121.
7. Niederman, p. 46.
8. Fischer, p. 157.
9. Quoted in Stratton, p. 53.
10. Quoted in Stratton, p. 55.
11. WPA, III, 48–49.
12. Ellis, p. 42.
13. Quoted in Levy, p. 62.
14. Hehn. Dakota Freie Press, n.d., translated by Erhardt R. Hehn.
15. Quoted in Schlissel, Gibbens, and Hampsten, p. 204.
16. Quoted in Anderson and Zinsser, p. 261.

Chapter Nine:
1. From Linda Allen, "Weaving and Quilting."
2. Ibid.
3. Hall, p. 13.
4. Linda Allen, op. cit.
5. C. E. Gettys, Bits and Pieces.
6. Stratton, p. 60.
7. Belknap, 1993, p. 48.
8. Lockley, 1981, p. 142.
9. Quoted in Jensen, p. 138.
10. Moynihan et al, p. 295.
11. Stewart, p. 175.
12. Butruille, 1993, p. 129.
13. Quoted in Moynihan, p. 55.
14. Lockley, 1928, p. 972.
15. Judson, p. 90.
16. Duncan, p. 71.
17. Grierson, p. 58.
18. Burt, p. 194.
19. Lee, p. 96.
20. Quoted in Jensen, p. 26.
21. Lockley, 1928, p. 980.
22. Judson, p. 244–245.
23. Hafen, p. 45.
24. WPA III, 169.
25. Butler, p. 346.
26. Glass and Singer, 1966, p. 44–45.
27. Anna Knight, Amelia Knight vf.
28. Quoted in Stratton, p. 61.
29. Mrs. Bowman's scrap book, p. 11.
30. Lincoln County Kitchen Memories, p. 42.
31. Judson, p. 245.
32. Bank, p. 79.
33. Astrov, p. 185–186

Chapter Ten:
1. Quoted in Stratton, p. 46.
2. Wagner, p. 65.
3. Wagner, p. 65–67.
4. Moynihan et al, p. 137.
5. Schlissel, Gibbens, and Hampsten, p. 146.
6. Remedies are adapted from Gedney, Graber, Hafen, and Merrifield.
7. Quoted in Stratton, p. 153.
8. Masterson, p. 60.
9. Holmes, I, p. 244.
10. Burt, p. 157.
11. Gilbert, p. 16.
12. Moynihan et al, p. 294.
13. Fischer, p. 53.
14. Holmes, II, p. 47.
15. Moynihan et al, p. 285–286.
16. Stratton, p. 105.
17. Quoted in Stallard, p. 37.
18. Attwell, p. 79.
19. Holmes III, p. 47.
20. Stratton, p. 97.
21. Helen Krebs Smith, p. 98.
22. Burt, p. 79–80.
23. Janet Sherlock Smith, p. 23.

24. "Song of the Great Blizzard of 1888," Mss B649–137, Nebraska State Historical Society, Lincoln.
25. Merrifield, p. 63.
26. WPA, III, p. 175.
27. Robbins Letters n.p.
28. Ellis, p. 99.
29. Moynihan et al, p. 287–288.
30. WPA, III, p. 184.
31. WPA, II, p. 168.
32. Burt, p. 38.
33. Burt, p. 146.

Chapter Eleven:
1. Schumacher, vf Esther Morris, Wyoming State Historical Library, Cheyenne.
2. Quoted in Massie, p. 21.
3. Huettl, p. 24.
4. *Daily Sentinel,* January 21, 1871.
5. Myres, p. 220.
6. Fleming, p. 68.
7. Elizabeth Knight, n.p.
8. Quoted in Friggins, p. 4.
9. Armitage and Jameson, p. 268.
10. Ellis, p. 36–37.
11. Bird, p. 169.
12. Ellis, p. 30–31.
13. Erdoes, p. 11.
14. Jeffrey, p. 185.
15. Lomax, xvi.
16. Lockley, 1981, p. 196–97.
17. Merrifield, p. 33.
18. Cooper, n.p.

Chapter Twelve:
1. Quoted in John D. Unruh, *The Plains Across: The Overland Emigrants and the Trans-Mississippi West, 1840–60,* University of Illinois Press, 1979.
2. Quoted in Bank, p. 94.
3. Lomax, p. 319.
4. Stewart, p. 100–101.
5. Stewart, p. 15.
6. Ellis, p. 135.
7. Lomax, p. 78.
8. Lyman et al, p. 872.
9. Markham, p. 5–6.
10. Ives, 1966, p. 100.
11. Quoted in Moynihan, p. 74.
12. Kate Robbins, September, 1981.
13. Moynihan et al, p. 83.
14. Judson, p. 235.
15. Judson, p. 267.
16. Lockley, 1981, p. 65–66.
17. Sandoz, p. 211.
18. Quoted in Reiter, p. 51.
19. Lockley, 1981, p. 7.
20. Schlissel, Gibbens, and Hampsten, p. 217.
21. Fischer, p. 52.
22. Moynihan et al, p.116.
23. Moynihan et al, p. 172.

24. Stewart, pp. 134, 191, 227.
25. Judson, p. 81.
26. Rebolledo and Rivero, p. 362.

Chapter Thirteen:
1. Astrov, p. 229
2. Judson, p. 224.
3. Blood-Patterson, p. 152.
4. Barbara G. Walker, 1983, p. 624–625.
5. Masterson, p. 84.
6. Sarah Winnemucca Hopkins, p. 47.
7. Astrov, p. 77.
8. Sarah Winnemucca Hopkins, p. 49.
9. Stratton, p. 135–136.
10. Quoted in Stratton, p. 137.
11. Gilbert, p. 33–34.
12. Gruening, p. 149.
13. Judson, p. 152.
14. Underhill, p. 10–11.
15. Astrov, p. 192.
16. Astrov, p. 238.
17. Niederman, p. 57.
18. Astrov, 224.
19. Astrov, p. 227.
20. Sarah Winnemucca Hopkins, p. 21.
21. Masterson, p. 126.
22. Ellis, p. 206.
23. Wall, p. 126.
24. WPA, II, p. 189.
25. Peredes, p. xxv.
26. Rebolledo, p. 9.
27. Peredes, p. xxix.
28. Niederman, p. 62.
29. Astrov, p. 233.
30. Barbara G. Walker, 1983, p. 166, and Frazer, p. 416.
31. Barbara G. Walker, 1983, p. 406, 662, and 1098; and 1988, p. 447.
32. Thomsen, p. 33.
33. Ellis, p. 520.
34. Stewart, p. 70–71.
35. Ellis, p. 34–35.
36. Tamura, p. 131.
37. Paula Gunn Allen, p. 56.

ACKNOWLEDGMENTS

The following have provided valuable information and assistance:

Kathryn Bogle
Centralia Timberland Library, Centralia, WA
Coronado State Monument, Museum of New Mexico
Barbara Drageaux
Fort Laramie National Historic Site, Fort Laramie, WY
Todd Guenther, South Pass City State Historic Site
Elizabeth Hazen
Erhardt Hehn
Cathy Luchetti
Ingeborg Nielsen MacHaffie
Katherine McCanna
Darrell Millner
Sally Morrissey
Multnomah County Library, Portland, OR
Oregon Historical Society, Portland, OR
Oregon Writers' Colony
Lillian Pitt
Duane Smith
Tigard Library, Tigard, OR
Ron Walp
Warm Springs Museum, Warm Springs, OR
Joella Werlin
Wyoming State Museum, Cheyenne, WY

ILLUSTRATIONS AND PHOTOGRAPHIC CREDITS

Center of Southwest Studies, Fort Lewis College, Durango, CO
Carol Claypool
Mary Cross
Eastern Washington State Historical Society, Cheney Cowles Museum,
      Spokane, WA
Madeline Edwards
Erhardt R. Hehn
Mike Griswold
Hood River County Museum, Hood River, OR
Idaho State Historical Society, Library and Archives, Boise, ID
Jefferson County Historical Society, Port Townsend, WA
Jennifer Joyce
Molalla Area Historical Society Dibble House, Molalla, OR
Museum of Western Colorado, Grand Junction, CO
Nebraska State Historical Society, Lincoln, NE
Nevada Historical Society, Reno, NV
Peter Palmquist
Mary Dodds Schlick
Molly Wullstein Van Austen
St. Vincent Hospital, Portland, OR
Washington County Museum, Portland, OR
Marcia Williams
Wyoming State Museum, Cheyenne, WY

BIBLIOGRAPHY

Adair, Bethenia Angelina Owens. "Speech for the Women's Congress (1920?)". Papers. Mss. 503. Oregon Historical Society, Portland, OR.

Aikman, Duncan. *Calamity Jane and the Lady Wildcats.* Lincoln and London: University of Nebraska Press, 1987.

Allen, Linda, singer and composer. "Overland 1852." *October Roses.* Nexus Records, Produced by Julian Smedley, 1984.

———. "Weaving and Quilting." *Washington Notebook: New Songs of the Northwest.* Victory Music, 1991.

Allen, Linda, Jennifer and Kristin Allen-Zito, singers and composers. "The Dandelion Song." *Washington Notebook,* op. cit. Rainbow Dancer Productions, PO Box 5881, Bellingham, WA 98227.

Allen, Paula Gunn. *The Sacred Hoop: Recovering the Feminine in American Indian Traditions.* Boston, MA: Beacon Press, 1986, 1992.

Anderson, Bertha Josephsen. "The Life History of Mrs. Bertha Josephsen Anderson." *The Bridge:* Journal of the Danish American Heritage Society, VI, No. 1, 20–79.

Anderson, Bonnie S. and Judith P. Zinsser. *A History of Their Own: Women in Europe from Prehistory to the Present,* Vol. I. NY: Harper & Row, 1988.

Anderson, Lavina Fielding. "Lucinda L. Dalton." Vicky Burgess-Olson, ed. Sister Saints. Studies in Mormon History, Vol. V. Salt Lake City: Brigham Young University, 1978.

Applegate, Shannon. "RX for Controversy: Two Early Day Feminist Physicians." An address in Portland, Oregon 26 March, 1991.

Armitage, Susan. "Western Women: Beginning to Come into Focus." *Montana The Magazine of Western History,* XXXII, No. 3 (Summer 1982), 3–9.

Armitage, Susan and Elizabeth Jameson, eds. *The Women's West.* Norman: University of Oklahoma Press, 1987.

Ashe, Geoffrey. *The Virgin.* London and New York: Arkana/Routledge & Kegan Paul Inc., 1976, 1988.

Ashmore, Ruth. "The Girl Who Uses Slang." *The Ladies' Home Journal.* November 1893, 20.

Astrov, Margot, ed. *The Winged Serpent: American Indian Prose and Poetry,* 1946, 1974; rpt. Boston: Beacon Press, 1992.

Attwell, Jim. *Early History of Klickitat County.* Skamania, WA: Tahlkie Books, 1977.

Axelrod, Alan. *Songs of the Wild West.* NY: Simon & Schuster, 1991.

Bancroft, Caroline. *Six Racy Madams of Colorado.* Caroline Bancroft, 1965, 1992.

Bank, Mirra. *Anonymous Was a Woman: A Celebration in Words and Images of Traditional American Art — and the Women Who Made It.* NY: St. Martin's Press, Inc., 1979.

Barnhart, Jacqueline Baker. *The Fair But Frail: Prostitution in San Francisco, 1849–1900.* Reno: University of Nevada Press, 1986.

Batdorf, Carol. *Northwest Native Harvest.* Surrey, B.C. and Blaine, WA: Hancock House Publishers, 1990.

Beard, Frances B. Letter 26 August, 1955 re. Esther Morris. Wyoming State Historical Library, Cheyenne.

Beckham, Steven Dow and Associates. *The Grande Ronde Valley and Blue Mountains; Impressions and Experiences of Travelers and Emigrants, The Oregon Trail, 1812–1880.* Lake Oswego, OR: Beckham & Associates, 1991.

Beecher, Catharine and Harriet Beecher Stowe. "Principles of Domestic Science," 1870; rpt. *Women and Womanhood in America.* Ronald W. Hogeland, ed. D.C. Heath and Company, 1973.

Belknap, Keturah. "Keturah Belknap's Chronicle of the Bellfountain Settlement." Robert Gatke, ed. *Oregon Historical Quarterly,* XXXVIII (September 1937), 265–299.

———. *On Her Way Rejoicing.* Keturah Belknap's Chronicles. Charlotte and John Hook, eds. Commission on Archives and History Oregon-Idaho Conference, United Methodist Church, 1993.

Bird, Allan G. *Bordellos of Blair Street: The Story of Silverton, Colorado's Notorious Red Light District.* Grand Rapids, MI: The Other Shop, 1987.

Bird, Isabella. *A Lady's Life in the Rocky Mountains.* New edition copyright ©1960 by the University of Oklahoma Press.

Bits and Pieces: Your Own Western History Magazine, V, No. 3, 1969. Wyoming State Library, Cheyenne.

Black, Martha. *Martha Black: Her Story from the Dawson Gold Fields to the Halls of Parliament.* Flo Whyard, ed. Edmonds, WA: Alaska Northwest Publishing Company, 1976, 1980.

Blair, Karen J., ed. *Women in Pacific Northwest History: An Anthology.* Seattle and London: University of Washington Press, 1988.

Blair, Kay Reynolds. *Ladies of the Lamplight.* Colorado Springs, CO: Little London Press,1971.

Blood-Patterson, ed. *Rise Up Singing.* Bethlehem, PA: Sing Out Corporation, 1988.

Bogle, Kathryn Hall. Telephone interview. 20 July, 1994.

Mrs. Bowman's scrap book #44, Crook County Museum, Prineville, OR.

Brier, Warren J. "Tilting Skirts & Hurdy-Gurdies: A Commentary on Gold Camp Women." *Montana the Magazine of Western History,* XIX, No. 4 (Autumn 1969), 58–67.

Brown, Dale and editors of Time-Life Books. *American Cooking.* NY: Time-Life Books, 1968.

———. *American Cooking:* The Northwest. NY: Time-Life Books, 1970.

Brown, Dee. *Bury My Heart at Wounded Knee: An Indian History of the American West.* NY: Holt, Rinehart & Winston, Inc., 1970.

———. *The Gentle Tamers.* University of Nebraska Press, 1958.

Brown, Robert L. *Ghost Towns of the Colorado Rockies.* Caldwell, ID: The Caxton Printers, Ltd., 1968.

Budapest, Zsuzsanna. *Grandmother of Time: A Woman's Book of Celebrations, Spells, and Sacred Objects for Every Month of the Year.* Harper & Row, 1989.

Burt, Elizabeth. Reminiscences. Typed manuscript. Fort Laramie, Wyoming.

Butler, Anne M. *Daughters of Joy, Sisters of Misery: Prostitutes in the American West, 1865–90*. University of Illinois Press, 1985.

———. Telephone interview. 19 October, 1993.

Butler, America Rollins. Oscar Osburn Winther and Rose Dodge Galey, eds. "Mrs. Butler's 1853 Diary of Rogue River Valley." *Oregon Historical Quarterly*, XLI, No. 4 (December 1940), 337–366.

Butruille, Susan G. "Inua: Spirit World of the Bering Sea Eskimo." Alaskafest, October 1982, 48–55+.

———. *Women's Voices From the Oregon Trail*. Boise, ID: Tamarack Books, Inc., 1993.

Butruille, Susan G. and Anita Taylor. "Women in American Popular Song." *Communication, Gender, and Sex Roles in Diverse Interaction Contexts*. Lea Stewart and Stella Ting-Toomey. ed. Norwood, NY: Ablex Publishing, 1987.

"Calamity Jane." *Democratic Leader*, 3 November, 1885, 3. Wyoming State Historical Library, Cheyenne.

Camas-Washougal *Post-Record*. "Area Indian Women had 'Equal Rights.'" "Ritual 'Warfare' Settled Quarrels." "Would You Rather Live in 'Tea Prairie?'" "Columbia Indians Lived the 'Good Life.'" Cenaqua-Bicentennial Issue, 1976, 13–17.

Canfield, Gae Whitney. *Sarah Winnemucca of the Northern Paiutes*. Norman and London: University of Oklahoma Press, 1983, 1988.

Carey, Margaret Standish and Patricia Hoy Hainline. *Brownsville: Linn County's Oldest Town*. Calapooia Publications, No. 1, 1976.

Cather, Willa. *O Pioneers!* 1913, 1941; rpt. Boston: Houghton Mifflin Company, 1988.

Chin-Hsin Yao Chen and Shih Hsiang Chen. *The Flower Drum and Other Chinese Songs*. NY: The John Day Company, 1943.

Clark, Ella E. "Indian Thanksgiving in the Pacific Northwest." *Oregon Historical Quarterly*, LXI, No. 4 (December 1960), 444–447.

Clark, Malcolm H., Jr. "The War on the Webfoot Saloon." *The War on the Webfoot Saloon & Other Tales of Feminine Adventures*. Portland, OR: Oregon Historical Society, 1969.

Claypool, Michael Eric, ed. *Heart of the Earth*, No. 1, 2, 3 (Spring, Summer, Fall, 1991). Durango, CO: Earth Craft.

———. Interview, June 1993.

Cooper, Arvazena Spillman. "An Address to the People of the Year 2000." 1908; rpt. The Dalles, OR: Klindts' Booksellers, n.d.

Cooper, Patricia and Norma Bradley Buferd. *The Quilters: Women and Domestic Art, An Oral History*. NY: Anchor Press, 1978.

Coronado State Monument, Bernalillo, NM. Display information, including descriptions by Pedro de Castaneda, 1540–41, and Gaspar Perez de Villagra, 1610.

Cox, Beverly and Martin Jacobs. "Spirit of the Harvest." *Native Peoples*, 7, No. 4 (Summer 1994), 14–16.

Cross, Mary Bywater. *Treasures in the Trunk: Quilts of the Oregon Trail*. Nashville, TN: Rutledge Hill Press, 1993.

Curtis, Natalie, ed. *The Indians' Book: Songs and Legends of the American Indians*. N Y: Dover Publications, Inc., 1907, 1950.

De Graaf, Lawrence B. "Race, Sex, and Region: Black Women in the American West, 1850–1920." *Pacific Historical Review,* 49, No. 2 (May 1980), 285–313.

De Pauw, Linda Grant. *Seafaring Women.* Boston: Houghton Mifflin Company, 1982.

Dewhurst, C. Kurt, Betty MacDowell and Marsh MacDowell. *Artists in Aprons: Folk Art by American Women.* NY: E.P. Dutton, 1979.

Dierdorff, Emma Ross. *Childhood Cookbook.* Mss 155. Washington County Museum, Portland, OR.

Dobler, Lavinia. *Esther Morris: First Woman Justice of the Peace.* Riverton, WY: Big Bend Press, 1993.

Duncan, Elizabeth Dahlen. *Skagit Schoolma'am: A Pioneer Teacher in the San Juans.* Lowell, WA: Lowell Printing and Publishing, 1990.

Duniway, Abigail Scott. *Path Breaking: An Autobiographical History of the Equal Suffrage Movement in Pacific Coast States,* 1914; rpt. NY: Source Book Press, 1970.

Ehrenreich, Barbara and Deirdre English. *For Her Own Good: 150 Years of the Experts' Advice to Women.* Garden City, NY: Anchor Press/Doubleday, 1978.

———. *Witches, Midwives, and Nurses: A History of Women Healers.* The Feminist Press, 1973.

Ellis, Anne. *The Life of an Ordinary Woman, 1929.* NY: Houghton-Mifflin Co., 1957.

Erdoes, Richard. *Saloons of the Old West.* NY: Alfred A. Knopf, 1979.

Estes, Clarissa Pinkola. *Women Who Run With the Wolves.* NY: Ballantine Books, 1992.

Evans, Bob. "Famous Hog Ranches Fade Into History." Casper *Star-Tribune,* 4 November, 1967.

Evans, Sara M. *Born for Liberty: A History of Women in America.* NY: The Free Press, 1989.

Ewers, John C. "Deadlier than the Male." *American Heritage* 16 (June 1965), 10–13.

Faragher, John Mack. *Women and Men on the Overland Trail.* New Haven and London: Yale University Press, 1979.

Ferrero, Pat, Elaine Hedges and Julie Silber. *Hearts and Hands: The Influence of Women & Quilts on American Society.* San Francisco: The Quilt Digest Press, 1987.

Fischer, Christiane, ed. *Let Them Speak for Themselves: Women in the American West, 1849–1900.* Hamden, CN: The Shoe String Press Inc., 1977.

Fisher, Vardis and Opal Laurel Holmes. *Gold Rushes and Mining Camps of the Early American West.* Caldwell, ID: The Caxton Printers, Ltd., 1968.

Fleming, Sidney Howell. "Solving the Jigsaw Puzzle: One Suffrage Story at a Time." *Annals of Wyoming,* 62, No. 1 (Spring 1990), 23–73.

Frazer, Sir James George. *The Golden Bough.* New York: Collier Books, 1922, 1950.

Friedman, Ralph. "Holmes vs. Ford: A Chapter in Ebony." *This Side of Oregon.* Caldwell, ID: The Caxton Printers, Ltd., 1983, 141–167.

Friggins, Paul. "What Wyoming Did For Women." *Reader's Digest* (September 1960). Condensed from the Denver *Post,* 14 August, 1960. Wyoming State Historical Library, Cheyenne.

Gaden, Elinor W. *The Once & Future Goddess.* HarperSanFrancisco, 1989.

The Gamblers. The Old West Series. Alexandria, VA: Time-Life Books, 1978.

Gear, Kathleen O'Neal. Interview. 29 June, 1994.

Gedney, Elizabeth. "Cross Section of Pioneer Life at Fourth Plains." *Oregon Historical Quarterly,* XLIII (March-December 1942), 14–36.

Gilbert, Fabiola Cabeza de Baca. *The Good Life: New Mexico Traditions and Food,* 1949; rpt. Santa Fe, NM: Museum of New Mexico Press, 1982, 1986.

Gillenwater, Beth. "Pioneer Recipes in a Bountiful Land." *Oregon Journal,* 29 May, 1974, 2M.

Gilman, Charlotte Perkins. *The Living of Charlotte Perkins Gilman: An Autobiography.* NY: Harper Colophon Books, 1975.

Glass, Paul and Louis C. Singer. *Songs of the West.* NY: Grosset & Dunlap, 1966.

———. *Songs of Hill and Mountain Folk.* NY: Grosset & Dunlop, 1967.

Glenn, Evelyn Nakano. *Issei, Nisei, War Bride: Three Generations of Japanese American Women in Domestic Service.* Philadelphia: Temple University Press, 1986.

Graber, Kay, compiler. *Nebraska Pioneer Cookbook.* Lincoln and London: University of Nebraska Press, 1974.

Green, Rayna. *Women in American Indian Society.* NY, Philadelphia: Chelsea House Publishers, 1992.

Greffenius, Ruth, director and producer. Women of the San Juan, a readers' theatre of women of Southwestern Colorado. Durango, CO, 1983.

Grierson, Alice Kirk. *An Army Wife's Cookbook.* Mary L. Williams, ed. Tucson: Southwest Parks and Monuments Association, 1972.

Grinnell, George Bird. *Blackfoot Lodge Tales: The Story of a Prairie People.* Lincoln: University of Nebraska Press, 1962.

Gruening, Ernest. *An Alaskan Reader.* NY: Meredith Press, 1966.

Hafen, Mary Ann. *Recollections of a Handcart Pioneer of 1860: A Woman's Life on the Mormon Frontier.* Lincoln and London: University of Nebraska Press, 1983.

Hall, Eliza Calvert Hall. *A Quilter's Wisdom: Conversations with Aunt Jane.* San Francisco: Chronicle Books, 1994.

Hansen, Barbara. "Mary Lesser, Quilt Maker and Collector." Student Folklore Collection, 1 FA 83/52. Idaho State Historical Society, Boise.

Harland, Marion. *House and Home: A Complete House-Wife's Guide.* Philadelphia and St. Louis: P.W. Ziegler & Co., 1889.

Head, Joseph Christopher. *Nights of Heaven: A Social History of Saloon Culture in Portland, 1900–1914.* Thesis, Division of History and Social Sciences, Reed College, 1980.

Hehn, Erhardt R., ed. Andreas Reimann and Katharina Höhn: from Russian Steppe to Dakota Plains. Unpublished family history, 1988.

Hickok, Jane Cannary. calamity jane's letters to her daughter. San Lorenzo, CA: shameless hussy press, 1976.

The High Altitude Cook Book. Ladies of the Methodist Episcopal Church, South, ed. 1896; rpt. Durango, CO: First United Methodist Church, n.d.

Hilton, Francis W. "Calamity Jane." Frontier Magazine, September 1925, 105–109.

Holmes, Kenneth L., ed. *Covered Wagon Women: Diaries and Letters from the Western Trails, 1840–1890,* I-XI. Spokane, WA: Arthur H. Clark, 1983–1993.

Holt family letters. Collected by Anna Grimes Calef. Transcribed by Elizabeth Calef Howells. From the private collection of Elizabeth Calef Howells.

Holy Bible, King James Version.

Hopkins, Sarah Winnemucca. Mrs. Horace Mann, ed. *Life Among the Piutes: Their Wrongs and Claims.* NY: G.P. Putnam's Sons, 1883.

Horner, Patricia V. "Mary Richardson Walker: The Shattered Dreams of a

Missionary Woman." *Montana the Magazine of Western History,* XXXII, No. 3 (Summer 1982), 20–31.

Hubbs, Joanna. *Mother Russia: The Feminine Myth in Russian Culture.* Bloomington and Indianapolis: Indiana University Press, 1988.

Huettl, Irene Arndt. *Esther Morris of Old South Pass & Other Poems of the West.* Francestown, NH: The Golden Quill Press, 1965.

Hughes, Phyllis, ed. *Pueblo Indian Cookbook: Recipes from the Pueblos of the American Southwest.* Albuquerque, NM: Museum of New Mexico Press, 1972, 1977.

Hungry Wolf, Beverly. *The Ways of My Grandmothers.* NY: Quill, 1982.

"Indians." American Guide Series, Wyoming, 52–57, n.d. Wyoming State Historical Library, Cheyenne.

Ives, Burl. *Burl Ives Song Book.* NY: Ballantine Books, 1953.

———. *More Burl Ives Songs.* NY: Ballantine Books, inc., 1966.

James, Edward T, ed. *Notable American Women 1607–1950: A Biographical Dictionary.* "Martha Cannary Burk," I, 267–268. "Marie Dorion," I, 502–503. "Alice Fletcher," I, 630–632. "Mary Ellen Pleasant," III, 75–77. "Anna Howard Shaw," II, 274–277. "Ann Eliza Webb Young," III, 696–697. Cambridge, MA and London: Belknap Press of Harvard University Press, 1971.

Jameson, Elizabeth. "Women as Workers, Women as Civilizers: True Womanhood in the American West." Armitage and Jameson, op. cit.

Jarvis, Marion. *Come on in Dearie or Prostitutes and Institutes of Early Durango.* Durango, CO: Durango Herald, 1976.

Jeffrey, Julie Roy. *Frontier Women: The Trans-Mississippi West, 1840–1880.* NY: Hill and Wang, 1979.

Jensen, Joan M. *With These Hands: Women Working on the Land.* The Feminist Press/ The McGraw-Hill Book Company, 1981.

Jordan, Philip D. "Come Back Soon, Honey." *The Westerners Brand Book,* XXVI, No. 1 (March, 1969), 1–8.

Judson, Phoebe Goodell. *A Pioneer's Search for an Ideal Home, 1925;* rpt. Lincoln and London: University of Nebraska Press, 1984.

Kalman, Bobbie. *Food for the Settler.* The Early Settler Life Series. NY: Crabtree Publishing Company, n.d.

Katz, William Loren. *The Black West.* Anchor Books, 1973.

Kaufman, Polly Welts. *Women Teachers on the Frontier.* Yale University Press, 1984.

Kimball, Stanley B. Historic Resource Study Mormon Pioneer National Historic Trail. U. S. Department of the Interior National Park Service, 1991.

Knight, Anna. "Things I Remember." As told to daughter Dula. Vf, Amelia Knight. Clark County Historical Society, Vancouver, WA.

Knight, Elizabeth. *Songs of the Suffragettes.* Booklet of Song: A Collection of Suffrage and Temperance Melodies. Folkways Records, 1958.

Kolodny, Annette. *The Land Before Her: Fantasy and Experience of the American Frontiers, 1630–1860.* Chapel Hill and London: The University of North Carolina Press, 1984.

Kroeber, Theodora. *Ishi in Two Worlds: A Biography of the Last Wild Indian in North America.* Berkeley and Los Angeles: University of California Press, 1962.

Lee, Katie. *Ten Thousand Goddam Cattle: A History of the American Cowboy in Song, Story and Verse.* Published by Katydid Books & Records, PO Box 395, Jerome, AZ 86331. 1976.

Leonard, Jonathan Norton and Editors of Time-Life Books. *American Cooking: The Great West.* NY: Time-Life Books, 1971.

Levy, Jo Ann. *They Saw the Elephant: Women in the California Gold Rush.* Norman and London: University of Nebraska Press, 1992.

Liberty, Margot. "Hell Came With Horses: Plains Indian Women in the Equestrian Era." *Montana the Magazine of Western History,* XXXII, No. 3 (Summer 1982), 10–19.

Lincoln County Kitchen Memories: A Taste of Yesterday. Florence Scott and Patricia Stone, editors and compilers. Newport, OR: Lincoln County Historical Society, 1985.

Lockley, Fred. *Conversations with Pioneer Women.* Mike Helm, compiler and ed. Eugene, OR: Rainy Day Press, 1981.

———. *History of the Columbia River Valley.* Vol. I. Chicago: S. J. Clarke, 1928.

Lomax, Alan. *The Folk Songs of North America.* NY: Doubleday & Company, Inc., 1960; rpt Dolphin Books, 1975.

Lomax, John A. and Alan. *Folk Song USA.* NY: Duell, Sloan, and Pearce, 1947.

Loomis, Reverend A.W. "Chinese Women in California." *Overland Journal,* II, No. 23 (April 1869).

Luchetti, Cathy and Carol Olwell. *Women of the West.* St. George, UT: Antelope Island Press, 1982.

Luchetti, Cathy. *Home on the Range: A Culinary History of the American West.* NY: Villard Books, 1993.

Lucia, Ellis. *Cornerstone: the Formative years of St. Vincent — Oregon's first hospital.* Portland, OR: St. Vincent Medical Foundation, 1975.

———. *Klondike Kate: The Life and Legend of Kitty Rockwell the Queen of the Yukon.* Sausalito, CA: Comstock Editions, Inc., 1962, 1977.

Lyman, Henry M., Christian Fanger, H. Webster Jones, and W.T. Belfield. *The Practical Home Physician.* Western Publishing House, 1885.

Mac Coll, Ewan, ed. *Folk Songs and Ballads of Scotland.* New York: Oak Publications, 1965.

Markham, Mrs. Elizabeth. *An Oregon Pioneer of 1847–1857.* Portland, OR: The J.K. Gill Company, 1921.

Martin, Cy. *Whiskey and Wild Women: An Amusing Account of the Saloons and Bawds of the Old West.* NY: Hart Publishing Company, Inc., 1974.

Massie, Michael A. "Reform is Where You Find It: The Roots of Woman Suffrage in Wyoming." *Annals of Wyoming,* 62, No. 1 (Spring 1990), 2–21.

Masterson, Martha Gay. Lois Barton, ed. *One Woman's West: Recollections of the Oregon Trail and Settling the Northwest Country 1838–1916.* Eugene, OR: Spencer Butte Press, 1986.

Mathes, Valerie Sherer. "Native American Women in Medicine and the Military." *Journal of the West.* American Folk Medicine: A Symposium. Hand, Wayland D., ed. University of California Press, 1976.

Matthews, R. P. "The Cult of True Womanhood and Women's Associational Activities on the Tualatin Plans, 1840–1880." Unpublished paper. Washington County Museum. Portland, OR, 1988.

McCunn, Ruthanne Lum. *Thousand Pieces of Gold.* San Francisco, CA: Design Enterprises of San Francisco, 1981.

McGrath, Roger D. *Gunfighters, Highwaymen & Vigilantes: Violence on the Frontier.* University of California Press, 1984.

McKee, Ruth Karr. *Mary Richardson Walker: Her Book.* Caldwell, ID: The Caxton Printers, Ltd., 1945.

Means, Russell. "Knowing Who You Are: Lessons from Native America." Denver Public Library, Boulder, Colorado, 11 October, 1993.

Megue, Abigal (sic) Franks. "Reminiscences of Early Life in Colorado." Mesa College, Grand Junction, CO: Journal of the Western Slope, II, No. 3 (Summer 1987).

Merrifield, Charlotte, with Suzy Kelly. *Memories of St. Elmo.* Evergreen, CO: Design by Shadow Canyon Graphics, 1992.

Mershon, Helen L. "The 'Oldest Profession' in the Old West." The *Oregon Journal,* 2 May, 1980, Living Section, 21.

Methodist Hymnal. Nashville: Whitmore & Smith, Methodist Publishing House, 1932, 1935, 1939.

Milner, Clyde A. II, Carol A. O'Connor, and Martha A. Sandweiss. *The Oxford History of The American West.* NY, Oxford: Oxford University Press, 1994.

Moynihan, Ruth B. *Rebel for Rights: Abigail Scott Duniway.* New Haven and London: Yale University Press, 1983.

Moynihan, Ruth B., Susan Armitage, and Christiane Fischer Dichamp, eds. *So Much to Be Done: Women Settlers on the Mining and Ranching Frontier.* Lincoln and London: University of Nebraska Press, 1990.

Mumford, Esther Hall, ed. *Seven Stars & Orion: Reflections of the Past.* Seattle: Ananse Press, 1986.

Murphy, Mary. "The Private Lives of Public Women: Prostitution in Butte, Montana, 1878–1917." Armitage and Jameson, op. cit.

Myres, Sandra L. *Westering Women and the Frontier Experience 1800–1915.* Albuquerque: University of New Mexico Press, 1982.

Nash, Tom and Twilo Scofield. *The Well-Traveled Casket: A Collection of Oregon Folklife.* Salt Lake City: University of Utah Press, 1992.

Nation, Earl F. "Fallen Angels in the Far West." *The Westerners Branding Iron,* No. 143 (June 1981), 2–9.

Niederman, Sharon. *A Quilt of Words: Women's Diaries, Letters & Original Accounts of Life in the Southwest, 1860–1960.* Boulder, CO: Johnson Books, 1988.

Niethammer, Carolyn. *Daughters of the Earth: The Lives and Legends of American Indian Women.* NY: Collier Books, 1977.

Norwood, Vera. "Women's Place: Continuity and Change in Response to Western Landscapes." Schlissel, Ruiz, and Monk, op. cit.

"O.D. Taylor Horse-Whipped." *Mountaineer,* Casper, WY, 21 July, 1893.

O'Faolain, Julia and Lauro Martines, eds. *Not in God's Image: Women in History from the Greeks to the Victorians.* Harper & Row, 1973.

Oregon Writer's Project. *Oregon: End of the Trail.* Portland, OR: Binfords & Mort, 1940.

Owen, Joyce. "Sister's History of Idaho County Tells Tale of Famous 'Poker Bride.'" *Statesman,* 29 April 1965, p. 2.

Paredes, Americo, ed. *Folktales of Mexico.* Chicago and London: The University of Chicago Press, 1970.

Parsons, Mark E. "Across Rushing Waters: A History of the Washougal River and Cape Horn." Camas, WA: Post-Record, 1982.

Patterson, Alex. *A Field Guide to Rock Art Symbols Of the Greater Southwest.* Boulder, CO: Johnson Books, 1992.

Paul, Rodman W. "When Culture Came to Boise: Mary Hallock Foote in Idaho." *Idaho Yesterdays,* 20, No. 2 (Summer 1976), 2–12.

Penson-Ward, Betty. *Idaho Women in History,* Vol. I. Boise, ID: Legendary Publishing Company, 1991.

Perrone, Bobette, H. Henrietta Stockel, and Victoria Drueger. *Medicine Women, Curanderas, and Women Doctors.* Norman: University of Oklahoma Press, 1989.

Petrik, Paula. *No Step Backward: Women and Family on the Rocky Mountain Mining Frontier, Helena, Montana 1865–1900.* Montana Historical Society Press, 1987, 1990.

———. "Prostitution in Helena, Montana, 1865–1900." *Montana, The Magazine of Western History,* XXXII, No. 3 (Summer 1982), 28–41.

Pioneers of the San Juan Country. D.A.R. Sarah Platt Decker Chapter, ed. Colorado Springs, CO: The Out West Printing and Stationery Company, Vol. I, 1942. Vol. II, 1946. Durango, CO: Durango Printing Company, Vol. III, 1952. Denver: Big Mountain Press, Vol. IV, 1961.

Pitt, Lillian. Interview. 21 July, 1994.

Pratt, Grace Roffey. Patience Willoleaf's Pioneer Receipt Book. n.p., 1976. Idaho State Historical Society, Boise, ID.

Primitive Indian Dress. Review. Susan Fecteau. *Annals of Wyoming,* 52, No. 1 (Spring 1980), 68.

Rebolledo, Tey Diana. *Nuestras Mujeres: Hispanas of New Mexico, Their Images and Their Lives, 1582–1992.* Albuquerque, NM: El Norte Publications/Academia, 1992.

Rebolledo, Tey Diana and Eliana S. Rivero. *Infinite Divisions: An Anthology of Chicana Literature.* Tucson & London: The University of Arizona Press, 1993.

Reiter, Joan Swallow. *The Women.* The Old West Series. Alexandria, VA: Time-Life Books, 1978.

The Revolution, V, No. 2 (13 January, 1870). Vf Esther Morris. Wyoming State Historical Library.

Richey, Elinor. *Eminent Women of the West.* Berkeley, CA: Howell-North Books, 1975.

Riley, Glenda. "Black Women in the West." *Black Women in American History: From Colonial Times Through the Nineteenth Century,* Vol. 4. Brooklyn, NY: Carlson Publishing Inc., 1990, 1–21.

———. *Women and Indians on the Frontier, 1825–1915.* Albuquerque: University of New Mexico Press, 1984.

Robbins, Kate and Eunice. Letters. File #628. Crook County Historical Society, Bowman Museum, Prineville, OR.

Robertson, Janet, ed. *The Magnificent Mountain Women: Adventures in the Colorado Rockies.* Lincoln and London: University of Nebraska Press, 1990.

Rorer, Mrs. S. T. *The Philadelphia Cook Book.* Philadelphia: George H. Buchanan and Company, 1886.

Royce, Sarah. Ralph Henry Gabriel, ed. *A Frontier Lady: Recollections of the Gold Rush and Early California.* Yale University Press, 1932; rpt Bison Book, 1977.

Sandoz, Mari. *Old Jules Country.* NY: Hastings House, 1965.

Schlick, Mary Dodds. *Columbia River Basketry: Gift of the Ancestors, Gift of the Earth.* Seattle: University of Washington Press, 1994.

Schlissel, Lillian. Telephone interview. 11 September, 1993.

Schlissel, Lillian. *Women's Diaries of the Westward Journey.* NY: Schocken Books, 1982.

Schlissel, Lillian, Byrd Gibbens and Elizabeth Hampsten, eds. *Far From Home: Families of the Westward Journey.* NY: Schocken Books Inc., 1989.

Schlissel, Lillian, Vicki L. Ruiz and Janice Monk, eds. *Western Women: Their Land, Their Lives.* Albuquerque: University of New Mexico Press, 1988.

Sharpe, J. Ed and Thomas B. Underwood. *American Indian Cooking & Herb Lore.* Cherokee, NC: Cherokee Publications, 1973.

Sheafer, Silvia Anne. *Women of the West.* Reading, MA: Addison-Wesley Publishing Company, Inc., 1978, 1980.

Shenton, James P., Angelo M. Pellegrini, Dale Brown, and Israel Shenker. *American Cooking: The Melting Pot.* NY: Time-Life Books, 1971.

Sherr, Lynn and Jurate Kazickas. *Susan B. Anthony Slept Here: A Guide to American Women's Landmarks.* Times Books, 1994.

Simmons, Alexy. *Red Light Ladies: Settlement Patterns and Material Culture on the Mining Frontier.* Anthropology Northwest, No. 4. Corvallis, OR: Oregon State University Department of Anthropology, 1984.

Smith, Helen Krebs. *With Her Own Wings: Anecdotes and Reminiscences about Pioneer Women and Life in the Oregon Territory.* Portland, OR: Beattie and Company, 1948.

Smith, Janet Sherlock. "'Dear Peter': The Letters of a Pioneer mother and Sister." Todd Guenther, ed. *Wind River Mountaineer,* VII, No. 2 (April-June 1991), 4–29.

Smith-Rosenberg. "The Female World of Love and Ritual: Relations between Women in Nineteenth-Century America." *Signs: Journal of Women in Culture and Society,* August 1975, 1–29.

Sochen, June. *Herstory: A Woman's View of American History.* NY: Alfred Publishing Company, 1974.

"Some Colorado Journalists: Caroline Westcott Romney." *The Southwest,* Official Paper of La Plata County (28 June, 1884), 1+.

Stallard, Patricia Y. *Glittering Misery: Dependents of the Indian Fighting Army.* Norman and London: University of Oklahoma Press, 1992.

Stark, Raymond. *Guide to Indian Herbs.* Surrey, B.C. and Blaine, WA: Hancock House Publishers, 1981, 1992.

Stegner, Wallace. *Mormon Country.* Lincoln: University of Nebraska Press, 1942, 1970.

Stewart, Elinore Pruitt. *Letters of a Woman Homesteader,* 1913, 1914, 1942; rpt. Boston: Houghton Mifflin Company, 1988.

Story of the Great American West. Pleasantville, NY: The Reader's Digest Association, Inc., 1977.

Stratton, Joanna L. *Pioneer Women: Voices from the Kansas Frontier.* NY: Touchstone, Simon and Schuster Inc.,1981.

Talmage, Rev. T. De Witt. "The Curiosity of Eve." *The Ladies' Home Journal,* February 1893, 14.

Tamura, Linda. *The Hood River Issei: An Oral History of Japanese Settlers in Oregon's Hood River Valley.* Urbana and Chicago: University of Illinois Press, 1993.

Theiss, Lewis Edwin. *Wyoming—The Pioneer.* Pictorial Review, October 1913, 14–15+. Wyoming State Historical Library, Cheyenne.

Thomsen, Dagmar. "Sketches From Our Family Life In The Early Nineties." *The Bridge,* Journal of the Danish American Heritage Society, III, No. 2 (August 1980), 23–47.

Toelken, Barre. "Northwest Regional Folklore." *Northwest Perspectives: Essays on the Culture of the Pacific Northwest.* Edwin R. Bingham and Glen A. Love, ed. Eugene: University of Oregon. Seattle and London: University of Washington Press, 1979.

Trager, James. *The People's Chronology.* NY: Henry Holt and Company, 1992.

Turner, Ann. *Grass Songs: Poems of Women's Journey West.* Harcourt Brace Jovanovich, 1993.

Turney-High, Harry Holbert. "The Flathead Indians of Montana." Memoirs of the American Anthropological Association. No. 48 (1937).

Underhill, Ruth. "The Autobiography of a Papago Woman." Memoirs of the American Anthropological Association, No. 46 (1936).

United States History Atlas. Maplewood, NJ: Hamond, Inc., 1975.

Utley, Robert. *The Indian Frontier of the American West 1846–1890.* Albuquerque: University of New Mexico Press, 1984.

Vander, Judith. "From the Musical Experience of Five Shoshone Women." Keeling, Richard, ed. *Women in Native American Indian Music: Six Essays.* Bloomington, IN: Society for Ethnomusicology, 1989.

Vogel, Virgil J. "American Indian Foods Used as Medicine." Hand, Wayland D., ed. *American Folk Medicine: A Symposium.* University of California Press, 1976.

Wagner, Sally Roesch, ed. *Daughters of Dakota,* Vol. II: Stories from the Attic. Yankton, SD: Daughters of Dakota, 1990.

Walker, Barbara G. *The Women's Dictionary of Symbols & Sacred Objects.* Harper & Row, 1988.

———. *The Woman's Encyclopedia of Myths and Secrets.* Harper & Row, 1983.

Walker, Barbara M. *The Little House Cookbook: Frontier Foods from Laura Ingalls Wilder's Classic Stories.* NY: HarperTrophy, 1979.

Walker, Mary Richardson. Papers. Mss. 503. Oregon Historical Society, Portland, OR.

Wall, Steve. *Wisdom's Daughters: Conversations with Women Elders of Native America.* Harper Collins, 1993.

Waters, Frank. *Book of the Hopi.* NY: Ballantine Books, 1963.

Webster's New Twentieth Century Dictionary of the English Language, Unabridged. Cleveland and N Y: The World Publishing Company, 1953.

Weigle, Marta. "Southwest Native American Mythology." Carolyne Larrington, ed. *The Feminist Companion to Mythology.* London: Pandora/HarperCollins, 1992.

Welsh, Roger. "Song for a Pioneer." *Reader's Digest,* March 1993, 75.

Welter, Barbara. "The Cult of True Womanhood, 1820–1860." *Women and Womanhood in America.* Ronald W. Hogeland, ed. D.C. Heath and Company, 1973.

Wertheimer, Barbara Mayer. *We Were There: The Story of Working Women in America.* NY: Pantheon Books, 1977.

West, Elliott. "Beyond Baby Doe: Child Rearing on the Mining Frontier." Armitage and Jameson, op. cit.

———. "Scarlet West: The Oldest Profession in the Trans-Mississippi West." *Montana, The Magazine of Western History,* XXXII, No. 3 (Summer 1982), 16–27.

Western Writers of America. *The Women Who Made The West.* NY: Doubleday, 1980.

The Wild West. Time-Life Books. NY: Warner Books, Inc., 1993.

Williams, Jacqueline. *Wagon Wheel Kitchens: Food on the Oregon Trail.* Lawrence, KS: University of Kansas Press, 1993.

Williams, Walter L. *The Spirit and the Flesh: Sexual Diversity in American Indian Culture.* Boston, MA: Beacon Press, 1986, 1992.

WPA, Washington Pioneer Project. Told by the Pioneers: Tales of Frontier life as Told by Those Who Remember the Days of the Territory and Early Statehood of Washington, Vol. 1,2,3. Project #5841, 1936–1938. Centralia Timberland Public Library, Centralia, Washington.

Wyoming Recreation Commission. *Wyoming: A Guide to Historic Sites.* Casper, WY: Westerner News, 1976, 1988.

Yung, Judy. *Chinese Women of America: A Pictorial History.* Seattle and London: University of Washington Press for the Chinese Culture Foundation of San Francisco, 1986.

Zauner, Phyllis. *Those Spirited Women of the Early West.* Sonoma, CA: Zanel Publications, 1989.

INDEX

A Contrast on Matrimony, 253
Adair, Dr. Bethenia Owens, 5,
    100, 239
Address to the People of the
    Year 2000, 239
Agave, 123
Akimel, 25 (see also Pima)
Alaska, 106; Ketchikan, 140
Amazon Guards, 108
American Board of
    Commissioners for Foreign
    Missions, 72
Anasazi, 30
Anderson, Bertha Josephsen, 15
Anthony, Susan B., 221, 235,
    241-242
Apache, 27, 32
Apodaca, Maria Duran, 158
Apple Tea, 192
Arapaho, 26
Arizona, 39, 158, 178, 185, 186,
    204, 205

Bald Mountain, 141
Ballou, Mary, 114
Bangston, Priscilla, 176
Bannock, 49
Beauty aids, 201
Beecher, Catharine, 79
Belknap, Keturah, 177
Bemis, Charles, 264
Bemis, Polly, 264 (see also
    Nathoy, Lalu)

Berdaches, 54
Berry-picking, 214-215
Bird, Isabella, 125
Black Elk, 57
Black Hills, 142
Black, Martha, 144
Blackfeet, 26, 49
Blackwell, Dr. Emily, 150
Blair Street, 121 (see Colorado,
    Silverton)
Bloomer, Amelia, 102
Bloomers, 102
Book of the Hopi, 52
Bowman, Mrs., 191
Bright, Colonel, 228
Bright, Nina, 171
Bright, William, 223
British Columbia, Vancouver,
    153
Brown, Angie Mitchell, 205-207,
    216
Brown, Clara, 107
Brown, Maggie Keller, 116, 201
Brown, Tabitha, 107
Buckingham, Harriet Talcott, 41,
    209
Buffalo Bird Woman, 4, 33, 36
Bulette, Julia, 141
Burt, Elizabeth, 185, 203, 210,
    218
Butler, America Rollins, 82, 189,
    197, 253-254

Calamity Jane, 4, 09, 105, 113
Calapooia, 287
California, 14, 69, 92, 102, 106,
    116, 123, 163, 177, 179, 203,
    253; Horseshoe Bar, 204, 260;
    Indian Creek, 213; Negrobar,
    114; Nevada City, 118, 159;
    Placerville, 120; Sacramento,
    117; San Francisco, 124, 129,
    141, 144, 153
Cannary, Martha Jane, 90 (see
    Calamity Jane)
Cardwell, Fannie, 140
Carnival, 112
Cashman, Nellie, 106
Catherine the Great, 165
Cattle queen, 95
Cayuse Indians, 259
Changing Woman, 22, 34
Chanukah, 291
Cheyenne, 26, 64
Chief, 47
Chief Truckee, 28
Chinese, 129, 153
Chinese Exclusion Act of 1882,
    129
Chippewa, 25, 272
Chona, Maria, 44, 46, 50, 54,
    279-280
Churchill, Carolyn, 234
Cipole School, 97
Code of the West, 126
Colorado, 16, 17, 83, 95, 103,
    113, 116, 136, 142, 162, 201,
    214, 233, 294; Bonanza, 147;
    Buckskin Joe, 133, 154; Canon
    City, 183; Central City, 107;
    Cripple Creek, 136, 142, 148;
    Denver, 18, 147, 152; Durango,
    104, 122-123, 137, 143, 149,
    275; Florence, 136; Greeley,
    197; Hermosa, 293; Montrose,
    120; Pueblo, 17; St. Elmo, 114,
    122, 152, 238; Silverton, 121
Colt, Miriam Davis, 103
Columbia River, 269
Columbia River Gorge, 208

Comanche, 26
Cook, Eliza Frances, 288
Cook, Louisa, 138
Cooper, Arvazena Spillman, 239
Cooper, Mrs. D.J., 241
Corn Maiden, 42
Corn Mother, 36
Corn Woman, 22
Corn-husking bee, 166
Coronado, 34
Coronado State Monument, 34,
    51, 53
Creek Street, 140 (see Alaska,
    Ketchikan)
Cribs, 152
Crow, 26, 32, 48, 49
Cult of Domesticity, 79, 87
Cult of Individualism, 77, 126
Cult of True Womanhood, 77, 90
Curandera, 99, 100, 203

Dahlen, Claribel Rathbone, 184
Dahlen, Inger, 9
Dakotas, 15
Dalton, Aggie, 276
Dawes Act, 102
De Casteneda, Pedro 35
De Villagra, Gaspar Perez, 33, 35
Delaney, Matilda Jane Sager, 259
Demimonde, 139
DeVere, Pearl, 142, 148
Diego, Juan, 289
Dine, 25 (see also Navajo)
Duniway, Abigail Scott, 181,
    233, 241, 255
Duniway, Harvey, 233

Earth Mother, 54
Earth Woman, 23
Eggs, 184
Ellis, Anne, 4, 16, 83, 111, 113,
    126, 147, 162, 189, 215, 235,
    236, 237, 248, 254, 265,286,
    294, 295, 296
Eostre or Eostara, 270
Estufa, 52
Evans, Laura, 142

Fannie's Flotilla, 140
Fellows, Elvira Apperson, 258
Festival of Flowers, 271
Fields, "Black Mary," 106
Finely, Laura Bangston, 163-165
First Woman, 23
Fisk, Elizabeth Chester, 199
Fitzhugh, George, 79
Flake, Lucy Hannah White, 178
Flathead Indians, 41
Fletcher, Alice, 101, 102
Four Virtues, 153
Freeman, Minnie, 211-212
Fremont, General John C., 28
Frizzell, Lodisa, 14

Gage, Matilda, 242
Gay deceivers, 147
Gay, Elizabeth Paschal, 155, 237
Gay, Jane, 102
Ghost Dance, 56
Gifford Pinchot National Forest, 38
Gilbert, Fabiola Cabeza de Baca, 100, 276
Gilbert, Marie Dolores Eliza Rosanna, 92 (see Montez, Lola)
Goodell, Dr. William, 81
Grandmother Spider, 23
Grasshopper Year, 207
Gray, Clara Smiley, 217
Great American Desert, 157
Great Blizzard of 1888, 211
Great Dakota Boom, 15
Great Plains, 211
Green, Annie, 197
Greffenius, Amalia Reimann, 175
Greffenius, Ruben J., 170
Grierson, Alice, 208
Gros Ventre, 49
Guerin, Elsa Jane Forest, 105
Gum San, 4, 11, 17, 152, 153

Hadley, Amelia, 278
Hafen, Mary Ann, 14, 188
Hangtown Fry, 120

Hang-Town, 120 (see California, Placerville)
Hart, Pearl, 106
Hester, Sally, 203
Hickok, Wild Bill, 91
Hidatsa, 32, 33, 36
History of Woman Suffrage, 242
Hitchcock, Harriet, 121
Hog ranches, 128, 154
Holmes, Julia Archibald, 5, 103
Holt, Della, 15
Holt, Julia, 251
Homestead Act of 1862, 157
Hookers, 139-140
Hoop skirts, 147
Hopi, 25, 54, 282, 284
Hornos, 37
Horse, 58
Huelsdonk, John and Dora, 263
Hurley, Pat, 238

Idaho, 101, 141, 264; Boise, 138; Warren, 264
Illinois, 222
Ishi: In Two Worlds, 11

Janney, Martha Jane Spencer, 104
Jenkins, Malinda, 93, 261
Johnson, Rhoda Quick, 62
Jones, Mary Isen, 182
Jones, Richard, 182
Josepha, 128
Judson, Phoebe, 13, 47, 60, 62, 63, 183, 187, 193, 256, 258, 263, 269, 278

Kachina, 53
Kansas, 103, 107, 157, 161, 176, 191, 195, 202, 207, 208, 209, 241, 274, 275; Bernard, 95, 159
Katcina, 53 , 268 (see Kachina)
Keres Pueblo, 36
Knight, Anna, 190
Kroeber, Theodora, 11

Kuaua Pueblo Kiva, 33, 34, 51, 52, 53
Kwa-Taka, 54

Labyrinth, 55
Lady in Blue, 96
Lakota, 23, 25, 55 (see also Sioux)
Lamb, George, 217
Laramie Daily Sentinel, 226
Laura, 18
Laverdure, Betty, 287
Le Roy, Kitty, 142
Leonard, Frances J., 189
Life Among the Piutes, 47, 65
Lummi, 47
Luther, Martin, 169
Lyon, Mary, 207

Maguey, 123
Maj or Mai, the Maiden, 270
Mandan, 32
Manifest Destiny, 12
Mansur, Abby T., 204, 260
Markham, Elizabeth, 253
Martin, Sadie, 178, 204
Martina, Sena, 203
Mason, Biddy, 102
Masterson, Martha Gay, 62, 202, 270, 285
McCrackan, John, 69
McGill, Frank, 276
McMeekin, Joseph Patrick, 171
McQuigg, Esther Hobart, 224 (see Morris, Esther)
McWhirter, Martha, 97
Megquier, Jennie, 131
Merrifield, Charlotte Vickerson, 122, 213, 238
Mescal, 281
Mexoga, 55
Mining, 115
Mires, Mrs. Austin, 213
Mohave, 55
Monaghan, Jo, 105
Montana, 15; Billings, 113; Butte, 148; Cascade, 106; Helena, 199

Montez, Lola, 92
Morgan, Mary Granger, 285
Mormons, 232
Morris, Catherine Thomas, 80
Morris, Esther, 221-231, 255
Morris, Kate, 187
Morrow, Peg Leg Annie, 141
Mother Joseph, 98, 99
Mother of Oregon, 107 (see Brown, Tabitha)
Mountain Charley, 106, (see Guerin, Elsa Jane Forest)
Mt. Silverheels, 154

Nadawe Sioux, 25
Nadle, 55
Nathoy, Lalu, 4, 17, 264 (see Polly Bemis)
National Board of Popular Education, 96
Navajo, 25, 27, 32, 50, 55
Nebraska, 101, 157, 259; Custer County, 18
Neher, Christina, 257
Nevada, Silver City, 124; Virginia City, 141, 261
New Mexico, 96, 98, 158, 203, 216, 276, 290; Santa Fe, 282
New Northwest, 233
New York, Seneca Falls, 221, 234
Newton, Phoebe, 77
Nez Perce, 41, 102
North Dakota, 169

O'Brien, Gertrude, E., 210
Ojibway, 50, 287
Omaha Indians, 55, 101
Oregon 13, 16, 62, 66, 74, 80, 155, 157, 187, 190, 197, 209, 239, 253, 255, 270, 274, 285; Eugene, 270; Lane County, 202; Ochoco, 200; Oregon City, 182; Portland, 153; Salem, 120; The Dalles, 241; Willamette Valley, 287

Oregon Donation Land Law, 156, 250
Oregon Historical Society, 112
Oregon Spectator, 253
Oregon Trail, 40, 100, 107, 177, 209, 221, 237, 258, 288
Oregonian, 233
Oyster Cocktail, 121
Oysters, 120-121

Pacific University, 107
Paiute, 27, 43, 65, 271, 272
Palmer, Louise, 261
Papago, 25, 44, 46, 50, 279
Parkhurst, Charley, 106
Parteras, 99
Pat Hurley Saloon, 122
"Patchwork Quilt," 171
Pearl DeVere's Homestead, 151 (see DeVere, Pearl)
Pemmican, 40
Picotte, Susan La Flesche, 101
Pike, Zeb, 247
Pilgi, 186
Pima, 25, 39, 186, 282
Pine Ridge Reservation, 57
Pitt, Lillian, 66
Plains Indians, 48
Plaisted, Emma, 259
Pleasant, Mary Ann, 141
Plumpers, 147
Polly, 63
Polygamy, 58, 232
Powers, Lillian, 136, 151
Prostitutes, 139
Pueblo Indian tribes, 27, 32
Puget Sound, 9
Pulque, 123, 281

Qaletaqa, 54

Raspberry Cobbler, 215
Read, Martha S. 70
Reimann, Andreas, 166-170
Reimann, Katharina Hohn, 166-170, 196

Richardson, Mary, see Walker, Mary Richardson
Ristras, 185
Rivers, Bessie, 137, 143
Robbins, Kate, 179-181, 189, 197, 200, 219, 255, 274
Romney, Caroline, 104
Row, 139
Royce, Sarah, 120
Running Eagle, 49

Saguaro cactus, 279-281
Saloon, 121
Segale, Sister Blandina, 97, 98
Seneca Falls Convention, 230
Seton-Thompson, Grace Gallatin, 89
Seven Golden Cities of Cibola, 11, 35
Shalako Mana, 42
Shaman, 55
Shaw, Anna Howard, 3, 39, 186
She Who Watches, 21, 61, 66, 67 (see also Tsagaglalal)
Shell Flower, 28 (see Sarah Winnemucca)
Sherlock, Maggie, 211
Shima, 32
Shipap, 26, 284
Shoshone, 26
Sikyatki, 42
Silver Heels, 133-35, 154
Sioux, 26
Sister of Charity, 97
Sister of Providence, 98
Sky Father, 54
Smith, Mrs. Robert, 161
South Dakota, 196, 257; Parkston, 167; Yankton, 167, 168
Souvenir Sporting Guides, 144
Speese, Moses, 18
Spiral, 55
Squaw, 47, 61, 66
Stagecoach Mary, 4
Stanton, Elizabeth Cady, 235, 241-242

Starving Time, 210
Stearns, Rev. Mr., 79
Stewart, Elinore Pruitt, 18, 82, 95, 179, 247, 262, 294
Stewart, Mary, 182
Stowe, Harriet Beecher, 79
Strater Hotel and Saloon, 143
Stright, Mary L., 282, 290
Strikes Two, 48
Sunday Baked Beans, 181
Swastika, 25

Talmage, Rev. T. De Witt, 80
Tatum Family, 95
Tatum, Rebecca Jane Brooks, 159
Tenderloin, 139
Tewa, 155
Thocmetony, 28 (see Sarah Winnemucca)
Thomsen, Dagmar, 292
Thought Woman, 22
Three Sacred Sisters, 36
Throwing the Ball, 50
Tiswin, or tulapai, 281
Tohono O'odam, 25 (see also Papago)
Tonantzin, 96, 99, 290
Toothaker, Lydia Murphy, 195
Townsend, Susanna, 163
Tsagaglalal, 21
Turner, Frederick Jackson, 6

Ukraine, 166
Utah, 14, 113, 188, 210, 231
Ute, 27

Virgin of Guadalupe, 96, 99, 289

Waheenee, 36 (see Buffalo Bird Woman)
Walker, Elkanah, 73-74
Walker, Mary Richardson, 71-76, 82, 86, 89, 96, 197, 256, 257
Warrior women, 48
Washerwomen's Bay, 129 (see California, San Francisco)

Washington, 14, 47, 60, 62, 63, 158, 161, 183, 193, 213, 217, 233, 259, 263, 269, 278, 288; Neah Bay, 171; Puget Sound, 184; Scow Bay, 39; Townsend, 140; Trout Lake, 38
Whipple-Haslam, Mrs. Lee, 116
White Buffalo Woman, 23
Whitman, Marcus, 75, 259
Whitman, Narcissa, 75, 259
Williams, Carrie, 82, 256
Wilson, Luzena Stanley, 117-119, 129, 159
Winkte, 55
Winnemucca, Sarah, 4, 28-30, 43, 47, 48, 63, 64, 65, 128, 271, 272, 284-285
Wiping of the Tears, 287
Woman Chief of the Crows, 49
Woman's Commonwealth, 97
Women's Congress, 100
Wounded Knee, 57
Wyoming, 82, 179, 210, 222-231, 247, 262, 294: Cheyenne, 227; Fort Laramie, 154; South Pass City, 211, 221-231

Yakama, 24, 65 (see also Yakima)
Yellow Woman, 23
Young, Ann Eliza Webb, 232-233
Young, Brigham, 232

Zeigler, Maude or Pearl, 107
Zieber, Eugenia, 278
Zuni, 268, 282, 291

ABOUT THE AUTHOR

Susan Greffenius Butruille grew up with a close-ness to the land in western Colorado, where her father was with the U.S. Forest Service and her mother was a teacher. Now a resident of Oregon, the author has lived with her forester husband and two sons in Wyoming, Alaska, and Washington, D.C. and has traveled extensively in foreign countries including Estonia, Russia, Turkey, Greece, Scandinavia, New Zealand, and Australia. Her award-winning, widely-published writing includes topics ranging from fishing to cowboys, needle artists to space women. A student and teacher of women's history, the author has edited two national publications and spoken to a variety of audiences. In this, her second book, Susan G. Butruille continues her commitment to making women's voices heard, and finding common roots among diverse peoples in their ancient ties to the land.

The author welcomes comments and suggestions for subsequent editions of *Women's Voices from the Western Frontier*. Please write c/o Tamarack Books, PO Box 190313, Boise, ID 83719-0313.

Additional copies of *Women's Voices from the Western Frontier* can be found in fine bookstores nationwide or directly from the publisher.

If ordering direct, please include a check for $19.95 (book @ $16.95 plus a shipping/handling charge of $3.00). Idaho residents should send $20.80 (book @ $16.95, shipping/handling $3.00, and Idaho tax $.85).

Send your name, address, and check to:

WVWF Orders
Tamarack Books, Inc.
PO Box 190313
Boise, ID 83719-0313

To place orders using MasterCard or Visa,
please call 1–800–962–6657.

If you liked this book, you might enjoy
Women's Voices from the Oregon Trail
also by Susan G. Butruille.

For information on these or other Tamarack titles
please call 1–800–962–6657.

Ask for our free catalog!